TEST YOURSELF MCSE

Designing Security for Windows 2000

(Exam 70-220)

TEST YOURSELF MCSE

Designing Security for Windows® 2000

(Exam 70-220)

Syngress Media, Inc.

Osborne/McGraw-Hill

Berkeley New York St. Louis San Francisco Auckland Bogotá
Hamburg London Madrid Mexico CityMilan Montreal New Delhi
Panama City Paris São Paulo Singapore Sydney Tokyo Toronto

Osborne/**McGraw-Hill**
2600 Tenth Street
Berkeley, California 94710
U.S.A.

For information on translations or book distributors outside the U.S.A., or to arrange bulk purchase discounts for sales promotions, premiums, or fund-raisers, please contact Osborne/**McGraw-Hill** at the above address.

Test Yourself MCSE Designing Security for Windows 2000 (Exam 70-220)

1234567890 CUS CUS 01987654321

ISBN 0-07-212930-1

KEY	SERIAL NUMBER
001	R7E38UJM9Q
002	F3CN2QY6XO
003	JLCCHN3AH2
004	JDLGJR81BH
005	BLLDED4AD7

Publisher
Brandon A. Nordin

Vice President and Associate Publisher
Scott Rogers

Editorial Director
Gareth Hancock

Associate Acquisitions Editor
Timothy Green

Editorial Management
Syngress Media, Inc.

Project Editor
Mark Listewnik

Project Manager
Laurie Stewart

Acquisitions Coordinator
Jessica Wilson

Technical Editor
Robert Aschermann

Copy Editors
Kathleen Faughnan,
Nancy Faughnan

Proofreaders
Kari Brooks,
Dann McDorman,
Alison Moncrieff

Computer Designer
Maureen Forys,
Happenstance Type-O-Rama

Illustrator
Jeff Wilson

Series Design
Maureen Forys,
Happenstance Type-O-Rama

Cover Design
Greg Scott

Cover Image
imagebank

This book was composed with QuarkXPress 4.11 on a Macintosh G4.

About Syngress Media

Syngress Media creates books and software for Information Technology professionals seeking skill enhancement and career advancement. Its products are designed to comply with vendor and industry standard course curricula, and are optimized for certification exam preparation. Visit the Syngress Web site at www.syngress.com.

Authors

Chris Rima (M.S., MCSE+I, and MCT) is the Technical Programs Administrator for the Southern Arizona Campus of the University of Phoenix, the nation's largest private university. Chris administers a Microsoft Authorized Academic Training Partner (AATP) program and teaches Windows NT, Windows 2000, A+ and Network+ courses. As a member of the University's MCSE steering committee, he develops MCSE teaching materials and provides overall program guidance. Chris is a master-certified instructor for Microsoft's New Employee Support Training (NEST), Windows 95/98 and FrontPage 98 support curriculums. Chris formerly worked at Microsoft and Keane Inc. in Tucson, Arizona, where he started a Microsoft Certified Technical Education Center (CTEC).

Susan Snedaker (MCSE, MCP+I, MCT, and MBA) has been involved with information systems technology for over ten years. She is currently President and CEO of Virtual Team (www.virtualteam.com), a consulting firm working with high-tech startups. During her career, Susan has worked for both hardware and software vendors. Prior to founding Virtual Team, Susan worked for a software startup firm as Vice President of Client Services. She has also worked for Microsoft, Honeywell, and Keane in key executive and technical roles.

Technical Editor

Robert Aschermann (MCSE, MCP, MCT, and MBA) has been involved with information systems as an IS professional for nearly ten years. During his career he has worked in technical support, systems design, consulting, and training. He has been an MCSE for almost five years now and has passed more than 15 Microsoft certification exams.

v

Currently Robert works for a large computer manufacturer based in Austin, Texas. His job responsibilities include systems engineering, project management, and business analysis. As a project manager, he has led large Windows 2000, Windows NT, and Windows 95 operating system migrations and many small- to medium-sized client/server development projects.

As a systems engineer and architect, his responsibilities include identifying business processes that need improvement, drafting design specifications for solutions, and building systems that meet those design specifications. He routinely works with Microsoft development tools such as Windows 2000, Microsoft SQL Server 7.0, Access, IIS 4.0, Visual InterDev, Visual Basic, and the Microsoft Solutions Framework.

Technical Reviewer

Stace Cunningham (CMISS, CCNA, MCSE, CLSE, COS/2E, CLSI, COS/2I, CLSA, MCPS, and A+) operates SDC Consulting in Biloxi, Mississippi. He has assisted several clients, including a casino, in the development and implementation of their networks, which range in size from 20 nodes to over 12,000 nodes. Stace has been heavily involved in technology for over 14 years. During that time he has participated as a Technical Contributor for the IIS 3.0 exam, SMS 1.2 exam, Proxy Server 1.0 exam, Exchange Server 5.0 and 5.5 exams, Proxy Server 2.0 exam, IIS 4.0 exam, IEAK exam, and the revised Windows 95 exam. Stace was an active contributor to The SANS Institute booklet "Windows NTSecurity Step by Step."

In addition, he has co-authored 18 books published by Osborne/McGraw-Hill, Microsoft Press, and Syngress Media. He has also served as technical editor for eight books published by Osborne/McGraw-Hill, Microsoft Press, and Syngress Media. Recently, an article written by Stace appeared in *Internet Security Advisor* magazine. His wife Martha and daughter Marissa are very supportive of the time he spends with the computers, routers, and firewalls in his "lab." He would not be able to accomplish the goals he has set for himself without their love and support.

ACKNOWLEDGMENTS

We would like to thank the following people:

- All the incredibly hard-working folks at Osborne/McGraw-Hill: Brandon Nordin, Scott Rogers, Gareth Hancock, Tim Green, and Jessica Wilson for their help in launching a great series and being solid team players.
- Monica Kilwine at Microsoft Corp., for being patient and diligent in answering all our questions.
- Laurie Stewart and Maureen Forys for their help in fine-tuning the project.

CONTENTS

This book's primary objective is to help you prepare for the Designing Security for a Microsoft Windows 2000 Network exam under the new Windows 2000 certification track. As the Microsoft program transitions from Windows NT 4.0, it will become increasingly important that current and aspiring IT professionals have multiple resources available to assist them in increasing their knowledge and building their skills.

At the time of publication, all the exam objectives have been posted on the Microsoft Web site and the beta exam process has been completed. Microsoft has announced its commitment to measuring real-world skills. This book is designed with that premise in mind; its authors have practical experience in the field, using the Windows 2000 operating systems in hands-on situations and have followed the development of the product since early beta versions.

In This Book

This book is organized in such a way as to serve as a review for the Designing Security for a Microsoft Windows 2000 Network exam for both experienced Windows NT professionals and newcomers to Microsoft networking technologies. Each chapter covers a major aspect of the exam, with an emphasis on the "why" as well as the "how to" of working with and supporting Windows 2000 as a network administrator or engineer.

In Every Chapter

We've created a set of chapter components that call your attention to important items, reinforce important points, and provide helpful exam-taking hints. Take a look at what you'll find in every chapter.

Test Yourself Objectives

Every chapter begins with a list of Test Yourself Objectives—what you need to know in order to pass the section on the exam dealing with the chapter topic. Each objective in this list will be discussed in the chapter and can be easily identified by the clear headings that give the name and corresponding number of the objective, so you'll always know an objective when you see it! Objectives are drilled down to the most important details—essentially what you need to know about the objectives and what to expect from the exam in relation to them. Should you find you need further review on any particular objective, you will find that the objective headings correspond to the chapters of Osborne/McGraw-Hill's *MCSE Designing Security for Windows 2000 Study Guide*.

Exam Watch Notes

Exam Watch notes call attention to information about, and potential pitfalls in, the exam. These helpful hints are written by authors who have taken the exams and received their certification; who better to tell you what to worry about? They know what you're about to go through!

Practice Questions and Answers

In each chapter you will find detailed practice questions for the exam, followed by a Quick Answer Key where you can quickly check your answers. The In-Depth Answers section contains full explanations of both the correct and incorrect choices.

The Practice Exam

If you have had your fill of explanations, review questions, and answers, the time has come to test your knowledge. Turn toward the end of this book to the Practice Exam where you'll find a simulation exam. Lock yourself in your office or clear the kitchen table, set a timer, and jump in.

About the Web Site

Syngress Media and Osborne/McGraw-Hill invite you to download one free practice exam for the Designing Security for a Microsoft Windows 2000 Network exam. Please visit www.syngress.com or www.certificationpress.com for details.

MCSE CERTIFICATION

This book is designed to help you prepare for the Designing Security for a Microsoft Windows 2000 Network exam. This book was written to give you an opportunity to review all the important topics that are targeted for the exam.

The nature of the Information Technology industry is changing rapidly, and the requirements and specifications for certification can change just as quickly without notice. Table 1 shows you the different certification tracks you can take. Please note that they accurately reflect the requirements at the time of this book's publication. You should regularly visit Microsoft's Web site at http://www.microsoft.com/mcp/certstep/mcse.htm to get the most up to date information on the entire MCSE program.

TABLE I	Core Exams
Windows 2000 Certification Track	**Track 1: Candidates Who Have _Not_ Already Passed Windows NT 4.0 Exams**
	All four of the following core exams are required:
	Exam 70-210: Installing, Configuring and Administering Microsoft Windows 2000 Professional
	Exam 70-215: Installing, Configuring and Administering Microsoft Windows 2000 Server
	Exam 70-216: Implementing and Administering a Microsoft Windows 2000 Network Infrastructure
	Exam 70-217: Implementing and Administering a Microsoft Windows 2000 Directory Services Infrastructure

Track 2: Candidates Who Have Passed Three Windows NT 4.0 Exams (Exams 70-067, 70-068, and 70-073)

Instead of the four core exams above, you may take the following:

Exam 70-240: Microsoft Windows 2000 Accelerated Exam for MCPs Certified on Microsoft Windows NT 4.0.

The accelerated exam will be available until December 31, 2001. It covers the core competencies of exams 70-210, 70-215, 70-216, and 70-217.

PLUS—All Candidates

One of the following core exams are required:

*Exam 70-219: Designing a Microsoft Windows 2000 Directory Services Infrastructure

*Exam 70-220: Designing Security for a Microsoft Windows 2000 Network

*Exam 70-221: Designing a Microsoft Windows 2000 Network Infrastructure

Two elective exams are required::

Any current MCSE electives when the Windows 2000 exams listed above are released in their live versions. **Electives scheduled for retirement will not be considered current.** Selected third-party certifications that focus on interoperability will be accepted as an alternative to one elective exam.

*Exam 70-219: Designing a Microsoft Windows® 2000 Directory Services Infrastructure

*Exam 70-220: Designing Security for a Microsoft Windows 2000 Network

*Exam 70-221: Designing a Microsoft Windows 2000 Network Infrastructure

Exam 70-222: Upgrading from Microsoft Windows NT 4.0 to Microsoft Windows 2000

* Note that some of the Windows 2000 core exams can be used as elective exams as well. An exam that is used to meet the design requirement cannot also count as an elective. Each exam can only be counted once in the Windows 2000 Certification.

Let's look at two scenarios in Table I-1. The first applies to the person who has already taken the Windows NT 4.0 Server (70-067), Windows NT 4.0 Workstation (70-073), and Windows NT 4.0 Server in the Enterprise (70-068) exams. The second scenario covers the situation of the person who has not completed those Windows NT 4.0 exams and would like to concentrate ONLY on Windows 2000.

In the first scenario, you have the option of taking all four Windows 2000 core exams, or you can take the Windows 2000 Accelerated Exam for MCPs if you have already passed exams 70-067, 70-068, and 70-073. (Note that you must have passed those specific exams to qualify for the Accelerated Exam; if you have fulfilled your NT 4.0 MCSE requirements by passing the Windows 95 or Windows 98 exam as your client operating system option, and did not take the NT Workstation Exam, you don't qualify.)

After completing the core requirements, either by passing the four core exams or the one Accelerated exam, you must pass a "design" exam. The design exams include Designing a Microsoft Windows 2000 Directory Services Infrastructure (70-219), Designing Security for Microsoft Windows 2000 Network (70-220), and Designing a Microsoft Windows 2000 Network Infrastructure (70-221). One design exam is REQUIRED.

You also must pass two exams from the list of electives. However, you cannot use the design exam that you took as an elective. Each exam can only count once toward certification. This includes any of the MCSE electives that are current when the Windows 2000 exams are released. In summary, you would take a total of at least two more exams, the upgrade exam and the design exam. Any additional exams would be dependent on which electives the candidate may have already completed.

In the second scenario, if you have not completed, and do not plan to complete the Core Windows NT 4.0 exams, you must pass the four core Windows 2000 exams, one design exam, and two elective exams. Again, no exam can be counted twice. In this case, you must pass a total of seven exams to obtain the Windows 2000 MCSE certification.

HOW TO TAKE A MICROSOFT CERTIFICATION EXAM

If you have taken a Microsoft Certification exam before, we have some good news and some bad news. The good news is that the new testing formats will be a true measure of your ability and knowledge. Microsoft has "raised the bar" for its Windows 2000 certification exams. If you are an expert in the Windows 2000 operating system, and can troubleshoot and engineer efficient, cost effective solutions using Windows 2000, you will have no difficulty with the new exams.

The bad news is that if you have used resources such as "brain-dumps," boot camps, or exam specific practice tests as your only method of test preparation, you will undoubtedly fail your Windows 2000 exams. The new Windows 2000 MCSE exams will test your knowledge, and your ability to apply that knowledge in more sophisticated and accurate ways than was expected for the MCSE exams for Windows NT 4.0.

In the Windows 2000 exams, Microsoft will use a variety of testing formats which include product simulations, adaptive testing, drag-and-drop matching, and possibly even "fill in the blank" questions (also called "free response" questions). The test-taking process will measure the examinee's fundamental knowledge of the Windows 2000 operating system rather than the ability to memorize a few facts and then answer a few simple multiple-choice questions.

In addition, the "pool" of questions for each exam will significantly increase. The greater number of questions combined with the adaptive testing techniques will enhance the validity and security of the certification process.

We will begin by looking at the purpose, focus, and structure of Microsoft certification tests, and examine the effect that these factors have on the kinds of questions you will face on your certification exams. We will define the structure of exam questions and investigate some common formats. Next, we will present a strategy for answering these questions. Finally, we will give some specific guidelines on what you should do on the day of your test.

Why Vendor Certification?

The Microsoft Certified Professional program, like the certification programs from Cisco, Novell, Oracle, and other software vendors, is maintained for the ultimate purpose of increasing the corporation's profits. A successful vendor certification program accomplishes this goal by helping to create a pool of experts in a company's software and by "branding" these experts so companies using the software can identify them.

We know that vendor certification has become increasingly popular in the last few years because it helps employers find qualified workers and because it helps software vendors like Microsoft sell their products. But why vendor certification rather than a more traditional approach like a college degree in computer science? A college education is a broadening and enriching experience, but a degree in computer science does not prepare students for most jobs in the IT industry.

A common truism in our business states, "If you are out of the IT industry for three years and want to return, you have to start over." The problem, of course, is *timeliness*; if a first-year student learns about a specific computer program, it probably will no longer be in wide use when he or she graduates. Although some colleges are trying to integrate Microsoft certification into their curriculum, the problem is not really a flaw in higher education, but a characteristic of the IT industry. Computer software is changing so rapidly that a four-year college just can't keep up.

A marked characteristic of the Microsoft certification program is an emphasis on performing specific job tasks rather than merely gathering knowledge. It may come as a shock, but most potential employers do not care how much you know about the theory of operating systems, networking, or database design. As one IT manager put it, "I don't really care what my employees know about the theory of our network. We don't need someone to sit at a desk and think about it. We need people who can actually do something to make it work better."

You should not think that this attitude is some kind of anti-intellectual revolt against "book learning." Knowledge is a necessary prerequisite, but it is not enough. More than one company has hired a computer science graduate as a network administrator, only to learn that the new employee has no idea how to add users, assign permissions, or perform the other day-to-day tasks necessary to maintain a network. This brings us to the second major characteristic of Microsoft certification that affects the questions you must be prepared to answer. In addition to timeliness, Microsoft certification is also job-task oriented.

The timeliness of Microsoft's certification program is obvious and is inherent in the fact that you will be tested on current versions of software in wide use today. The job task orientation of Microsoft certification is almost as obvious, but testing real-world job skills using a computer-based test is not easy.

Computerized Testing

Considering the popularity of Microsoft certification, and the fact that certification candidates are spread around the world, the only practical way to administer tests for the certification program is through Sylvan Prometric or Vue testing centers, which operate internationally. Sylvan Prometric and Vue provide proctor testing services for Microsoft, Oracle, Novell, Lotus, and the A+ computer technician certification. Although the IT industry accounts for much of Sylvan's revenue, the company provides services for a number of other businesses and organizations, such as FAA pre-flight pilot tests. Historically, several hundred questions were developed for a new Microsoft certification exam. The Windows 2000 MCSE exam pool is expected to contain hundreds of new questions. Microsoft is aware that many new MCSE candidates have been able to access information on test questions via the Internet or other resources. The company is very concerned about maintaining the MCSE as a "premium" certification. The significant increase in the number of test questions, together with stronger enforcement of the NDA (Non-disclosure agreement) will ensure that a higher standard for certification is attained.

Microsoft treats the test-building process very seriously. Test questions are first reviewed by a number of subject matter experts for technical accuracy and then are presented in a beta test. Taking the beta test may require several hours, due to the large number of questions. After a few weeks, Microsoft Certification uses the statistical feedback from Sylvan to check the performance of the beta questions. The beta test group for the Windows 2000 certification series included MCTs, MCSEs, and members of Microsoft's rapid deployment partners groups. Because the exams will be normalized based on this population, you can be sure that the passing scores will be difficult to achieve without detailed product knowledge.

Questions are discarded if most test takers get them right (too easy) or wrong (too difficult), and a number of other statistical measures are taken of each question. Although the scope of our discussion precludes a rigorous treatment of question analysis, you should be aware that Microsoft and other vendors spend a great deal of time and effort making sure their exam questions are valid.

The questions that survive statistical analysis form the pool of questions for the final certification exam.

Test Structure

The questions in a Microsoft form test will not be equally weighted. From what we can tell at the present time, different questions are given a value based on the level of difficulty. You will get more credit for getting a difficult question correct, than if you got an easy one correct. Because the questions are weighted differently, and because

the exams will likely use the adapter method of testing, your score will not bear any relationship to how many questions you answered correctly.

Microsoft has implemented *adaptive* testing. When an adaptive test begins, the candidate is first given a level three question. If it is answered correctly, a question from the next higher level is presented, and an incorrect response results in a question from the next lower level. When 15 to 20 questions have been answered in this manner, the scoring algorithm is able to predict, with a high degree of statistical certainty, whether the candidate would pass or fail if all the questions in the form were answered. When the required degree of certainty is attained, the test ends and the candidate receives a pass/fail grade.

Adaptive testing has some definite advantages for everyone involved in the certification process. Adaptive tests allow Sylvan Prometric or Vue to deliver more tests with the same resources, as certification candidates often are in and out in 30 minutes or less. For candidates, the "fatigue factor" is reduced due to the shortened testing time. For Microsoft, adaptive testing means that fewer test questions are exposed to each candidate, and this can enhance the security, and therefore the overall validity, of certification tests.

One possible problem you may have with adaptive testing is that you are not allowed to mark and revisit questions. Since the adaptive algorithm is interactive, and all questions but the first are selected on the basis of your response to the previous question, it is not possible to skip a particular question or change an answer.

Question Types

Computerized test questions can be presented in a number of ways. Some of the possible formats are used on Microsoft certification exams and some are not.

True/False

We are all familiar with True/False questions, but because of the inherent 50 percent chance of guessing the correct answer, you will not see questions of this type on Microsoft certification exams.

Multiple Choice

The majority of Microsoft certification questions are in the multiple-choice format, with either a single correct answer or multiple correct answers. One interesting variation on multiple-choice questions with multiple correct answers is whether or not the candidate is told how many answers are correct.

> **EXAMPLE:**
>
> Which two files can be altered to configure the MS-DOS environment? (Choose two.)
>
> or
>
> Which files can be altered to configure the MS-DOS environment? (Choose all that apply.)

You may see both variations on Microsoft certification exams, but the trend seems to be toward the first type, where candidates are told explicitly how many answers are correct. Questions of the "choose all that apply" variety are more difficult and can be merely confusing.

Graphical Questions

One or more graphical elements are sometimes used as exhibits to help present or clarify an exam question. These elements may take the form of a network diagram, pictures of networking components, or screen shots from the software on which you are being tested. It is often easier to present the concepts required for a complex performance-based scenario with a graphic than with words.

Test questions known as *hotspots* actually incorporate graphics as part of the answer. These questions ask the certification candidate to click on a location or graphical element to answer the question. For example, you might be shown the diagram of a network and asked to click on an appropriate location for a router. The answer is correct if the candidate clicks within the *hotspot* that defines the correct location.

Free Response Questions

Another kind of question you sometimes see on Microsoft certification exams requires a *free response* or type-in answer. An example of this type of question might present a TCP/IP network scenario and ask the candidate to calculate and enter the correct subnet mask in dotted decimal notation.

Simulation Questions

Simulation questions provide a method for Microsoft to test how familiar the test taker is with the actual product interface and the candidate's ability to quickly implement a task using the interface. These questions will present an actual Windows 2000 interface that you must work with to solve a problem or implement a solution. If you are familiar with the product, you will be able to answer these questions quickly, and they will be the easiest questions on the exam. However, if you are not accustomed to working with Windows 2000, these questions will be difficult for you to answer. This is why actual hands-on practice with Windows 2000 is so important!

Knowledge-Based and Performance-Based Questions

Microsoft Certification develops a blueprint for each Microsoft certification exam with input from subject matter experts. This blueprint defines the content areas and objectives for each test, and each test question is created to test a specific objective. The basic information from the examination blueprint can be found on Microsoft's Web site in the Exam Prep Guide for each test.

Psychometricians (psychologists who specialize in designing and analyzing tests) categorize test questions as knowledge-based or performance-based. As the names imply, knowledge-based questions are designed to test knowledge, while performance-based questions are designed to test performance.

Some objectives demand a knowledge-based question. For example, objectives that use verbs like *list* and *identify* tend to test only what you know, not what you can do.

EXAMPLE:

Objective: Identify the MS-DOS configuration files.

Which two files can be altered to configure the MS-DOS environment? (Choose two.)

A. COMMAND.COM

B. AUTOEXEC.BAT

C. IO.SYS

D. CONFIG.SYS

Correct answers: B, D

Other objectives use action verbs like *install*, *configure*, and *troubleshoot* to define job tasks. These objectives can often be tested with either a knowledge-based question or a performance-based question.

EXAMPLE:

Objective: Configure an MS-DOS installation appropriately using the PATH statement in AUTOEXEC.BAT.

Knowledge-based question:

What is the correct syntax to set a path to the D: directory in AUTOEXEC.BAT?

A. SET PATH EQUAL TO D:

B. PATH D:

C. SETPATH D:

D. D:EQUALS PATH

Correct answer: B

Performance-based question:

Your company uses several DOS accounting applications that access a group of common utility programs. What is the best strategy for configuring the computers in the accounting department so that the accounting applications will always be able to access the utility programs?

A. Store all the utilities on a single floppy disk and make a copy of the disk for each computer in the accounting department.

B. Copy all the utilities to a directory on the C: drive of each computer in the accounting department and add a PATH statement pointing to this directory in the AUTOEXEC.BAT files.

C. Copy all the utilities to all application directories on each computer in the accounting department.

D. Place all the utilities in the C: directory on each computer, because the C: directory is automatically included in the PATH statement when AUTOEXEC.BAT is executed.

Correct answer: B

Even in this simple example, the superiority of the performance-based question is obvious. Whereas the knowledge-based question asks for a single fact, the performance-based question presents a real-life situation and requires that you make a decision based on this scenario. Thus, performance-based questions give more bang (validity) for the test author's buck (individual question).

TESTING JOB PERFORMANCE

We have said that Microsoft certification focuses on timeliness and the ability to perform job tasks. We have also introduced the concept of performance-based questions, but even performance-based multiple-choice questions do not really measure performance. Another strategy is needed to test job skills.

Given unlimited resources, it is not difficult to test job skills. In an ideal world, Microsoft would fly MCP candidates to Redmond, place them in a controlled environment with a team of experts, and ask them to plan, install, maintain, and troubleshoot a Windows network. In a few days at most, the experts could reach a valid decision as to whether each candidate should or should not be granted MCDBA or MCSE status. Needless to say, this is not likely to happen.

Closer to reality, another way to test performance is by using the actual software and creating a testing program to present tasks and automatically grade a candidate's performance when the tasks are completed. This *cooperative* approach would be practical in some testing situations, but the same test that is presented to MCP candidates in Boston must also be available in Bahrain and Botswana. The most workable solution for measuring performance in today's testing environment is a *simulation* program. When the program is launched during a test, the candidate sees a simulation of the actual software that looks, and behaves, just like the real thing. When the testing software presents a task, the simulation program is launched and the candidate performs the required task. The testing software then grades the candidate's performance on the required task and moves to the next question. Microsoft has introduced simulation questions on the certification exam for Internet Information Server 4.0. Simulation questions provide many advantages over other testing methodologies, and simulations are expected to become increasingly important in the Microsoft certification program. For example, studies have shown that there is a very high correlation between the ability to perform simulated tasks on a computer-based test and the ability to perform the actual job tasks. Thus, simulations enhance the validity of the certification process.

Another truly wonderful benefit of simulations is in the area of test security. It is just not possible to cheat on a simulation question. In fact, you will be told exactly what tasks you are expected to perform on the test. How can a certification candidate cheat? By learning to perform the tasks? What a concept!

Study Strategies

There are appropriate ways to study for the different types of questions you will see on a Microsoft certification exam.

Knowledge-Based Questions

Knowledge-based questions require that you memorize facts. There are hundreds of facts inherent in every content area of every Microsoft certification exam. There are several keys to memorizing facts:

Repetition   The more times your brain is exposed to a fact, the more likely you are to remember it.

Association   Connecting facts within a logical framework makes them easier to remember.

Motor Association   It is often easier to remember something if you write it down or perform some other physical act, like clicking on a practice test answer.

We have said that the emphasis of Microsoft certification is job performance, and that there are very few knowledge-based questions on Microsoft certification exams. Why should you waste a lot of time learning filenames, IP address formulas, and other minutiae? Read on.

Performance-Based Questions

Most of the questions you will face on a Microsoft certification exam are performance-based scenario questions. We have discussed the superiority of these questions over simple knowledge-based questions, but you should remember that the job task orientation of Microsoft certification extends the knowledge you need to pass the exams; it does not replace this knowledge. Therefore, the first step in preparing for scenario questions is to absorb as many facts relating to the exam content areas as you can. In other words, go back to the previous section and follow the steps to prepare for an exam composed of knowledge-based questions.

The second step is to familiarize yourself with the format of the questions you are likely to see on the exam. You can do this by answering the questions in this book, or by using Microsoft assessment tests. The day of your test is not the time to be surprised by the construction of Microsoft exam questions.

At best, performance-based scenario questions really do test certification candidates at a higher cognitive level than knowledge-based questions. At worst, these questions can test your reading comprehension and test-taking ability rather than your ability to use Microsoft products. Be sure to get in the habit of reading the question carefully to determine what is being asked.

The third step in preparing for Microsoft scenario questions is to adopt the following attitude: Multiple-choice questions aren't really performance-based. It is all a cruel lie.

These scenario questions are just knowledge-based questions with a story wrapped around them.

To answer a scenario question, you have to sift through the story to the underlying facts of the situation and apply your knowledge to determine the correct answer. This may sound silly at first, but the process we go through in solving real-life problems is quite similar. The key concept is that every scenario question (and every real-life problem) has a fact at its center, and if we can identify that fact, we can answer the question.

Simulations

Simulation questions really do measure your ability to perform job tasks. You must be able to perform the specified tasks. One of the ways to prepare for simulation questions is to get experience with the actual software. If you have the resources, this is a great way to prepare for simulation questions.

SIGNING UP

Signing up to take a Microsoft certification exam is easy. Sylvan Prometric or Vue operators in each country can schedule tests at any testing center. There are, however, a few things you should know:

- If you call Sylvan Prometric or Vue during a busy time, get a cup of coffee first, because you may be in for a long wait. The exam providers do an excellent job, but everyone in the world seems to want to sign up for a test on Monday morning.

- You will need your social security number or some other unique identifier to sign up for a test, so have it at hand.

- Pay for your test by credit card if at all possible. This makes things easier, and you can even schedule tests for the same day you call, if space is available at your local testing center.

- Know the number and title of the test you want to take before you call. This is not essential, and the Sylvan operators will help you if they can. Having this information in advance, however, speeds up and improves the accuracy of the registration process.

TAKING THE TEST

Teachers have always told you not to try to cram for exams because it does no good. If you are faced with a knowledge-based test requiring only that you regurgitate facts, cramming can mean the difference between passing and failing. This is not the case, however, with Microsoft certification exams. If you don't know it the night before, don't bother to stay up and cram.

Instead, create a schedule and stick to it. Plan your study time carefully, and do not schedule your test until you think you are ready to succeed. Follow these guidelines on the day of your exam:

- Get a good night's sleep. The scenario questions you will face on a Microsoft certification exam require a clear head.

- Remember to take two forms of identification—at least one with a picture. A driver's license with your picture and social security or credit card is acceptable.

- Leave home in time to arrive at your testing center a few minutes early. It is not a good idea to feel rushed as you begin your exam.

- Do not spend too much time on any one question. You cannot mark and revisit questions on an adaptive test, so you must do your best on each question as you go.

- If you do not know the answer to a question, try to eliminate the obviously wrong answers and guess from the rest. If you can eliminate two out of four options, you have a 50 percent chance of guessing the correct answer.

- For scenario questions, follow the steps we outlined earlier. Read the question carefully and try to identify the facts at the center of the story.

Finally, we would advise anyone attempting to earn Microsoft MCDBA and MCSE certification to adopt a philosophical attitude. The Windows 2000 MCSE will be the most difficult MCSE ever to be offered. The questions will be at a higher cognitive level than seen on all previous MCSE exams. Therefore, even if you are the kind of person who never fails a test, you are likely to fail at least one Windows 2000 certification test somewhere along the way. Do not get discouraged. Microsoft wants to ensure the value of your certification. Moreover, it will attempt to so by keeping the standard as high as possible. If Microsoft certification were easy to obtain, more people would have it, and it would not be so respected and so valuable to your future in the IT industry.

MCSE

MICROSOFT CERTIFIED SYSTEMS ENGINEER

1

Analyzing the Existing and Planned Business Models

T his chapter reviews company models and geographic scope, as well as company processes and life cycles in relation to security planning. How a company is organized, both logically (company model) and physically (geographical scope) will be the foundation of any network plan. This will impact domain planning, sites, site links, and organizational units (OUs).

Company processes cover a broad scope including how companies manage network resources, how companies hire or manage staff, and how companies manage products or services. Network security must take company processes into account to ensure that security plans support those processes. Implementing security for local and remote users, utilizing data encryption, delegating network administration through OUs, and applying Group Policies to computers in the domain are all components related to how your company runs.

Finally, understanding life cycles is also important in designing a secure network. Products, services, and even companies have discrete life cycles that impact cost, technology, and security. Total cost of ownership (TCO) and the life cycle of aging applications or hardware impact network planning.

TEST YOURSELF OBJECTIVE 1.01

Analyzing the Company Model and Geographical Scope

One of the most critical processes in designing a secure network is to analyze and understand the organizational structure and locations where business computing activity takes place. The information garnered from this analysis should be organized into documents that will assist in the overall design of the network and security components. These documents can include an organizational chart, a network resource diagram that describes the physical sites and their links speeds, and descriptions of administrative roles and responsibilities.

- Research and document the composition of workers in the organization. This documentation can be used to create organizational charts that will ease the creation of user accounts, OUs, and domains.

- Research and document the physical locations of the company. An understanding of the locations can assist in the creations of OUs and is useful for network diagrams.

- Research and document the network topology. This is used for the creation of sites.

Understanding how geographic locations impact network security is critical to passing the exam. Companies often are geographically disbursed and a network infrastructure can be created in many different ways. Understanding how companies' networks can be designed and implemented when they are centrally located, campus-based, regional, national, or international is critical on this exam. When several answers appear to be correct on the exam, select the answer(s) that contain the newest Microsoft Windows 2000 technologies such as using Layer Two Tunneling Protocol (L2TP) with Internet Protocol Security (IPSec), public keys, and certificates.

QUESTIONS

1.01: Analyzing the Company Model and Geographical Sc

1. You have been t̲ ationnal units based on your company's struct would be most useful to you?

A. Annual report

B. Organizational

C. Articles of incorporation

D. Company address book

2. Based on the information provided in the following organizational chart, what items would be relevant in planning your network security?

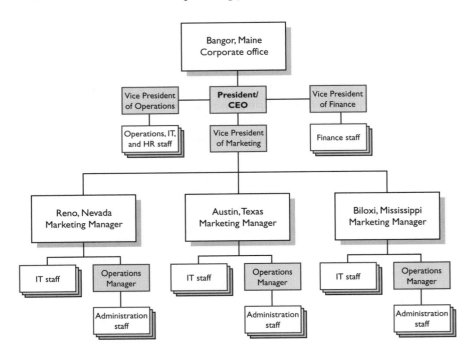

A. Geographic location: server location, IT staff, and site links

B. Geographic location: server location, IT staff, site links, and business model—headquarters with all functions replicated at each branch site

C. Business model: distributed business functions across branches

D. Geographic location: server location, IT staff, site links, and business model—headquarters with centralized finance and HR functions

3. **Current Situation:** Your company, Valley Flying Brigade, has 300 employees and is located in three U.S. cities (Minneapolis, Des Moines, and Boulder) and two cities in Europe (Paris and Rome). Each location has its own IT staff and Windows 2000 server(s). Each location runs distributed business applications and requires real-time data from all branches 24/7.

   Required Result: You must organize your company into OUs to optimize network administration.

Optional Desired Results: Branches should be able to manage all distributed business applications independently. Users at branch offices should have local support so that they effectively have 24/7 access and support provided by local staff.

Proposed Solution: Create five OUs. Delegate administration of each OU to the IT manager at each branch. Provide application support to end users via local branch office IT staff with on-call backup provided by central IT staff at headquarters.

What results are produced from the proposed solution?

A. The proposed solution produces the required result and all of the optional results.

B. The proposed solution produces the required result and only some of the optional results.

C. The proposed solution produces the required result only.

D. The proposed solution does not produce the required result.

Questions 4–6   This scenario should be used to answer questions 4, 5, and 6. Read the case study below and answer the questions that follow.

Coyote Consulting is a national company with 3,000 employees nationwide. Coyote Consulting uses Windows 2000 Server and has configured Active Directory Services. The headquarters are located in New York, with regional offices located in San Francisco, Dallas, and Boise. Each site has a 10MB LAN. The regional offices are connected by T1 connections.

The company is in talks to acquire one of their regional competitors, Roadrunner Consulting, within the next six months. Roadrunner Consulting has two locations, their headquarters in Dallas and their branch office in Boise. These two locations are running Novell networks and are not connected to each other at this time.

4.   How many sites should be created in Active Directory?

A. One

B. Two

C. Four

D. Six

5. Based on the information in the case study, how many OUs would you have to create?

    A. One

    B. Two

    C. Three

    D. Cannot be determined

6. Based on the information in the case study, once the acquisition of Roadrunner Consulting is complete, what planning considerations would have to be made to integrate Roadrunner Consulting into Coyote Consulting?

    A. Determine how many branches the company will have and how many total staff will be on board. Once headcount is assessed, the domain structure can be finalized. Then, servers and sites can be set up to reflect total staff as well as staff per branch.

    B. Determine how many branches the company will have and how many servers per branch will be used. Determine whether to create OUs for the acquired branches or to delegate administration of the new branches to existing IT staff in current company branches in same city.

    C. Determine how many IT staff will remain with the company. Assess the Windows 2000 skills of the acquired IT staff and assign roles for each IT member based on site location and network type.

    D. Have each branch IT administrator create OUs for their site then replicate those OUs through the organization.

TEST YOURSELF OBJECTIVE 1.02

Analyzing Company Processes

It is important to understand how a company is organized, what the political and functional divisions are and how information flows through the organization. This information should be incorporated into network planning to ensure that each group or division has proper access to resources, that delegation of administration for network resources is optimized, and that the overall network remains secure while providing adequate access to resources.

Each company uses processes to manage daily business functions. These may include the process used to hire new employees, the process used to analyze market conditions for products and services, or processes used to manage network resources. This data is used when creating security policies for access to and control of company resources and information. It is critical to understand how the business units, divisions, and departments use the various types of data and resources.

- Identify and understand the political and functional divisions in the company and the associated roles and responsibilities for various groups. This will be used for creating group policies, determining if multiple domains are necessary, and delegation of administration.

- Identify and document the unique naming convention for a domain. This will be used to provide a common identifiable and unique structure for users, computers, and groups.

- Identify and understand the core competencies of the business. This will be useful in determining data access levels, global and local groups, and policies.

- Understand the flow of information that enables your business to sell products or services. This will allow for a better architecture in terms of the location of resources, what the most likely requirements are for access to data, the redundancy of operations, and how data should be secured.

exam
ⓦatch

Most of the case studies on the exam focus on providing information about the location and the business processes of a hypothetical company. Understanding how business processes impact access and security design is fundamental to passing the exam. Questions will focus on how end users connect to company resources, what company objectives are, and what business processes must be supported. Watch for questions using proposed solutions with required and optional results. Check first to determine if the solution meets required results. If it does not, there is no need to assess the optional results of the question. This may reduce the time it takes to answer these sometimes lengthy questions.

QUESTIONS

1.02: Analyzing Company Processes

7. Delegation of administration is managed through which feature of Windows 2000?

   A. Organizational units

   B. Group policies

   C. Organizational Wizard

   D. Group units

8. Based on the following diagram, what is the relationship between NA.company.com and Sales.EU.company.com?

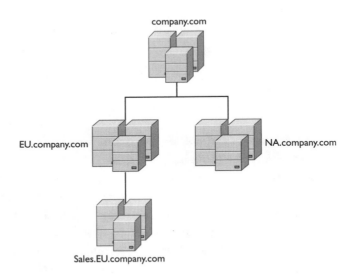

company.com

EU.company.com   NA.company.com

Sales.EU.company.com

   A. NA.company.com is the parent domain of Sales.EU.company.com.

   B. NA.company.com is the trusted partner of Sales.EU.company.com.

C. NA.company.com and EU.company.com are peer domains; each is a child of the root domain, company.com; Sales.EU.company.com is a child of EU.company.com.

D. There is not relationship between NA.company.com and Sales.EU.company.com; they cannot communicate with one another due to the hierarchy in place.

9. **Current Situation:** You are responsible for designing a new, Windows 2000–based network solution for your company.

    The company has three separate divisions. The sales representatives work with the engineering division and are selling a highly competitive, market-leading chip set, which requires strict confidentiality. Some of the sales representatives have laptops. The laptops range from 486s to P133s, all running Windows 95.

    The HR group works with a line-of-business application, but they travel frequently among the various branches. They do not need access to company resources during non-work hours. The third division is the finance division, which tallies all reports from the sales group and manages the finances for the company from headquarters.

    Required Results: Ensure that all sales reps have access to network resources when needed. Ensure that network security is as strong as possible without compromising ease of use or efficiency. Ensure that confidential data remains secure.

    Optional Desired Results: Provide a method of monitoring network access that ensures resources are being properly utilized, reducing costs for the company wherever possible without compromising quality or ease of use for end users.

    Proposed Solution: Create a group for the sales representatives that provides dial-in access for all representatives. Allow 24/7 access, but require strong passwords and data encryption. Create a group for the HR group that allows them remote access during working hours from the branch offices. For members of this group, require callback so that users not calling from a branch office will be denied access. Create a group for all finance people that allows them access to sales data but does not allow for remote access of any kind.

What results are produced from the proposed solution?

A. The proposed solution produces the required results and all of the optional results.

B. The proposed solution produces the required results and some of the optional results.

C. The proposed solution produces the required results only.

D. The proposed solution does not produce the required results.

Questions 10–12   This scenario should be used to answer questions 10, 11, and 12. Read the case study below and answer the questions that follow.

Your firm, Global Enterprises, is planning a migration to a Windows 2000–based network. Your firm currently has a Windows NT 4.0–based network with servers located in each of eight branch offices. Global Enterprises has just acquired three new companies. These three new companies each provide an expansion of existing services within your company. Company A, the first company you acquired, did not have an Internet presence but was using email for internal and external communications among its three branch locations. Company B, headquartered in Brussels, has strong name recognition throughout Europe.

Your company is hoping to capitalize on their strong name recognition to expand European sales of Global Enterprises' products and services. Company B has been a leader in e-commerce products for the past three years. Company B also has very strong corporate leaders who have been assured significant autonomy in running their soon-to-be new division of Global Enterprises. Company C is a regional company with one office located in Red Rock, Arizona, with a small but loyal customer base in the Southwestern United States. Company C has used the Internet to expand sales, but Internet sales are not yet a significant part of Company C's revenues or their overall business strategy. Company C's management team is happy to be acquired since their business had been running into extremely stiff competition lately and cash reserves were running low.

10. Based on the information in the case study, how many domains would you create for your firm, assuming all acquisitions are successfully completed?

A. 1

B. 2

C. 3

D. 11

11. If you wanted to create a domain structure that allowed each company to maintain a somewhat unique identity, what domain naming conventions could you use?

A. globalenterprises.com, companyA.globalenterprises.com, companyC.globalenterprises.com, companyB.com

B. globalenterprises.com, globalenterprises.com/companyA, globalenterprises.com/companyC, companyB.com

C. gloablenterprises.com, companyA\globalenterprises.com, companyB\globalenterprises.com, companyC\globalenterprises.com

D. globalenterprises.com, companyB.com

12. Based on the information in the case study, how many sites would you create in the globalenterprises.com domain?

A. 8

B. 10

C. 12

D. 14

TEST YOURSELF OBJECTIVE 1.03

Understanding Life Cycles

Products and services for a company go through distinct stages of life cycles, as do companies themselves. Understanding the life cycles of your company's products and services will enable you to design and manage a network that meets the changing needs of the company. Understanding how technology can be used to maximize profits, minimize losses, or increase efficiencies will ensure that the network plan is well aligned with corporate goals.

■ Understand and identify the life cycles for products. This will allow you to prepare for the changes that occur from one stage to another as a product goes from its initial release to retirement.

■ Understand the life cycles for service. This will allow you to prepare for the various steps that the service process goes through, from the initial event to a solution.

■ Understand how decisions are made for technology implementation. This will allow you to understand how often time management decisions are based on the business principles of profit. It will be your job to explain how the technology is aligned with the business strategy and how this new technology will enable it to maximize revenues or minimize losses.

exam
Ⓦatch

The exam is oriented toward case studies. Life cycle issues within a question will typically be addressed indirectly. For instance, the question may state that a company is retiring a particular technology or is migrating to a new technology. Factors related to life cycle that you may see on an exam are

■ *Products/technologies being retired have a lower cost in terms of book value but may have a higher cost in terms of keeping them running.*

■ *Products/technologies being acquired have a higher cost in terms of acquisition and implementation but may have a lower cost in terms of ongoing maintenance and support.*

■ *Products/technologies being acquired typically provide increases in efficiency that can partially or wholly offset cost of acquisition.*

QUESTIONS

1.03: Understanding Life Cycles

13. Which is a legitimate reason for implementing new technology? (Choose all that apply.)

    A. Lower cost of ownership

    B. Higher cost of maintenance and support

    C. Higher cost of maintaining older technology

    D. Increased security

14. Based on the following illustration, what statement describes the relationship of the graphic and the life cycle of an application?

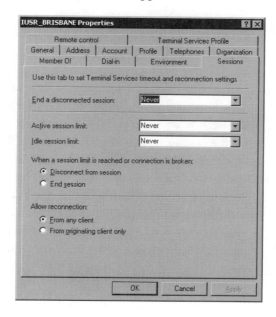

A. Only used with new applications written specifically for Terminal Services

B. Only used with new applications written to run on Transmission Control Protocol/Internet Protocol (TCP/IP)

C. Only used with older applications written specifically for Windows NT 4.0 Service Pack 4 or below

D. Can be used with any application and can extend the life of an older application by providing Internet access to applications that are not Web-enabled

15. **Current Situation:** Your company currently manufactures parts of telecom switches used in telephone company central offices to improve line conditions. Your company is also nearing final design for a new part for telecom switches that enables voice-over data on the same phone line. Your job is to review company-wide software applications and provide a three-year plan.

Required Results: Migrate entire organization to a Windows 2000–based network environment. Ensure that all applications will run in the Windows 2000 environment. Lower total cost of ownership and minimize all costs.

Optional Desired Results: Provide secure access to applications for those requiring remote access. Reduce number of applications supported while improving operational efficiencies.

Proposed Solution: Create a testing lab and run all applications on Windows 2000 in the lab to ensure that each application will run properly in the Windows 2000 environment. Evaluate applications and how they are used in the organization to determine if there are any duplications (such as running Word in one division and Corel WordPerfect in another division). Eliminate duplication wherever possible by forming a standardized suite of applications for the enterprise. Any application that will not run in Windows 2000 should be either updated or retired. Any applications that cannot be updated or retired and are critical to the company should be placed on a server with the most current operating system possible. Applications that are not Web-enabled but will run on Windows 2000 and require remote access should be made available via Terminal Services. Any computer that can connect to the Internet can be used to connect to the application via Terminal Services.

What results are produced from the proposed solution?

A. The proposed solution produces the required results and all of optional results.

B. The proposed solution produces the required results and some of the optional results.

C. The proposed solution produces the required results only.

D. The proposed solution does not produce the required results.

Questions 16–18   This scenario should be used to answer questions 16, 17, and 18.

You are the CIO for an Internet start-up company. Your company plans to be involved with e-commerce, selling a cutting edge product that is innovative and needed by every consumer in the United States. Your investors want a technology plan from you to help justify the $30 million investment they are about to make. Your strategy is fairly simple: implement a Windows 2000–based network for internal company needs running a line-of-business application and several standard office automation applications. Create a Web server that utilizes Windows 2000–based security features and integrates with Microsoft Internet Information Services (IIS) and other Microsoft Internet e-commerce solutions.

Hire an IT manager to oversee the design and implementation of the e-commerce Web site and launch the Web site within 180 days, after load testing and design testing are complete. Hire an outside consulting firm to attempt to breach security to ensure the site cannot be easily hacked or compromised.

16. Based on the information in the case study, which life cycle is most relevant to your plans?

   A. Windows 2000 is based on proven technology. This makes it stable, reliable and proven, similar to midlife cycle products. The risks for technology failure are low.

   B. E-commerce is an unproven concept and therefore early in its life cycle. The risks for technology failure are high.

   C. Outside consultants testing Web security is a maturing industry where costs are primarily based on maintaining technology.

   D. Windows 2000 is based on emerging technology. This makes it unstable, unreliable, and very cutting edge. However, it is desirable for a start-up company. The risks for technology failure are high, primarily due to hardware incompatibilities.

17. Your investors want an estimate of the costs for your plan. What would you take into consideration when developing your cost analysis? (Choose all that apply.)

   A. Network infrastructure costs

   B. Web development costs

   C. Protocols needs for secure Web implementation

   D. Age of equipment used by current staff

18. Part of your plan must delineate the service you would provide your e-commerce customers. Which is not a step in the life cycle of a service request?

   A. The end user cannot log on the secure site for purchasing company product.

   B. The end user emails the webmaster that the secure connection cannot be established.

   C. The webmaster determines a service has halted on the server, restarts service, and notifies the user.

   D. The end user notifies the webmaster that the issue has been resolved.

LAB QUESTION

Objectives 1.01–1.03

The following is a description of a company that needs to develop a network security plan. After reviewing the information, describe the likely concerns the company may have that will impact the network security plan.

GoFast.com has four divisions: HR, finance, marketing, and engineering. The company has three locations: headquarters, where HR, finance, and engineering are located; and two branch locations. At each branch, there is one HR and one finance person as well as four marketing staff and 25 sales representatives. The marketing and sales representatives travel within their region as well as attend national and international trade shows. The company just completed a merger with a company that was well established but falling far behind in the marketplace. The sales representatives of both GoFast.com and the merged company have been tasked with increasing sales significantly in the next 24 months, with emphasis on gaining a competitive edge and sales momentum in the next two quarters. Recently, confidential sales data was published on the Internet. This was very damaging to the company. It seems several of the sales representatives' laptops were stolen during a recent trip.

QUICK ANSWER KEY

Objective 1.01

1. B
2. D
3. A
4. C
5. D
6. B

Objective 1.02

7. A
8. C
9. D
10. B
11. A
12. C

Objective 1.03

13. A, C, and D
14. D
15. A
16. A
17. A and B
18. D

IN-DEPTH ANSWERS

1.01: Analyzing the Company Model and Geographical Scope

1. ☑ **B.** The organizational chart would assist you in designing OUs since they typically are created to reflect the way the company's staff is organized.

    ☒ **A** is not correct. The annual report will give you an overview of the company's goals and objectives but will not assist with the OU planning. **C** is not correct. The articles of incorporation will tell you how the company is organized for legal and accounting purposes but will not assist in OU planning. **D** is not correct. The company address book would tell you where people are located but would not give you an overview of the way departments and staff are organized.

2. ☑ **D.** With branch locations (national company), you need to consider which staff is at the branches. In this case, you have IT staff at each branch. You will need to consider how these branches are connected to headquarters for planning domains and sites. You also need to consider that headquarters contains at least two functions that are needed by the branches (finance and HR).

    ☒ **A** is not correct. Geographic location only accounts for part of the business issue to be analyzed. **B** is not correct. All functions at headquarters are not replicated at the branches. **C** is not correct. The business functions are only partially distributed (marketing) and this solution does not account for the geographic model as it relates to network topology requirements (for example, sites, site links, replication planning, and OUs).

3. ☑ **A.** By delegating full control of the resources at each branch to the local IT staff, you meet the requirement to optimize network administration. Delegating control provides end users with local access to service and support such as resetting locked out accounts and troubleshooting connectivity issues. Therefore, the solution meets both the required and the optional requirements.

☒ **B, C,** and **D** are not correct as the solution meets both the required and the optional requirements.

4. ☑ **C.** The company currently has four locations: New York, Dallas, Boise, and San Francisco. Each one is connected via a wide area network (WAN) connection (T1). Sites are defined as a network or collection of subnets connected by high-speed connections. Therefore, each branch would be a site.

☒ **A** and **B** are not correct because each branch is a separate site linked by a WAN connection. **D** is not correct. Even though you may eventually create two more sites to accommodate the two branches being acquired, you would not create them until you had developed an integration plan. It is possible that the two branch locations in both Boise and Dallas would merge, eliminating the need for additional sites.

5. ☑ **D.** The case study does not tell you anything about how the company is organized beyond its geographic scope. Without more information about how the company's employees are organized, it is impossible to design OUs.

☒ **A, B,** and **C** are incorrect because there is insufficient information to assess OUs.

6. ☑ **B.** The company may acquire the branch offices and end up with six offices. Since the company would have two offices in both Boise and Dallas, the company may consolidate and still only have four branch offices. Since the two acquired branches are running Novell servers, determining how (or if) those servers will be incorporated into the network will be key in determining the OU structure. If the acquired branches do not have sufficient Windows 2000 skills to effectively administer their resources, an OU could encompass both branches in Boise, for example, to ease administration.

☒ **A** is not correct. Total headcount (number of user and computer accounts) does not impact domain planning in Windows 2000. A site is defined by the network connection, not by the number of users. **C** is not correct. While you may assess skills of your IT staff, your network planning should look at the company's structure and processes to design network plans. **D** is not correct. Creating OUs is done at the organizational level. A person with authority over an OU may create additional OUs within that parent OU structure, but they would not be replicated across the organization.

1.02: Analyzing Company Processes

7. ☑ **A.** Organizational units, or OUs, are a new feature of Windows 2000 created to provide the ability to easily delegate administration of network tasks while maintaining a secure network environment.

   ☒ **B** is not correct. Group policies help administer network policies but do not assist in the delegation of administration. **C** is not correct; the wizard used for network administration delegation is the Delegation of Control Wizard. **D** is not correct. Windows 2000 does not have a Group Units option.

8. ☑ **C.** NA.company.com is a child of the root domain, company.com. EU.company.com is also a child of the root domain. Sales.EU.company.com is a child of EU.company.com.

   ☒ **A** is not correct. EU.company.com is the parent of Sales.EU.company.com. **B** is not correct. A trusted partner refers to an external firm your company works with closely. A *trust relationship* or simply *trust*, refers to the relationship between domains. **D** is not correct. NA.company.com and Sales.EU.company.com are related through the room domain, company.com.

9. ☑ **D.** The sales representatives all have older laptops but they are dealing with very sensitive data. Without upgrading their laptops, the data on their laptops and the types of security that can be used is limited. The proposed solution does not discuss the data on laptops. Therefore, the required result that confidential data remains secure is not met.

   ☒ **A, B**, and **C** are incorrect because the proposed solution does not meet required results, although it partially meets the optional results. The proposed solution would allow for callbacks to the HR group. This monitors their usage and can help lower phone charges. However, it does not provide a method for monitoring other access. It does not matter if answers A, B, and C meet the optional results because they do not meet the required results.

10. ☑ **B.** You would likely create two domains, one for Global Enterprises and one for Company B, which has created a strong Internet presence and has strong management. Company A does not have an Internet presence and does not appear to have a sophisticated IT infrastructure in place and therefore could be incorporated into Global Enterprises' domain. Similarly, Company C has made a few attempts to get out on the Internet, but they also could be incorporated into Global Enterprises' domain.

☒ **A**, **C**, and **D** are wrong because only Global Enterprises and Company B require a distinct Internet presence and have strong management. Only two domains are required.

11. ☑ **A.** The domain naming structure is hierarchical. Therefore, Company A and Company C could still maintain their unique identity as child domains of globalenterprises.com, while Company B could remain a unique domain to preserve the strong name brand identity it has created in the marketplace.

☒ **B** and **C** are not correct because they do not use legitimate domain naming conventions. **D** is not correct because it does not provide for a unique identity for Company A or C.

12. ☑ **C.** Global Enterprises has eight branch locations. Company A has three branch locations. Company C has one location. Therefore, you would likely have 12 branches connected by a WAN connection. Each of these branches would then be a site. Company B is a separate domain, so you would create domain trust relationships, not sites, between these domains.

☒ **A** would account only for the branches within the existing corporate structure, not the acquired companies. **B** and **D** do not provide for a logical number of sites corresponding to the number of branches or local, high-speed networks the company will have once all acquisitions are completed.

1.03: Understanding Life Cycles

13. ☑ **A**, **C**, and **D** are correct. Newer technology can lower the total cost of ownership through increased efficiency, lower maintenance and support costs, or lower cost of the technology itself. Maintaining older technologies can be expensive if legacy systems must be maintained that do not provide efficiency if the older systems break more often or if repairs are more costly. Finally, increased security technologies can be incorporated with products and services designed with security in mind.

☒ **B** is not correct. A higher cost to maintain and support a newer technology would not be a legitimate reason to implement new technology. While implementing new technology may be more expensive in some cases, this would have to be offset or justified rather than being used as a reason in itself.

14. ☑ **D.** Any application that can run on Windows 2000 can be run via Terminal Services. This can extend the life cycle of an application by providing access to the application via the Internet even if the application is not specifically Internet- or browser-enabled.

    ☒ **A** is not correct. Newer applications can be used with Terminal Services but do not need to be written specifically for that use. **B** is not correct. Applications do not need to be written to utilize TCP/IP since Terminal Services handles all aspects of remote data communication for the application. **C** is not correct. Older applications can be used, but they do not need to be written specifically for the operating system (although they must be able to run on the operating system).

15. ☑ **A.** The solution produces all of the required and optional results. By testing applications, you ensure that they are Windows 2000 compliant. You can assess applications for upgrade or retirement or you can extend their serviceable life by implementing them via Terminal Services. Terminal Services lowers total cost of ownership by allowing any computer that can connect to the Internet access to enterprise software applications, even if the hardware and software resources on that computer are not compliant with application requirements. Terminal Services provides a secure method of connecting to an application via the Internet and extends the life cycle of older applications. By reducing duplication, you improve operational efficiencies, ease support requirements, and may lower costs.

    ☒ **B, C,** and **D** are not correct because the proposed solution addresses all of the required and optional results.

16. ☑ **A.** Windows 2000 is a new technology, but it is based on proven Windows NT technologies. While new features make it leading edge, it is a stable, reliable product. The risks of the network going down due to the relative immaturity (life cycle) of the product is lower.

    ☒ **B** is not correct. While the business model for making a profit in e-commerce may be new, many of the technologies surrounding e-commerce such as Web servers and transaction servers have been tested and proven for many years. The risk for technology failure specifically related to Web technologies is not particularly high except in cases of intentional disruption—denial of service attacks, for instance. **C** is not correct. Consultants who test Web site and network security make up a fairly new, growing industry. Costs are primarily associated with staying current on new and emerging technologies. **D** is not correct. Although there are new components in Windows 2000 that are leading edge, the underlying technology has a solid basis in Windows NT. This leads to a new product that is stable and reliable. Hardware incompatibilities do exist but can be minimized by examining the Hardware Compatibility List (HCL) for Windows 2000 and testing in a lab environment prior to implementation.

17. ☑ **A** and **B** are correct. Since the company is new, you must evaluate the cost of the network infrastructure. It must be designed to meet the needs of your growing company and be cost efficient. You must evaluate how you will implement your e-commerce strategy and determine all the costs surrounding that. Since this is a new company and there are many emerging e-commerce technologies (early-life cycle), it may be more difficult to give an accurate assessment of the cost of technology for this segment.

☒ **C** is not correct. The choice of protocols used for Web implementation typically is part of a tactical plan and will not impact costs directly. **D** is not correct. Since the company is a start-up, it is safe to assume equipment is being purchased at current market standards.

18. ☑ **D.** In the life cycle of a service, the provider typically closes the issue after determining that the end user's issue is resolved. While the webmaster may contact the end user to ensure resolution, it is not the end user's responsibility to notify the webmaster of resolution.

☒ **A** is not correct. The end user would notify your company of problems with your site. **B** is not correct. The end user would either email or call your company to notify you of a problem, assuming the end user was interested enough to notify you rather than go to a competitor. **C** is not correct. The webmaster (or someone) from your organization would analyze the problem, determine and test a resolution, and notify the end user of the resolution.

LAB ANSWER

Objectives 1.01–1.03

There are several different ways to approach this matter. However, based on the information in the description, the company plan will have to address the following concerns:

- When merging technologies from two companies, some technology may be older because one company was not doing well financially. Identifying life cycles of technology, applications, products, and services for each company will be important in reducing duplication and lowering TCO.

- Remote branches will require a method of interconnecting sites and maintaining security. Reviewing how branches and divisions are interrelated will provide a good starting point for evaluating applications, access needs, group policies, and the physical topology of the network.

- Security is obviously a concern. The company that was acquired was falling behind in the marketplace. Was that due to security breaches, confidential data being leaked to competitors, or other issues not related to technology? Reviewing security issues that may have been present in the merged company would be wise. In addition, the recent theft of laptops indicates that the company may be targeted for industrial espionage. Since the data ended up on the Internet, there is little indication that the laptops were stolen by common thieves looking to resell the hardware for a quick dollar.

- Lowering or maintaining costs is important. With the merged company losing market share, it was likely losing money also. Mergers require capital expenditures to get both organizations aligned and working together.

- It is critical to implement effective technology solutions, especially with regard to remote users. The branch locations have marketing and sales representatives who travel. Providing secure, effective remote access will improve efficiency and security for all remote users.

- Creating OUs to delegate administration will improve efficiency, provide a faster resolution to local problems (such as remote users unable to access the network), and improve overall network security.

MICROSOFT CERTIFIED SYSTEMS ENGINEER

2

Analyzing Business Requirements

TEST YOURSELF OBJECTIVES

This chapter covers the analysis of the existing and planned business models, organizational structures, factors influencing company strategies, and the structure of the IT group in the organization. Analyzing the current and future business models includes a current and planned geographic scope, the number of business units within the company, and the autonomy of each business unit, as well as planned acquisitions and strategic alliances. The management of the company can be centralized, decentralized, or a combination of the two. Established company processes range from how new employees are hired to how applications are distributed across the enterprise. Factors that influence company strategies include strategic partnerships, planned acquisitions, changing customer needs, changing technologies, competitors, and the current and future financial health of the company. The IT group can be centralized and managed by one group within the organization or decentralized, with each branch or location managing its own resources.

TEST YOURSELF OBJECTIVE 2.01

Analyzing the Existing and Planned Business Models and Organizational Structures

This section reviews the analysis of existing and planned business models and organizational structures. Business models include how companies are organized by department function (such as engineering, IT, human resources, and finance) or by branch location where each branch has its own distinct functions. The business model may depend on whether management is centralized or decentralized. When management is centralized, there is typically a standard set of procedures for documenting and executing company policies. When management is decentralized, there can be a number of procedures (by location, department, or other criteria) for documenting and executing company policies. Pinpointing these differences is critical both to passing the exam and to your success as an IT professional on the job.

- Companies can be organized by department, site, branch, unit function, or other criteria. Identify how your company is organized to ensure network solutions map with the company's current and future organizational structure.

- Management models for networks are generally defined by whether they are centralized (on the same domain) or decentralized (loosely connected or separate from other branches).

- Understand your company's organization methods. Is there a standard protocol for documenting, processing, and executing company directives, or are these protocols different between divisions, branches, or groups?

- Hierarchical company networks are broken into three main categories: domains, trees, and forests. These should reflect the logical organization of the company.

- Methods of providing secure communication among sites, branches, remote locations, or traveling employees are virtual private networks (VPNs), Routing and Remote Access Service (RRAS), strong authentication, and data encryption.

exam
⚠atch

The exam covers a number of different scenarios that test your knowledge of communications between various company locations. Having a strong understanding of various remote communication terminology such as T1, T3, dial-up, packet switched, Frame Relay, VPN, Layer Two Tunneling Protocol (L2TP), Internet Protocol Security (IPSec), and Kerberos will help you decipher the scenario questions and answers. Designing a secure network solution is the focus of the exam and understanding secure remote communications is one of the keys to navigating successfully through the scenario-based questions.

QUESTIONS

2.01: Analyzing the Existing and Planned Business Models and Organizational Structures

1. Which of the following is not a standard business model?

   A. Divisions

   B. Branches

   C. Unit function

   D. Administrative

2.   Based on the illustration below, how would you characterize this company's structure?

Indigo Designs

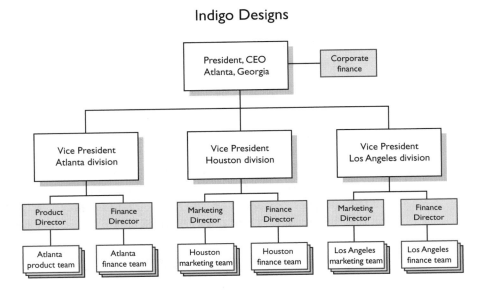

A.   Centralized

B.   Decentralized

C.   Combination of centralized and decentralized

D.   Cannot determine from diagram

3.   **Current Situation:** Your company has three separate divisions all in one location. Your company has announced plans to merge with another company, eliminating one division while creating a new division. The company will maintain two locations, one in the United States and one in Europe. You have been tasked with identifying the high-level Windows 2000–based network structure that will accommodate both your current and planned structure.

Required Results: Your plan must accommodate your current business structure and your future business structure.

Desired Optional Results: If possible, reduce administrative overhead for network-related tasks and increase security.

Proposed Solution: Create one forest with one domain: company. When the new company comes online, create a second domain: newcompany. Within the company domain, create three organizational units (OUs), one for each current division. Assess the impact of the elimination of one division and the addition of a new division and create an OU, if needed, to accommodate that new division. Review whether or not to implement Kerberos authentication on your native Windows 2000 network for added security.

What results are produced from the proposed solution?

A. The proposed solution produces the required results and all of the optional results.

B. The proposed solution produces the required results and some of the optional results.

C. The proposed solution produces the required results only.

D. The proposed solution does not produce the required results.

4. If a company has a Windows NT 4.0 network and has five domains with 25,000 users at two locations, what is the number of domains needed to handle this number of users and locations in Windows 2000?

A. One

B. Two

C. Five

D. Cannot determine from data given

5. What methods are used to connect users at remote branches of an organization to centrally located corporate network resources? (Choose all that apply.)

A. Dial-up connection via modem to RRAS

B. L2TP virtual hosted connection

C. Dedicated R1/T3 host connection

D. VPN connection via Internet

6. Data encryption can be used for which types of communications?

A. Between remote sites and headquarters

B. Between remote users and network resources

C. On a local network

D. All of the above

Analyzing Factors That Influence Company Strategies

In this section, we'll review factors that influence company strategies as they relate to network security. Factors analyzed typically include the company's risk tolerance and costs related to network resources. While there are a many factors that can influence a company, such as economic conditions or political situations, this section focuses primarily on risk tolerance and technology costs. Assessing a company's risk tolerance is vital to ensuring that the network security addresses the level of risk a company is willing to accept. Understanding that increasing security can increase costs is part of assessing risk tolerance. Total cost of ownership (TOC) and the changing technological landscape are also important in designing a secure network. These topics are covered in this section and are found in many of the scenario-based questions on the exam.

- Understanding your company's tolerance for risk will help you decide what type of encryption to use.
- The TCO is an elaborate method used to understand the true value of your company's network infrastructure.
- When developing future plans for security, you should factor in your company's short- and long-term plans and what level of risk they carry if the data is insecure.

exam
Ⓦatcⓗ

The exam contains several scenarios that involve external partners—remote branch locations, including international branches. At first glance, the concepts seem simple enough. However, the exam tests your ability to put these factors together for an optimal solution. Being able to assess the level of risk a company faces as well as the level of risk the company can tolerate will help you choose the best solution to exam questions. Also remember, these questions often throw superfluous facts into the scenario, so watch for "red herrings."

QUESTIONS

2.02: Analyzing Factors That Influence Company Strategies

7. A bank has branches in each state in the United States as well as branches in 24 major European and South American locations. What factors would impact the company's risk profile? (Choose all that apply.)

   A. Political climate in each country

   B. Financial transactions across networks, locations, time zones, and countries

   C. Changes to e-commerce regulations requiring taxation on products shipped across state boundaries

   D. Tight job market in the United States and Europe

8. What could be changed in the settings shown below to increase security while still providing remote access? (Choose all that apply.)

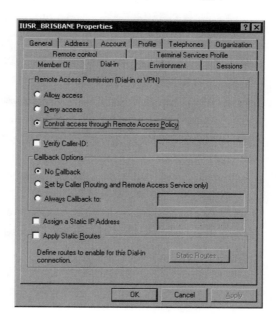

A. Deny Access

B. Verify Caller-ID

C. Always Callback to

D. Assign a Static IP Address

9. **Current Situation:** Your firm, PayMeNow, is a national payroll processing firm. You have been tasked with creating a plan to reduce network operations costs. The company has no plans to expand for the foreseeable future. Due to increasing competition, management expects to realize significant cost savings over the next two years. The migration to Windows 2000 is still slated for next quarter, but equipment upgrades for most computers have been postponed indefinitely. Your company currently is assessing using a new Web-based application that will be available in about ten months. Right now, the application your entire company relies upon is an older application. In the past, only employees from one division used the application, but due to a recent change in management structure, almost 90 percent of your employees will require access to this application. Many employees work at client sites using laptops or from home.

Required Results: You must reduce or maintain IT costs. You must maintain security at its existing level. You must provide a secure, reliable method for a new group of employees to use the older application.

Optional Desired Results: Improve security and provide an integrated migration path for moving to a new Web-based application once development is complete.

Proposed Solution: Once Windows 2000 is installed, make the older application available via Terminal Services. Place all new employees who require access to this application in a group and give that group permission to connect to the application via the Internet using Terminal Services. Provide information on how to connect to the application via Terminal Services to employees who currently use the application in a local mode. Negotiate with a reputable ISP for Internet access for all employees who require remote access. Ensure the ISP can provide local phone numbers for all employees using remote connection capabilities.

What results are produced from the proposed solution?

A. The proposed solution produces the required results and all of the optional results.

B.   The proposed solution produces the required results and some of the optional results.

C.   The proposed solution produces the required results only.

D.   The proposed solution does not produce the required results.

Questions 10–12   This scenario should be used to answer questions 10, 11, and 12.

HireMeNow, a temporary staffing agency, has 25,000 employees nationwide. They have their headquarters in Milwaukee, WI. They have 30 servers, all running Windows 2000. The accounting, IT, and HR functions are all managed from this location. They also have 150 branch offices located throughout the United States Currently, applicants fill out a form on the company's Web site via a Web-based application. This data is stored in a database and staff at the branch offices query the database to determine if there are any applicants who meet their specific staffing needs. Payroll is handled in two offices, the Sacramento, CA, office and the Billerica, MA, office. Each branch has about 20 employees including a branch manager, an IT person, and one administrative assistant. There are fractional T1 (128 Kbps) connections between the branches and headquarters. Headquarters is connected to the Internet via a T1 connection.

10.   Based on the information provided in the case study, what is the greatest security risk to the organization?

A.   Unauthorized use of network resources at branch locations

B.   Unauthorized use of network resources at headquarters

C.   Employees using the Internet for unauthorized purposes

D.   Database corruption via Internet attack

11.   Which is a viable strategy for upgrading the payroll servers at the Sacramento, CA, and Billerica, MA, locations?

A.   Assess future payroll processing needs. Determine location of all employees to be paid. Ensure payroll application can handle all future employees. Provide appropriate permissions to each payroll processor who requires access to the application. Use data encryption on payroll files.

B.   Assess current and future payroll processing needs. Determine suitability of application for long-term use. Determine who requires access to the application. Set up test lab. Migrate application to Windows 2000. Implement group policies. Use public key infrastructure (PKI) or certificates to authenticate users.

C.   Assess current and future payroll processing needs. Determine stability of servers. Require digital signatures for all users authorized to use the application. Set up a test lab. Migrate the application to Windows 2000. Implement Kerberos authentication.

D.   Assess RAM and processor requirements of application. Ensure servers meet those specifications. Set up a test lab, install Windows 2000 Professional, and install the application. Set up automated backups and data encryption.

12.   Which method could be implemented to reduce the company's risk with regard to payroll and application processing? (Choose all that apply.)

A.   Certificate authorities

B.   L2TP with IPSec for secure communications

C.   Callback policies to cause the dial-up connection to disconnect and call the user back at a specified location

D.   Daily backups of critical data

TEST YOURSELF OBJECTIVE 2.03

Analyzing the Structure of IT Management

IT management refers both to the organization of the IT group as well as to how IT resources are managed within an organization. The IT management can be centralized, where all IT planning and implementation is managed from a central location. It can be decentralized, where each branch or location is responsible for managing its IT functions, including connectivity to other branches or to headquarters. IT management also refers to the management of network resources. As such, it includes strategic management decisions such as whether to outsource any or all components of network administration, how to implement security, connectivity, and support functions, as well as network topology design.

- IT management can be centralized or decentralized. It can also be divided by department or by function.

- Outsourcing is a potentially useful way of getting expert help on issues that affect your business.

- Recognize that your most serious security risks can happen internally. Designing effective security policies and procedures can reduce internal security risks.

exam
Ⓦatch

The MCP exam emphasizes remote connectivity: employees, trusted partners, and Web sites. However, it's also very important to recognize that most security threats come from within the organization. Threats within the organization don't necessarily mean that an employee is trying to hack into the network. It can mean that employees with remote access privileges or even trusted partner employees who have been granted limited access to your network could pose the biggest risk. Keep this in mind on the exam; it's sometimes easy to forget the internal risks.

QUESTIONS

2.03: Analyzing the Structure of IT Management

13. The IT Department at your company is located at corporate headquarters. The IT director decides to hire SecurePro, an outside firm, to assess security on the corporate network. This is an example of what?

A. Decentralized IT management

B. Outsourcing

C. Security authentication

D. Centralized IT management

14. Assuming all servers in the following illustration are Windows 2000–based, what security protocols would the IT group likely implement? (Choose all that apply.)

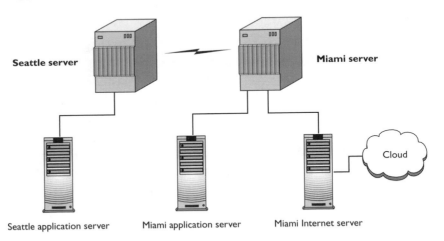

A. L2TP with IPSec

B. Kerberos

C. SLIP

D. MS-CHAP

15. **Current Situation:** Your firm is expanding rapidly and has been unable to hire qualified technical staff fast enough to meet the requirements of the IT Department. One project, being watched by competition and investors alike, is mission critical and is falling behind schedule. You have two locations, Calgary and Vancouver, each with full IT staff.

Required Results: Increase staff capacity quickly while providing a long-term solution. Get the lagging project completed on time or ahead of schedule.

Optional Desired Results: Reduce IT costs, improve communications infrastructure, and decentralize IT operations.

Proposed Solution: Hire an external consulting firm to assist with completing the project that has fallen behind. Assess whether this firm should be retained for ongoing IT support or whether certain help desk functions should be outsourced. Have Calgary assume responsibility for all daily network operations and have Vancouver assume responsibility for all IT projects.

What results are produced from the proposed solution?

A. The proposed solution produces the required results and all of the optional results.

B. The proposed solution produces the required results and some of the optional results.

C. The proposed solution produces the required results only.

D. The proposed solution does not produce the required results.

16. Why is TCO a major factor in business strategy?

A. TCO reveals the annual total cost of a network.

B. CEOs and other executive staff can refer to TCO data for a general understanding of the network architecture.

C. TCO helps you understand and expose hidden costs in products and services during their life cycles.

D. IT administrators only use TCO data when making security decisions.

17. The greatest security risk to your network comes from which source?

A. Anonymous Internet hackers

B. Internal users

C. External remote users

D. Industrial espionage

18. Which of the following factors are business factors that should be considered when choosing a connectivity medium? (Choose all that apply.)

A. Speed. In business, time is money and a slow connection means lost work time.

B. Some connection media leave your system vulnerable to hackers if files are left open on the desktop.

C. Many media require special modems or equipment that can be very expensive.

D. Local printing slows things down by adding connection options.

LAB QUESTION

Objectives 2.01–2.03

You have been tasked with developing a high-level migration plan for your Windows NT 4.0 network. You must migrate to a Windows 2000–based network and you must address security elements as they relate to your business model, company strategies, and IT management. Based on this information, list the elements you would include in your plan.

QUICK ANSWER KEY

Objective 2.01

1. D
2. B
3. B
4. A
5. A and D
6. D

Objective 2.02

7. A, B, and D
8. B and C
9. A
10. D
11. B
12. A, B, and D

Objective 2.03

13. B
14. A and B
15. B
16. C
17. B
18. A and C

IN-DEPTH ANSWERS

2.01: Analyzing the Existing and Planned Business Models and Organizational Structures

1. ☑ **D.** Administrative is not a standard business model.

   ☒ **A** is not correct. Divisions are a standard manner in which businesses are organized. **B** is not correct. Some companies are organized by branches or by physical locations. **C** is not correct. Companies often define their structure by the function of a unit or department.

2. ☑ **B.** The diagram depicts functions at each branch without a central headquarters or management team.

   ☒ **A** is not correct. A centralized company would have a headquarters or branch location where decisions are made and disseminated out into the rest of the organization. **C** is not correct. A combination would have management functions both at a central location and within the branch locations. **D** is not correct. From the diagram, it is possible to determine that the organization is decentralized since key management functions are located at each branch.

3. ☑ **B.** The proposed solution produces the required results. By creating one domain with three OUs, you have addressed the current needs of the organization. By planning for a second domain for newcompany and by planning for the new division, you have addressed the future needs of the organization as well. Creating OUs is one step you can take to reduce administrative overhead, but you have not taken steps to improve security. In Native Windows 2000 mode, Kerberos authentication is implemented by default. Therefore, you have not improved security.

   ☒ **A** is incorrect because not all optional results were produced. **C** is incorrect because some optional results were produced. **D** is incorrect because the required result was produced.

4. ☑ **A.** Windows 2000 removes many of the size limitations that were present in Windows NT 4.0 and below. Therefore, with two locations and 25,000 users, one domain could easily accommodate these resources in Windows 2000.

☒ **B** is not correct. Domains are not specific to locations. Within Windows 2000, locations are often considered sites, which map to the physical structure of the organization. **C** is not correct. It is no longer necessary in Windows 2000 to create multiple domains for the sole purpose of managing large number of resources. **D** is not correct. Although additional data may provide the rationale for creating multiple domains, given the data provided, one domain would be sufficient.

5. ☑ **A** and **D** are correct. Two common methods of connecting remote users to a central location are dial-up connections and VPN connections. Dial-up connections connect the user's computer and modem to a corporate RRAS server. VPN is the method of connecting the user through an Internet service provider (ISP) and the Internet to corporate resources.

☒ **B** is not correct. L2TP is a tunneling protocol that can be used in VPN connections but is not itself a connection method. **C** is not correct. A dedicated connection may use a T1 or T3 line, but it is not considered a hosted connection and there is no R1/T3 type connection.

6. ☑ **D.** Data encryption can be used on a local network or for remote communications. When companies have branches or remote users dealing with sensitive information, data encryption can be implemented in both local and remote situations. Although performance will likely be degraded using strong encryption, it ensures that both local and remote communications remain secure.

2.02: Analyzing Factors That Influence Company Strategies

7. ☑ **A, B,** and **D** are correct. A is correct. The political climate can certainly affect business in any country. Some countries have relatively stable political environments; others are more volatile. These impact the company's overall risk. B is correct. Financial transactions traveling over the Internet or other

network resources are vulnerable to capture and attack. Therefore, the company must assess the cost or impact of compromised financial data. Network security plans should address both the risks and the costs of security breaches to determine the optimal solution. **D** is correct because tight labor markets can cause companies to recruit strongly, taking employees with strategic corporate knowledge. Safeguarding against this possibility enhances network and corporate security.

☒ **C** is not correct. While e-commerce regulations may change taxation, banks typically are not involved in these transactions. They may receive or disburse funds from e-commerce transactions, but they generally are not selling taxable products.

8. ☑ **B** and **C** are correct. If your telecommunications equipment can provide caller-ID, you can set your system to recognize the ID of the caller for whom access is granted. You can also set the properties always to call the user back at a specified number. Once the RRAS service handles a call initiated by the user, it drops the call and re-establishes the connection at the specified phone number.

☒ **A** is not correct. This would not satisfy the requirement of still providing remote access. Although denying remote access is the most secure environment, it is not a practical solution in most companies. **D** is not correct. This does not enhance security, but is used to meet certain hardware or software requirements for a set IP address.

9. ☑ **A.** The solution produces the required and all of the optional results. The required results are as follows: maintain IT costs, maintain security, and expand application access. Optional results are as follows: improve security and provide integrated migration path. By providing access to the application via Terminal Services, you have addressed several needs. First, Terminal Services allows users with older hardware and software to connect to an application securely. Therefore, you are helping to maintain IT costs by eliminating the need for users to upgrade equipment. Terminal Services will extend the life of the application, thereby reducing upgrade costs for the near term. Second, Terminal Services provides very secure communication options that can be implemented. This meets the requirement to maintain security and meets the optional result of improving security. Terminal Services can provide wider access to an application, especially if user systems do not meet application hardware or software requirements for local installation. This expands the availability of the application to the required group of users. By implementing Terminal Services, users are becoming accustomed to accessing an application via the Internet. This will be useful

when the fully Web-enabled application is implemented in ten months. This meets the optional result of providing a seamless migration to the new application.

☒   **B, C,** and **D** are not correct because the solution produces all the required and all the optional results.

10.   ☑   **D.** The company's entire structure is based on utilizing the database into which applicants place their employment data. This database must remain secure. Employees are using the application via the Web and anonymous users (applicants) are entering data via the Web. Therefore, this is the greatest security risk to the company.

☒   **A** is not correct. Unauthorized use of the network resources can be a security risk, but since all employees are currently using the network, it appears that security has adequately addressed this risk. **B** is not correct for the same reasons. The only significant difference between the branch locations and headquarters is a faster Internet connection. **C** is not correct. Employees may use the Internet for unauthorized purposes, but this creates less of a security threat than does database corruption.

11.   ☑   **B.** Assessing the changing needs of the Payroll Department will ensure you account for all current and future needs of the organization. Assessing the application will help determine whether to implement the application as is, to upgrade the application to a newer version, to implement the application via Terminal Services, or to assess alternative applications that may be based on newer technologies or provide enhanced features. Determining who will require access to the application will help determine access methods such as local installation, remote installation, or Web-based installation. In planning major changes (and sometimes minor ones), setting up a test lab avoids costly system outages and downtime. Determining how you want users to be authenticated is an important planning task. When dealing with payroll and other sensitive data, you should consider strong authentication methods such as PKI or certificates.

☒   **A** is not correct. The location of employees paid via the payroll application is not germane to the topic. Permissions can be assigned to individuals, but assigning permissions to groups and placing users in groups is the preferred method of assigning permissions. **C** is not correct. Digital signatures are used to authenticate the source of a program or application such as an ActiveX component downloaded via the Internet. This is not a method of authenticating users.

12. ☑ **A**, **B**, and **D** are correct. Using certificates, users can be authenticated at a more secure level than the default Kerberos authentication in Windows 2000. Kerberos provides a very secure authentication method, but can be augmented when critical data is at risk. L2TP with IPSec provides secure communications in a VPN environment. If the branches connect to corporate resources using VPN, implementing L2TP with IPSec will enhance security. Daily backups of critical data reduce the risk of loss of data via hardware or software failures and can provide a method of restoring data that becomes corrupt.

☒ **C** is not correct. Callback policies do reduce security threats of impersonation, but there is no data in the case study to indicate remote users are dialing in to corporate resources.

2.03: Analyzing the Structure of IT Management

13. ☑ **B.** Outsourcing is defined as a firm outside your company being hired to perform specific tasks. Often outsourcing is used to provide specific expertise to a problem or to quickly expand the capabilities of an organization.

☒ **A** is not correct. The IT Department is located at corporate headquarters only; this is an example of centralized IT management. **C** is not correct. Although the firm is auditing security, authentication is provided by various technology components such as Kerberos, certificates, and public keys. **D** is not correct. Although this question does include central IT management, the process of hiring an outside firm is referred to outsourcing.

14. ☑ **A** and **B** are correct. L2TP with IPSec are tunneling and data encryption protocols used to secure remote communications. Kerberos is used to authenticate users in a native Windows 2000 environment.

☒ **C** is not correct. Unlike Windows NT 4.0 and below, Serial Line Internet Protocol (SLIP) is not supported in Windows 2000. **D** is not correct. MS-CHAP is the acronym used for Microsoft Challenge Handshake Authentication Protocol.

15. ☑ **B.** The required results are as follows: increase staff capacity, find a long-term solution, and get the project back on track. The solution addresses these by working with a consulting firm that will immediately increase capacity, may be a viable long-term solution, and will, in the short term, get the project

back on track. The optional results are as follows: reduce IT costs, improve communication infrastructure, and decentralize IT operations. This solution may or may not reduce IT costs. Outsourcing can often save money by using a more focused, effective approach to a project. This solution does not address improving communications. However, by dividing the work between Calgary and Vancouver, the IT operations have become decentralized to some degree.

☒ **A, C,** and **D** are not correct because the solution meets all required and some optional results.

16. ☑ **C.** The main reason for TCO analysis is to expose the hidden costs of a product over its life cycle. TCO is not limited to Windows 2000 software. TCO is an all-encompassing view of the network that includes the costs of hardware, training, labor, and installations and maintenance.

☒ **A** is not correct. TCO is not limited to annual costs. **B** is not correct. Although CEOs and other executive staff in an organization look at TCO data, it is not used to understand the network architecture in any direct way. **D** is not correct. Reviewing TCO data does not directly result in security decisions, although it is recommended that TCO data be utilized when discussing security policy and the costs of implementing various security measures.

17. ☑ **B.** Internal users are more likely to breach security because they already have physical access to the network, they understand naming and password schemes, and they may have an in-depth understanding of network security.

☒ **A** is not correct. Although hackers receive a lot of publicity, the threat they pose to your network security is lower than internal threats. **C** is not correct for the same reason. **D** is not correct. Industrial espionage is not a common occurrence. Although the damage that can be done can be significant, the greater threat is internal.

18. ☑ **A** and **C** are correct. With more availability of bandwidth options than ever before, organizations can choose connection speeds based on company requirements, including budget constraints.

☒ **B** is not correct. If your network has file and print sharing turned on, your network will be more vulnerable to hackers when using DSL, cable, and dial-up access. However, simply having folders open on the desktop will not cause any major security hazards in you system. **D** is not correct. Printing speed is not related to connectivity unless you are printing at a remote site and your bandwidth is low.

LAB ANSWER

Objectives 2.01–2.03

1. Determine the company structure, including how divisions, departments, and locations interact.

2. Identify any planned mergers, acquisitions, and restructuring of corporate resources.

3. Map out current network topology and resources.

4. Identify current and planned network connectivity such as remote sites or remote access.

5. Determine if servers meet minimum (or optimal) hardware and software requirements.

6. Identify total cost of ownership for the network, or begin to collect data to quantify various costs.

7. Identify budget guidelines or constraints.

8. Identify security needs for users, departments, data types, and access types.

9. Identify current or planned technology strategies (for example, remote access, Internet, Web-based applications, and e-commerce).

10. Identify IT structure: centralized, decentralized, or outsourced.

Clearly, there are many factors that should be assessed in any network plan. The items listed are high-level factors that relate to the topics in this chapter and should be assessed when creating a migration plan.

MCSE
MICROSOFT CERTIFIED SYSTEMS ENGINEER

3

Analyzing End User Computing Requirements

T his chapter focuses on analyzing the business and security requirements for end users. It also reviews analysis of current physical and information security models for the network. Business requirements are defined by executives, administrators, and technical groups. End users can be comprised of employees, contractors, trusted partners, or the public. Each user group has specific needs that must be addressed while maintaining high levels of security. Users need to connect to network resources with a high degree of availability and reliability while working locally or remotely.

The analysis of current physical and information security includes reviewing the physical security of the building, server rooms, and equipment. Information security models are concerned with how files, printers, servers, and other network resources can be secured.

TEST YOURSELF OBJECTIVE 3.01

Analyzing Business and Security Requirements for the End User

Business requirements include executive perspectives on competitors, market conditions, financial conditions, and other high-level company needs. Administrator perspectives include the overall design of the network and of IT strategies. These should fit strategically with the high-level needs expressed by the executives of the company. The technical group is concerned with implementing these plans. The exam will test your skills in deciding whether proposed solutions meet the needs of these diverse groups.

End users require various kinds of access: local, remote, secure, and anonymous. The exam will focus on meeting end user computing needs while maintaining a highly secure network. Balancing the needs of end users and security measures is key. This section will review the security concerns of executives, administrators, and technicians. It will also cover the security requirements for users and applications, both local and remote.

- Executives view the business at the highest level, including competitors and the industry.
- Administrators view the business in terms of designing the network (domains, topology) and security policies.
- Technicians implement the plans and policies, and administer and manage the day-to-day network operations.
- User communities include Everyone (anonymous access), Staff (employees), Users (grouped by function), and Partners (members of other companies).

- Local users connect to the network via the local area network (LAN) and are physically present at the company's facility.

- Remote users are outside the facility and can connect via Routing and Remote Access Service (RRAS)—direct dial-up—or VPN—via an ISP through the Internet.

- Public users access information via corporate Internet Web sites.

- Trusted partners access data either locally or remotely, similar to company employees.

- Applications can be classified by user group to ease installation and administration.

- Applications can be made available via Windows 2000 Terminal Services, which provides ease of installation and administration and bandwidth-efficient computing for end users on a variety of hardware platforms.

exam !
⚙atch *Many of the scenario-based questions include interviews with various company stakeholders such as executives, administrators, and end users. You will need to find the optimal solution given the requirements of these groups. When taking the exam, it's a good practice to write down a phrase for each requirement for each group. This will assist in focusing in on the problem. These phrases can be used as a checklist when reading proposed solutions, ensuring that you address each of the concerns on your list. When several solutions appear to be correct, choose the one that utilizes the newest features of Windows 2000.*

QUESTIONS

3.01: Analyzing Business and Security Requirements for the End User

1. "Our competitor just announced that their application was completely browser-based and will be available on their Web site next month." This statement reflects the concerns of which group?

   A. End user

    B. Administrator

    C. Technical

    D. Executive

2. What security need is addressed by the following illustration?

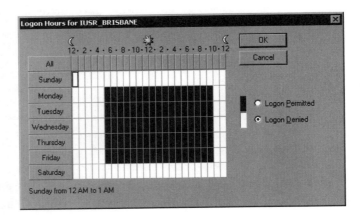

    A. Network availability policy

    B. Group security settings

    C. Restricting end user access

    D. Domain logon hours settings

3. **Current Situation:** Your company has just increased its sales force by 60 percent. Each representative has been given a P800 laptop and an account with a national ISP for Internet connectivity. Representatives are expected to use a new Web-based application for recording customer contacts and the status of various deals. They also are accustomed to using a Web-based email system for communicating with corporate and client contacts.

    Required Results: You must identify the concerns of the executive, administrator, technical, and end user.

    Optional Desired Results: Identify at least two areas that are new security risks for your company and two methods of mitigating those risks.

Proposed Solution:

Executive Increase sales and return on investment of increased staff and laptops.

Administrator Design secure access to Web application and email.

Technical Implement secure access to Web application. Ensure that application and data are secure. Ensure that end users can connect as needed to Web application and email.

End user Ease-of-use with ISP account, on-demand access to application and email, and backups of critical data on laptop.

New security risks Internet access of Web application and email.

Mitigate risks Enable event auditing for all successful logon attempts. Install antivirus software to avoid virus infection from email attachments.

What results are produced from the proposed solution?

A. The proposed solution produces the required results and all of the optional results.

B. The proposed solution produces the required results and some of the optional results.

C. The proposed solution produces the required results only.

D. The proposed solution does not produce the required results.

Questions 4–9 This scenario should be used to answer questions 4, 5, 6, 7, 8, and 9.

Your CEO tells you the following information: Due to changes in regulations enforced by the SEC, our company may have to start charging sales tax on all sales generated from our Web site. This could have a tremendous impact on our financial reporting.

Your CIO tells you the following information: Our Web site sales have increased to the point that four servers are being overwhelmed between 11:00A.M. and 2:00P.M. almost every day. Three days ago, the Web site was so bogged down that users were getting denial of service (DOS). We're putting together a plan right now to deal with that.

Your vice president of sales tells you the following information: In the past month or so, my sales representatives have had trouble logging onto the Web site to do their jobs. Several times, it appeared as though the servers were down because some of the representatives got very strange, garbled messages. We need better access to resources in order to continue to increase our sales.

4. As the IT director, what security risks do you see? (Choose all that apply.)

   A. Possible virus on sales representatives' laptops

   B. Possible attack on Web site

   C. Loss of critical data on laptops

   D. Unauthorized access to network resources

5. Rank the following business risks to your organization from highest to lowest.

   A. Loss of revenue from Web site sales

   B. Loss of productivity for sales representatives attempting to use site

   C. Changing SEC regulations

   D. Loss of consumer confidence

6. Which solution would best address end user concerns?

   A. Bring another server online that is dedicated solely to sales representatives.

   B. Analyze traffic on four existing servers and enable auditing and event logging.

   C. Increase bandwidth to Internet for all four servers.

   D. Increase RAM on all sales representatives' laptops.

7. Which methods can be used to manage connections to an application deployed using Terminal Services? (Choose all that apply.)

   A. Distribution groups

   B. Group policies

   C. Remote access policies

   D. Built-in groups

8. An executive of the company is concerned about network security. The technician in charge of security is asked to provide information about the total cost of various security implementations. In terms of cost vs. security, which solutions provide the highest security for the lowest cost? (Choose two.)

   A. Smart cards using EAP-TLS security

    B. L2TP with IPSec for VPN connections

    C. PPTP with IPSec using 128-bit encryption for VPN connections

    D. Digital certificates

9. The administrative group within your organization would be involved with which of the following tasks? (Choose all that apply.)

    A. Placing users in security groups

    B. Implementing subnets

    C. Transitioning from an X.25 to a Frame Relay connection

    D. Reviewing the competitors' Web site capabilities

TEST YOURSELF OBJECTIVE 3.02

Analyzing the Current Physical Model and Information Security Model

The physical security model is defined by the physical aspects of the network: the facility, the server rooms, desktop computers, printers, and even cables. These can be secured via limiting physical access to an area or a specific piece of equipment. The security model describes how information is secured. Files and folders, hard drives, and data storage media can be secured both physically and logically, and data communication can be encrypted. Determining the best way to secure the physical environment and critical data for your company is the focus of this section.

- Physical security must involve the facility, the data center (servers), and user workstations.

- Data can be protected by authenticating users at logon, New Technology File System (NTFS) file permissions, and Encrypting File System (EFS) encryption methods.

- Security risks are both internal and external to the organization. Internal threats typically involve authorized users attempting to gain unauthorized access to data on the network.

- External threats include intentional and unintentional attacks. Trojan horses and viruses are the most common external threats.

exam
Ⓦatch

The exam emphasizes external and mobile computing concerns. Understanding external concerns such as the differences among a virus, a Trojan horse, and a DOS attack, as well as methods to counteract these attacks are important aspects of successfully passing the exam. Mobile computing security risks are also highlighted on the exam. Typically, questions focus on how mobile users can connect securely to corporate resources and how data can be protected on mobile devices. Be familiar with dial-up vs. VPN connections as well as the protocols and methods used for authentication and securing data communications.

QUESTIONS

3.02: Analyzing the Current Physical Model and Information Security Model

Questions 10–12   This scenario should be used to answer questions 10, 11, and 12.

You've started a new job and have been told by another system administrator that the following security measures are currently being implemented:

■ Physically securing servers within locked cabinets

■ Encrypting shared folders on servers

■ Requiring keycard access to server rooms

■ Removing all backup media to an offsite location daily

10.   Which would not be a legitimate security measure for corporate servers?

A.   Physically securing servers within locked cabinets

B.   Encrypting shared folders on servers

C.   Requiring keycard access to server rooms

D.   Removing all backup media to an offsite location daily

11. In addition to the security measures listed, what other method could be used to secure the servers? (Choose all that apply.)

    A. Requiring the use of smart cards for all server logons

    B. Implementing Certificate Services on each server

    C. Renaming the administrator account

    D. Auditing all successful logons for the administrator account

12. Which security risks are addressed by using the settings highlighted in the following illustration? (Choose all that apply.)

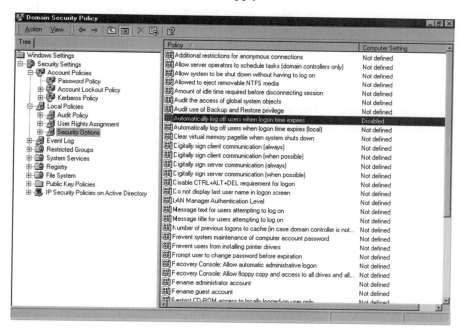

    A. Physical security

    B. Information security

    C. Desktop configuration security

    D. External security

13. **Current Situation:** You are responsible for security for all network resources at your company. A recent theft resulted in the loss of eight laptops and two laser printers from employee work areas.

    Required Results: Secure network equipment in the facility from theft. Provide a method of monitoring physical access to equipment. Ensure that security measures do not unduly restrain legitimate users.

    Optional Desired Results: Ensure that data communications are secure for laptop users outside the facility and that data is secure.

    Proposed Solution: Require all employees to check in with security and to sign in and out during standard and non-working hours. Require all to have a property removal form signed by management each time equipment is brought in or out of the building. Install video cameras in areas where theft is likely to occur such as secluded areas or areas near exit doors. Provide cable locks for docking stations and for employees using laptops in the building. Install printers in locking cabinets. Use NTFS on all laptops and use EFS encryption on the My Documents folder on laptops.

    What results are produced from the proposed solution?

    A. The proposed solution produces the required results and all of the optional results.

    B. The proposed solution produces the required results and some of the optional results.

    C. The proposed solution produces the required results only.

    D. The proposed solution does not produce the required results.

14. Which are components of strong password policies? (Choose all that apply.)

    A. Set password history to remember last eight passwords.

    B. Require complex passwords comprised of letters, numbers, and special characters.

    C. Require passwords to be at least six characters long.

    D. Encourage the use of common words so users will not write down their passwords in order to remember them.

15. How often should Incremental backups be performed?

    A. Daily on all servers and desktops

B. Weekly on servers only

C. Daily on servers only

D. Weekly on all servers and desktops

16. What are the three recommended ways to manage trusted partner access to your corporate network?

A. Create a separate domain for the partner organization, create a one-way trust relationship, and require the use of strong passwords.

B. Create a separate domain within the organizational unit, create a one-way explicit trust relationship between the networks (both must be Windows 2000–based networks), and require the use of EFS file encryption.

C. Create an organizational unit for each partner organization, create a one-way explicit trust relationship between networks (both must be Windows 2000–based networks), and require the use of third-party certificates for user authentication.

D. Create an organizational unit for each user in the partner organization, create a two-way explicit trust (so users on both networks can communicate with one another), and install a Certificate Server on your network.

17. Your network currently allows users to dial in to access email. What solution could you implement to ensure greater security for email?

A. Implement SSL with TLS.

B. Implement SGC.

C. Implement X.509 digital certificates and PKI technology.

D. Implement Authenticode Services in Exchange.

18. Your company has set a group policy that performs several different audits. The first audit event set is the success and failure for file access and object access. What will this help detect?

A. Random password hacks

B. Improper access to sensitive files

C. Misuse of privileges

D. Virus outbreak

19. The second audit event set is the success and failure of write access for program files. What will this help detect?

    A. Random password hacks

    B. Improper access to sensitive files

    C. Misuse of privileges

    D. Virus outbreak

20. A user changes the security settings for the root folder on a database server. This action would be logged if you were auditing what type of events?

    A. Failure audit for logon/logoff

    B. Success audit for changes to user rights, user and group management, security change policies, system shutdown

    C. Success audit for logon/logoff

    D. Failure audit for changes to user rights, user and group management, security change policies, system shutdown

LAB QUESTION

Objectives 3.01–3.02

You are the network administrator for an expanding pet food distribution firm, Jawbone, Inc. Jawbone wants you to devise a solution so that nationwide sales representatives can gain access to the financial application required to do their jobs. Currently, these sales representatives are running a number of different financial applications on their individual desktops and laptops. The cost of supporting and upgrading multiple applications that perform the same function is becoming prohibitive. One of these same applications is used by the Finance group at Jawbone headquarters. They access the application via the LAN. Additionally, the sales representatives need to send their weekly sales data to the director of sales at Jawbone headquarters. These typically large Excel spreadsheets average 50KB to 100KB per file. A sales representative may have to send two to four of these per week, depending on various business factors.

The president of the company has specifically told you that she expects this application deployment to be seamless. She has a meeting with the industry analysts in 90 days, and this application must be up and running by then. The CIO mentioned to you in the hallway yesterday that he expected you to use the latest technologies and to ensure that the financial data transmitted by the sales representatives is absolutely secure. He also mentioned that he didn't want to see a large financial expenditure to get this done, since the company was in its last fiscal quarter of the year and is over budget on a number of items. In fact, he mentioned cutting costs as a way to help ensure that your pending promotion comes through.

What solution would you recommend for deploying this financial application? Support your recommendation with specific data.

QUICK ANSWER KEY

Objective 3.01	
1.	D
2.	C
3.	B
4.	A and B
5.	B, A, D, C
6.	A
7.	B, C
8.	B and D
9.	C and D

Objective 3.02	
10.	B
11.	A and C
12.	B
13.	D
14.	A and B
15.	C
16.	C
17.	C
18.	C
19.	D
20.	B

IN-DEPTH ANSWERS

3.01: Analyzing Business and Security Requirements for the End User

1. ☑ **D.** The executive group is concerned with high-level issues surrounding the environment in which the company operates, including regulatory, competitive, and market conditions.

   ☒ **A** is not correct. End users are concerned with utilizing network resources to accomplish their jobs. **B** is not correct. Administrators are responsible for planning and designing network solutions that reflect the needs of the company. **C** is not correct. The technical group is responsible for the implementation and daily operations of the network technology components.

2. ☑ **C.** End-user access can be set by specifically permitting or denying logon any time. This enhances security by ensuring that legitimate users are not abusing logon rights at times they should not be connected to the network.

   ☒ **A** is not correct. The network is always available (or should be), but access can be controlled on a per-user or per-group basis. **B** is not correct. Restricting logon hours can, and should, be set by placing users in groups and then restricting the logon hours of an entire group. However, the illustration does not reflect a group setting. **D** is not correct. Logon hours are not set for the domain but for users or groups.

3. ☑ **B.** The proposed solution produces the required results by addressing the concerns of the executive, administrative, technical and end user groups. The proposed solution identifies one new security risk: Web-based application. Email is not a new security risk for the company as end users are "accustomed to using a Web-based email system." Enabling successful logon attempts will not mitigate risk for the Web-based application. Therefore, the proposed solution only produces one of the two optional results.

   ☒ **A** , **C**, and **D** are not correct. The proposed solution produces the required results and only one of the two optional results.

4. ☑ **A** and **B** are correct. The strange garbled messages could indicate a virus. Both the garbled messages and the slow Web response with servers being overwhelmed could indicate an attack on the Web site. Notice the executive concerns about collecting sales tax are important, but do not pose a security threat. If you are responsible for network planning, you will need to begin contingency planning for handling state sales tax, should the regulations go through, but this is superfluous information in light of possible security risks.

   ☒ **C** is not correct. There is no indication that data on laptops is being lost. **D** is not correct. There is no indication that anyone has breached the firewall. It is possible an attack to slow or halt the Web site is occurring, but there is no indication that any unauthorized use of network resources has occurred.

5. ☑ **B, A, D**, and **C** is the correct order. Loss of productivity seems to be the highest business risk. In this business model, revenue is generated from both Web sales and from sales representatives. These reps need access to the Web site in order to conduct business. While the Web site has slowed and been overwhelmed, there is no evidence presented that indicates sales have slowed, although this is a significant risk. Therefore, loss of revenue from Web sales is listed as second. Due to the slowing of servers, loss of consumer confidence is the third risk, as it ties directly with loss of revenue. When servers slow or stop, consumers quickly lose confidence in the company's products and services. The lowest risk is changing SEC regulations, primarily because it is less immediate. Plans must be made to address pending regulatory changes, but it is important to deal with the immediate problem of the Web servers being overwhelmed first.

6. ☑ **A.** One solution would be to bring a dedicated Web server online that is used for sales representatives. This would allow the existing four servers to be dedicated to Web sales. This would improve throughput for end users and customers.

   ☒ **B** is not correct. Analyzing traffic on the four servers might assist in determining whether the company's Web site is being attacked; auditing could also assist in this process. However, auditing tends to slow down servers by logging various events. This could actually make the situation worse for the end users. **C** is not correct. If servers are being overwhelmed at current bandwidth, increasing bandwidth will only make the problem worse. If server capacity is significantly increased, increasing bandwidth can improve the end user experience by providing faster response times. **D** is not correct. The problem appears to be with corporate servers, not laptops.

7. ☑ **B** and **C** are correct. Group policies can be used to manage computers on the network, including computers running Terminal Services. Remote access policies also can be used to manage connections to a Terminal Services server. Management of the connection can include security requirements and logon duration, among other things.

   ☒ **A** is not correct. Distribution groups are used only for purposes of distribution lists such as email or company information. **D** is not correct. Built-in groups are default groups within Windows 2000 such as Power Users. While these groups could be given permissions related to a Terminal Services application, this is not the primary purpose of built-in user groups in Windows 2000.

8. ☑ **B** and **D** are correct. L2TP with IPSec provides a very high level of security. L2TP creates a secure tunnel connection. IPSec provides end-to-end data encryption. This is a very secure solution and can be implemented without additional hardware or software. A VPN Server must be established as part of this solution. This capability is built into Windows 2000. Digital certificates can be a low-cost solution in many cases. Internal certificates can be generated by Certificate Services within the domain as part of a Windows 2000 solution. However, third-party certificates can add cost to this solution.

   ☒ **A** is not correct. Although smart cards provide a very secure solution, it requires the purchasing of the smart cards as well as smart card readers for every computer that will require this type of logon. This provides very high security but at a higher cost than L2TP with IPSec. **C** is not correct. PPTP is an implementation of the PPP protocols but cannot utilize IPSec. In order to utilize IPSec in Windows 2000, you must use L2TP.

9. ☑ **C** and **D** are correct. Transitioning from an X.25 to a Frame Relay connection for a branch or location would fall under the administrative function. This is a high-level decision based on both strategic and tactical information. The actual implementation of this transition would be handled by the technical group. Reviewing competitors' Web sites would also be an administrative function. While portions of this task may be delegated to technicians, this is part of the administrative function—to ensure that the company's technology helps the company remain competitive based on decisions made at the executive level.

   ☒ **A** is not correct. Placing users in groups would be done by the technical group with guidance from the policies and procedures defined by the executive and administrative groups. **B** is not correct. Implementing subnets is a task that would be performed by the technical group. The administrative group may identify the need for subnets to optimize network performance (although this could also be done by the technical group), but the implementation of any physical changes would be handled by the technical group.

3.02: Analyzing the Current Physical Model and Information Security Model

10. ☑ **B.** Encrypting shared folders on servers would not provide an added measure of security. Although sharing files creates a security risk, corporate networks are typically in place for exactly that purpose—to share information easily. Data in shared folders should not be encrypted because only the person who owns the file can decrypt that file. This defeats the purpose of shared files and folders. In addition, encryption can significantly degrade performance, if applied inappropriately.

   ☒ **A** is not correct. Securing the servers in locked cabinets is a legitimate security measure a company can take to limit physical access to equipment. **C** is not correct. Requiring keycard access to server rooms limits the physical access to servers. **D** is not correct. Removing backup media daily can ensure that unauthorized personnel do not take the media and use it on another machine to gain access to data.

11. ☑ **A** and **C** are correct. Smart cards require the user to place a card into a card-reading device at the computer in order to log on. This requirement can be enforced through Group Policies so that if the smart card reader is detached or if the card is removed, the computer is locked. This strong enforcement can secure computers, including servers. Renaming the administrator account is a recommended policy. This secures the administrator account, which can be used to manage all network resources, including servers.

   ☒ **B** is not correct. Certificates can provide additional security, but Certificate Services would not be implemented on each server. **D** is not correct. Successful logons for the administrator account would tell you if an unauthorized user had managed to gain access to the administrator account, but this is not used to secure a server.

12. ☑ **B.** The illustration shows that the option to forcibly disconnect users is disabled. This means that users whose logon hours have expired can continue to work with resources to which they have already established a connection but cannot establish new connections. Restricting logon hours or forcibly disconnecting users is a method of information security. These options can be enabled, for instance, if backups require files to be closed and the network administrator wants to ensure that all users are off the system prior to initiating backups.

☒ **A** is not correct. Logon hour restrictions or forcible disconnects do not physically protect computers or servers. **C** is not correct. Desktop configuration is not impacted by user logon hours policies. Group policies can be implemented to configure or protect the configuration of the desktop. **D** is not correct. Most security breaches occur within the organization. External security is not directly addressed via logon hour or forcible disconnect policies. It is assumed that the user, whether connected locally or remotely, is a legitimate user during normal logon hours and therefore is not considered an external security risk.

13. ☑ **D.** Required results are as follows: secure equipment from loss, monitor physical access, and take measures that do not hamper legitimate users. The proposed solution meets the first two required results. By requiring security check in as well as sign in/out, physical access is monitored. By securing laptops with cable locks, equipment is secured from loss. However, locking printers in cabinets will impede the use of those printers by making print outs inaccessible. In addition, requiring a signed form each time a user brings a laptop in or out of the building poses an undue burden for laptop users and encourages circumvention of the rules. If this type of monitoring is desired, have users and managers sign a form that covers a period of time (such as a month or a quarter, depending on how laptops are used). If needed, have security check bags each time users leave and reference the signed forms for authorization.

☒ **A**, **B**, and **C** are not correct because the solution does not produce the required results. The solution does address one of the two optional results by using NTFS and EFS. It does not address secure communications.

14. ☑ **A** and **B** are correct. Password history prevents a user from re-using a password too often, making guessing passwords more difficult. Requiring the use of letters, numbers, and special characters (such as #, $, @) makes dictionary attacks and guessing of passwords more difficult.

☒ **C** is not correct. In order to be considered a strong password, it should contain at least eight characters. **D** is not correct. Although strong password policies should not be so complex as to cause users to write down passwords, using common words, such as names of children or pets, is not a practice that should be encouraged as it leaves the system vulnerable to brute force, dictionary, and other password-breaking attacks.

15. ☑ **C.** Incremental backups provide a copy of data that has changed since the last backup. Typically, a Full backup is performed weekly (depending on your company's data needs) and an Incremental backup is performed each day in between.

☒ **A** is not correct. There is generally no reason to perform backups on desktops daily. If critical data is being used, it should be saved to a network location to be backed up when servers are backed up. **B** is not correct. Performing a weekly Incremental backup on servers would leave the company vulnerable to data loss. If the backup is performed on Saturdays and a hardware failure wipes out a RAID system on a Friday, all data for the preceding week would be lost. **D** is not correct. A weekly Incremental backup for servers, as stated, would leave the company vulnerable to data loss. Weekly Incremental backups of desktops could be used, but saving critical data to servers is a more efficient and cost-effective solution.

16. ☑ **C.** Place each partner in an organizational unit for ease of administration. If both firms are running Windows 2000–based networks, a one-way trust can be implemented. Finally, requiring the use of third-party certificates will ensure the authentication of remote partner access.

☒ **A** is incorrect. It is not necessary to create a domain for your partner organization. Strong passwords are not enough to ensure remote access authentication, though they can be used as part of an overall strategy. **B** is incorrect. You cannot create a domain within an organizational unit. Also, EFS will secure data on local drives, but is not involved in remote user authentication. **D** is incorrect. You do not create organizational units for individual users. You do not want to create a two-way trust with a partner organization; communication among domains is bi-directional, even with one-way trusts. Finally, a Certificate Services server can be installed on your network, but you should require third-party certificates for all external partners so your organization is not burdened with maintaining and administering all certificates. In cases where a limited number of partner organizations or employees needs to gain network access, a stand-alone certificate authority in your network could provide the needed certificates rather than a third-party certificate authority.

17. ☑ **C.** X.509 digital certificates used in S/MIME (Secure/Multipurpose Internet Mail Extensions) systems provide secure email communications. Senders can digitally sign email messages to provide data integrity and email cannot easily be decrypted without proper credentials.

　☒ **A** is not correct. SSL is associated with security on Web sites. **B** is not correct. SGC (Server Gated Cryptography) is used to secure financial transactions via Web sites. **D** is not correct. Authenticode is used to digitally sign software to ensure users that the code has not been tampered with. This technology also uses X.509 technology but is used to sign software, not email.

18. ☑ **B.** Improper access can be monitored by auditing the success and failure for file and object access. Auditing sensitive files or objects will help detect improper access without bogging down the system with auditing events.

　☒ **A** is not correct. Auditing file and object access will not help you determine that a password has been compromised. **C** is not correct. Misuse of privileges would not be detected by auditing file and object access. Privileges are the rights users are given based on their user account and group membership. **D** is not correct. A virus outbreak would not be detected using this method.

19. ☑ **D.** A virus often will attempt to modify program files. However, because this auditing will monitor programs using .EXE and .DLL extensions, the log file could quickly become huge. Run the suspected programs with monitoring enabled. Examine security logs for unexpected attempts to modify program files or create unexpected processes. Run only when actively monitoring the system log.

　☒ **A** is not correct. Auditing write access of program files will not assist in detecting random password hacks. **B** is not correct. Improper access to sensitive files could be a result of a virus or a person gaining improper access to resources. This is better detected using success and failure audit for file and object access. **C** is not correct. Misuse of privileges will not be detected by auditing success and failure of write access for program files. Typically, program files (files with .EXE and .DLL extensions) can only be modified through programming or other software, not through user access.

20. ☑ **B.** Successful use of user rights such as changing user rights, user or group account information, or security changes would indicate misuse of user privileges. Users in groups such as Backup Operators group or Power Users group may use their privileges in an unauthorized manner. Auditing successful changes enables the network administrator to monitor changes and the users implementing those changes.

☒ **A** is not correct. A failure audit for logon/logoff would help you detect possible password hacks. **C** is not correct. Success audit for logon/logoff would help detect stolen passwords. **D** is not correct. Failure audit for changes to user rights is less useful than a success audit. Failure in these events could be caused by a number of harmless incidents such as typing errors on the part of the user. Successful changes, however, would be far more important to monitor. To minimize the size of the audit log, limit auditing to meaningful events.

LAB ANSWER

Objectives 3.01–3.02

- Eliminate the use of multiple applications and standardize on one financial application. Deploy the application using Terminal Services.

- Put all remote sales representatives in a Sales group. Allow VPN access for all sales representatives in this group.

- Have sales representatives use the financial application via Terminal Services, and use VPN (using L2TP with IPSec for end-to-end encryption) via local ISPs for their remote access.

- Have all sales representatives using laptops install Windows 2000 Professional, and use NTFS and EFS to encrypt critical data. For all desktop users with adequate hardware requirements, install Windows 2000 Professional and use NTFS and EFS as well.

- For all files to be sent to the director of sales, save files in an encrypted folder (My Documents) on the laptop, transmit files via VPN to restricted network share for access by director.

- All internal members of the Finance group can access the financial application via the Terminal Services or via a network installation, depending on intranet and Internet access at headquarters.

MICROSOFT CERTIFIED SYSTEMS ENGINEER

4

Analyzing Technical Requirements

T his chapter examines evaluation of existing and planned technical environments and the impact of security design on that environment. The technical environment includes the size of a company, the current and planned network design and infrastructure, and issues such as scalability, administration, and connectivity. Analyzing the impact of security on the technical environment includes assessing the current security model, current and future corporate security needs, and the impact of security on users, network resources, and corporate resources. In planning the technical requirements and the security model, it is important to find a balance between security and accessibility; between reasonable measures and excessive measures. For example, if your company has five employees, utilizing end-to-end encryption with IPSec on the network may not make sense. This chapter prepares you for exam questions related to planning security in the technical environment.

TEST YOURSELF OBJECTIVE 4.01

Evaluating the Company's Existing and Planned Technical Environment

The technical environment at a company has many facets. The size of a company and how it is organized will influence how the network components are organized. Branches and sites will influence network topology and connectivity. Number of users and number of resources will influence logical structures, such as domains and organizational units, as well as physical structures, such as sites, site links, servers (number and capacity), and desktops/laptops for users. Understanding the company's future plans that may impact the technical environment is also important. Transitioning to new technologies, such as Windows 2000–based networks, supporting handheld devices, or expanding services for wireless connections, all impact the technical environment.

- The number of users and computers, the number of locations, and the connection methods are three important factors in determining the level of security necessary for your network.

- Building a scalable network is critical for allowing quick growth in a network capable of supporting local and remote users as well as users at branch locations.

- As an administrator, a homogeneous network is of great assistance to you for accomplishing your work. Knowing the hardware and software configurations for your network makes network administration and security more consistent.

- Many companies are beginning to use their connections for a wide array of applications such as voice-over IP (VoIP), teleconferencing, application service providers (ASPs), and full service providers (FSPs).

- Whenever possible, connect separated departmental LANs into the corporate network.

exam
⚠️atch

The MCP exam for designing security uses scenario-based questions that involve multiple company locations in the United States and abroad. Typical questions involve the following: using Windows 2000–based networks and one or two Windows NT 4.0 servers; developing site links and connectivity; securing communication technologies for branches and remote users; and assessing the technical requirements for secure, Web-based solutions. Remember that Native mode uses all Windows 2000–based servers and Mixed mode uses Windows 2000 and other servers (typically Windows NT 4.0). Certain features of Windows 2000 cannot be used in a mixed environment. Scenario questions that involve non–Windows 2000–based technology should be reviewed carefully to assess the limitations of a mixed network in the technology environment.

QUESTIONS

4.01: Evaluating the Company's Existing and Planned Technical Environment

1. You were recently promoted to IT director. You have been asked to evaluate your company's entire IT strategy. What should be considered when evaluating your company's technical environment? (Choose all that apply.)

    A. The roles and responsibilities of administrators and users

    B. The cost of equipment and labor for all technology components

    C. The size of the organization and number of users and locations

    D. B and C only

2. As part of the existing technical environment at your company, what does the following diagram illustrate? (Choose all that apply.)

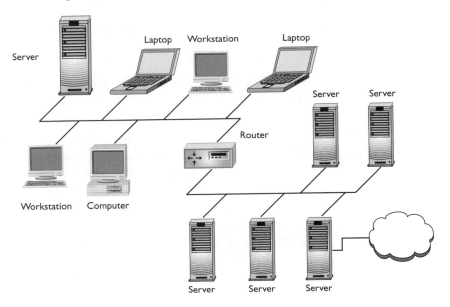

A. Heterogeneous environment

B. Homogeneous environment

C. Web server with firewall or DMZ components

D. Inadequate network bandwidth

3. For server clusters, the ability to incrementally add a server to an existing cluster when the demand exceeds the capacity of the cluster is an example of what?

A. Processor expansion slot

B. Scalability

C. Cluster fail over

D. Cluster Port Extensibility (CPE)

4. **Current Situation:** Your company has eight locations. Two are in the United States, two in Australia, two in France, and two in Russia. Your network has 50,000 users worldwide, approximately 15,000 of whom travel extensively. Your company headquarters is located in New York City.

Required Result: Develop a plan to provide effective support for all locations worldwide.

Optional Desired Result: Improve efficiency of network administration and lower costs.

Proposed Solution: Hire an outsourcing firm with international locations to manage help desk calls from users. Hire an external firm to supplement the local IT staff by providing on-site network support to each of the eight locations. Create domains based on whether the sites can complete replication reliably and in an acceptable time frame. Decentralize administration through the use of OUs. Provide 24/7 second-tier support at headquarters for all locations worldwide. Contract with ISPs to provide local access numbers worldwide to traveling users. Allow users to connect via VPN rather than dial-up access.

What results are produced from the proposed solution?

A. The proposed solution produces the required result and all of the optional results.

B. The proposed solution produces the required result and some of the optional results.

C. The proposed solution produces the required result only.

D. The proposed solution does not produce the required result.

5. You have a friend who owns a business with 16 employees. He's seeking a cost-effective, higher bandwidth communications option. What is an ideal connection choice for his business? (Choose all that apply.)

A. Cable

B. DSL

C. Fiber optic

D. T1

6. Your company would like to allow users to have remote access to corporate resources. Under what circumstances would you most likely choose to implement IAS?

A. If you have no Remote Access Servers (RAS) currently in place

B. If you have a small number of Remote Access Servers in place

C. If you have a large number of Remote Access Servers in place

D. If you cannot utilize RADIUS due to bandwidth constraints

7. When planning a full migration to Windows 2000 for the network seen in the following illustration, what would be three main concerns?

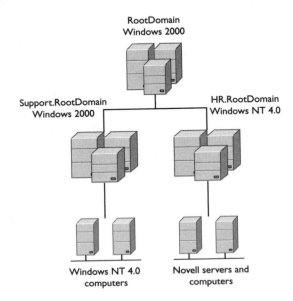

A. Capacity of current Novell servers, planning domain structure, and upgrading LAN capacity

B. Planning domain structure, reviewing HCL for Windows 2000, and planning and implementing secure authentication protocols

C. Capacity of current Novell servers, capacity of network, and planning and implementing secure authentication protocols

D. Planning domain structure, planning and implementing secure authentication protocols, and reviewing server and desktop group policies

8. If your company plans to expand overseas, what is the primary communications security limitation you'll face?

A. Cannot use 128-bit encryption for communications outside the United States

B. Cannot use 56-bit encryption for communications outside the United States

C. Cannot use 128-bit encryption for communications outside North America

D. Cannot use 128-bit encryption for communications in North America

9. Your company has a Web site that uses SSL. You'd like to create a secure section of your Web for registered users. What protocol could you implement to ensure secure user authentication?

A. HTTPS

B. WAP

C. SLIP

D. MS-CHAP

TEST YOURSELF OBJECTIVE 4.02

Analyzing the Impact of the Security Design on the Existing and Planned Technical Environment

Security design must include internal security, external security (including remote users and Internet connections), and intersite security for communication between sites or locations of a company. This section reviews the impact of security design on current and existing technology solutions. Security must reflect the needs of the organization and the capabilities of the technology, both current and planned. Over-engineering a security solution can lead to excessive costs, degraded system performance, and frustrated users.

- ■ Prioritize connectivity between satellite field offices or telecommuters and the corporate network.

- ■ If only a limited or deficient amount of service is made available, your users will become dissatisfied with your network's operations.

- ■ Software piracy is any occurrence in which an original computer program is copied without authorization from the author or publishing company.

■ It is critical to update your company servers' virus patterns as often as possible.

■ Whenever possible, management should schedule maintenance and upgrades during windows of time that will cause minimal service disruption.

■ In some cases, the strongest security possible is unnecessary. If data sensitivity is low, high-level security is an unjustified and costly solution.

exam***!***
Ⓦatch
Prioritizing connectivity with remote locations and remote users is a topic that comes up frequently on this exam. Remote considerations are speed of connection, data sensitivity, and user requirements. Speed of connection will dictate how often replication occurs among sites, how an application should be deployed, and how much network traffic can be handled. Data sensitivity will dictate user authentication methods and data encryption requirements. User requirements will influence decisions regarding 24/7 access, dial-in or VPN connectivity, access to line-of-business applications, and Web access. A clear understanding of each of these areas will help you assess the best answer for each exam question related to technology and security.

QUESTIONS

4.02: Analyzing the Impact of the Security Design on the Existing and Planned Technical Environment

10.   Your new CIO is performing a cost/benefit analysis of all network security currently implemented. What are costs associated with implementing strong security policies? (Choose all that apply.)

A.   Increased administration and technical support

B.   Loss of ability to perform packet filtering and content monitoring

C.   Loss of productivity

D.   Increased RAID drive capacity

11. Refer to the following illustration. Your company is acquiring a new firm with one location (Site 4). That site has 25 servers, which will be added to the existing domain. The existing domain has servers as follows: Site 1 (35 servers), Site 2 (48 servers), and Site 3 (23 servers). Given the speed of the connections between the sites, what is the most important technology issue you will have to deal with?

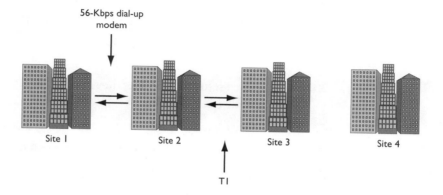

A. Security risk via Site 1 dial-up access.

B. Slow link between Site 1 and Site 2 means replication traffic may never complete.

C. Site 4 can only be connected to Site 3 via a dial-up 56-Kbps connection to mirror the site link between Site 1 and Site 2.

D. Adding Site 4 to the domain exceeds the maximum number of servers (128) allowed in a domain.

12. **Current Situation:** Data security has become a concern at your growing, international company. Your CEO has asked you to develop a plan for improving data security.

Required Results: Improve overall security and encrypt transmissions for all sensitive data. Implement virus detection and correction capabilities.

Optional Desired Results: Improve overall network performance, improve end user satisfaction, and lower or maintain costs.

Proposed Solution: Use end-to-end data encryption for all internal and external network traffic. Install virus-scanning software purchased in last quarter but never installed. Obtain virus updates from software manufacturer via Web site. Upgrade network from 10MB to 100MB Ethernet. Create policies to restrict user logon hours and forcibly disconnect when logon hours expire.

What results are produced from the proposed solution?

A. The proposed solution produces the required results and all of the optional results.

B. The proposed solution produces the required results and some of the optional results.

C. The proposed solution produces the required results only.

D. The proposed solution does not produce the required results.

Questions 13–15   This scenario should be used to answer questions 13, 14, and 15.

Your small, fast-growing company has one location. All employees, until recently, worked in that one location. Your company's business model recently changed. For the first time, you have employees who will be working from home. They require secure access to network resources. All work-from-home employees have Pentium-class computers with 56-Kbps modems at their homes. The data they work with is fairly sensitive. Files are shared among these employees regularly.

13. Based on the information presented in the situation, what is the greatest concern from the employee perspective? (Choose all that apply.)

A. Secure data communications

B. Ease of use with remote connection

C. Speed of connection

D. Cost-effective connection

14. Based on the information presented in the situation, what solution would you recommend to provide the highest security at the least cost?

    A. Place all employees in a security group. Provide that group with dial-in access via RRAS. Set all accounts to call back the user at a specified number. Require strong passwords. Implement IPSec for end-to-end data security.

    B. Place all employees in a security group. Provide that group with access via local ISP accounts using VPN connections to the network. Require strong passwords. Create a share on a network server, and use EFS to encrypt all files on that share.

    C. Place all employees in a security group. Provide that group with access via direct dial-in accounts. Implement MS-CHAP for secure data communications and require strong passwords.

    D. Place all employees in a security group on the RRAS server. Provide that group with permission to log on locally. Provide access numbers for direct dial-in. Require strong passwords, and implement EAP for secure communications.

15. Based on the information presented in the situation, what is the greatest risk the company faces?

    A. Denial of service attacks

    B. Viruses introduced by work-from-home employees

    C. Unauthorized access to sensitive files on network shares

    D. Unauthorized access to network resources

16. Your company has decided to increase security for all data related to company sales. What would be the impact of encrypting all sales data on the network?

    A. Network performance may suffer.

    B. Some users may not be able to access the data they need.

    C. Sales representatives would have to remember encryption passwords in addition to user passwords.

    D. Sales data does not need to be encrypted on the network.

17. You are preparing a 30-minute presentation for new hire orientation sessions. You've been asked to talk about viruses and how and why employees should avoid them. What would you tell new employees is not a behavior of a virus?

    A. Reformats hard drive

    B. Creates drive partitions

    C. Often attacks boot sectors of hard drives

    D. Has a signature that can be identified

18. You have recently implemented several new security measures on your network. What could you monitor to determine whether server capacity was adequately handling the new demands?

    A. Unsuccessful user logons

    B. Network counters

    C. % User Time

    D. System: processor queue length

LAB QUESTION

Objectives 4.01–4.02

Based on the information presented in this chapter, develop a high-level network security checklist. Include all factors that are relevant to designing and implementing security based on current and future technology.

QUICK ANSWER KEY

Objective 4.01	
1.	**A, B**, and **C**
2.	**A** and **C**
3.	**B**
4.	**A**
5.	**A** and **B**
6.	**C**
7.	**B**
8.	**C**
9.	**D**

Objective 4.02	
10.	**A, B**, and **C**
11.	**B**
12.	**B**
13.	**B** and **C**
14.	**A**
15.	**B**
16.	**A**
17.	**B**
18.	**B** and **D**

IN-DEPTH ANSWERS

4.01: Evaluating the Company's Existing and Planned Technical Environment

1. ☑ **A**, **B**, and **C** are correct. The roles and responsibilities of network administrators and users is an important part of assessing current and future technology environments. The cost of equipment and labor—from servers to routers to Internet connectivity to cable installation—must be accounted for in all technology assessments. The size of the organization, both in terms of number of users and number of locations, is another component. The current technology environment may be meeting the needs of today's users, it may contain excess capacity for growth, or it may be lagging current demand. Taken together, these are the three key components of assessing the technology environment.

   ☒ **D** is not correct because it excludes roles and responsibilities of administrators and users, which is a key component of planning.

2. ☑ **A** and **C** are correct. The various computers on the network create a heterogeneous environment, which is typical of most companies. A homogeneous network with standard (or similar) computers or servers can ease administration and support requirements but is not always feasible or desirable. The four servers connected to the "cloud" indicate an Internet presence. With four servers, there is likely a firewall or demilitarized zone (DMZ) set up to protect internal network resources from external threats.

   ☒ **B** is not correct. A homogeneous environment is defined by the same or very similar computers on the network. **D** is not correct. There is no indication as to the speed or capacity of the network.

3. ☑ **B.** Scalability is defined as the ability to incrementally add capacity to a system. Whether it involves server clusters or network bandwidth, the ability to add units with relative ease is a key component of any network plan.

☒ **A** is not correct. A processor expansion slot would allow you to add processors. The ability to add processors is an example of scalability. **C** is not correct. Cluster fail-over occurs when a server (or any component belonging to a cluster) fails and operations or responsibilities are picked up by another member of the cluster. In this question, adding a server to meet increasing demand is an example of scalability. **D** is not correct. This is not a legitimate term in Windows 2000.

4. ☑ **A.** The required result is to develop a plan for effective support. The optional results are as follows: improve administration and lower costs. The proposed plan delivers effective support by outsourcing local support and providing expert assistance from headquarters. The proposed solution also improves administration through the creation of domains and OUs. If site links are slow, separate domains can be created to eliminate replication traffic. OUs delegate administration to local network administrators who can more easily manage a subset of resources. Costs are lowered through using a local ISP for Internet connections rather that incurring phone charges via dial-up connections.

☒ **B**, **C**, and **D** are not correct because the proposed solution produces the required results and all of the optional results.

5. ☑ **A** and **B** are correct. Both cable and DSL offer fairly inexpensive solutions for reasonably fast connection bandwidth. As an added convenience, both cable and DSL offer full-time connectivity—eliminating delays.

☒ **C** is incorrect. Fiber optic is an expensive solution, although it does provide high throughput and secure communications. **D** is not correct. T1 connections are also relatively expensive for a small company, although competition in the communications market is helping drive costs down.

6. ☑ **C.** IAS (Internet Authentication Services) provides the ability to manage multiple remote access servers to provide a single point of administration. Therefore, when the organization has a large number of RAS servers, implementing IAS would ease administration and provide a more consistent application of authentication and Internet access policies for the organization.

☒ **A** is not correct. You must have RAS implemented in order to utilize IAS. **B** is not correct. IAS and RAS share the same remote access policies and authentication capabilities. With a small number of RAS servers in place, the

additional administration for IAS would likely not benefit your organization.
D is not correct. RADIUS (Remote Access Dial-In User Service) is an industry
standard for dial-in services. When RAS is configured as a RADIUS client to
an IAS server, the policies of the IAS server are used. RADIUS standards are
implemented via IAS in Windows 2000.

7. ☑ **B.** The domain structure currently supports three domains. Reviewing the
current domains and the domain structure needed in Windows 2000 would be
one of three tasks. Another task would be to review the Hardware Compatibility
List (HCL) for Windows 2000 to ensure that the existing Windows NT 4.0
controllers and the Novell servers meet Windows 2000 requirements. If they
do not, the decision to upgrade or maintain the current operating system must
be made based on company guidelines and priorities. Finally, in the current
mixed environment, there are likely to be several methods of user authentication
in place. If users are logging onto Novell servers, Windows NT servers, and
Windows 2000 servers, there are several authentication methods in use.
Streamlining this with the use of standard user authentication (Kerberos v5)
or with more secure authentication will ensure that all user authentication is
secure and consistent.

☒ **A** is not correct. There is no indication that the LAN capacity needs to
be changed. There are no specific LAN requirements for Windows 2000. **C** is
not correct. Again, there are no specific network capacity requirements for
Windows 2000 and no indications that capacity is an issue. **D** is not correct.
Group policies are dependent upon Active Directory, and, therefore, are only
implemented on RootDomain and Support.RootDomain.

8. ☑ **C.** United States laws prohibit companies from using 128-bit encryption
for communications outside of North America. You can implement 40-bit or
56-bit encryption for locations outside North America.

☒ **A** is not correct. 128-bit can be used in Canada. **B** is not correct. 56-bit
encryption can be used in Canada and other countries as well. **D** is not correct.
128-bit encryption can be used for all communications limited to North America.

9. ☑ **D.** MS-CHAP (Microsoft Challenge Handshake Authentication Protocol)
can be implemented to provide secure user authentication on your Web site.

☒   **A** is not correct. HTTPS (Hypertext Transfer Protocol Secure) provides similar features as SSL (Secure Sockets Layer) and secures communication between a Web application and a user, but does not authenticate the user. **B** is not correct. WAP (Wireless Application Protocol) is a protocol used for various wireless applications but does not authenticate users. **C** is not correct. SLIP (Serial Line Internet Protocol) is a remote access protocol supported in Windows NT 4.0 and below. It is not supported in Windows 2000.

4.02: Analyzing the Impact of the Security Design on the Existing and Planned Technical Environment

10.   ☑   **A**, **B**, and **C** are not correct. Stronger security policies can increase administration and support costs. When users frequently forget passwords, leave smart cards at home, or get locked out of their accounts, support costs increase. With data encryption, the ability to perform packet filtering and content monitoring can be impaired. When set to disallow protocols or content, a firewall may not be able to distinguish those packets when encrypted with IPSec. Productivity can be lost when users get locked out of accounts, forcibly disconnected from resources, or when system performance is degraded due to heavy security traffic. (End-to-end encryption, for instance, can contribute to slower network response.)

☒   **D** is not correct. Increased hard disk capacity does not directly correlate to increased security measures. System performance, as it relates to security, will typically be impacted by additional processors or RAM rather than drive capacity.

11.   ☑   **B.** Site replication between Site 1 and Site 2 is 56-Kbps. Given the number of servers at both sites, replication may be so slow as to degrade network performance. Scheduling replication during off-peak hours is optimal. However, if there are numerous changes that must be replicated, it is possible replication may never complete. Therefore, the biggest risk is the slow link between Site 1 and Site 2. Adding Site 4 will only increase replication traffic. Upgrading the link between Site 1 and Site 2 is the biggest improvement you could make to the network.

☒ **A** is not correct. With proper settings, dial-up access can be very secure. **C** is not correct. Site 4 can be connected using as fast a connection as possible given cost constraints. **D** is not correct. There is no practical limit to the number of servers that can be in a Windows 2000 domain. You may choose to create multiple domains for a number of reasons, but the number of users and servers that can be in a Windows 2000 domain is virtually unlimited.

12. ☑ **B.** The required results are as follows: improve overall security, encrypt sensitive data, and implement virus protection. The optional results are as follows: improve network performance, improve end user satisfaction, and lower or maintain costs. The proposed solution encrypts all data (not just sensitive data), so it exceeds that requirement. By installing and updating the virus software, the solution produces the second required result. The solution produces one of the optional results of improving network performance. Increasing the network from 10MB to 100MB will certainly improve network performance. However, applying encryption to all data may degrade performance, so the net gain is significantly smaller than might be anticipated. However, moving from a 10MB to a 100MB network requires the purchase and installation of new hardware on the network; it may include replacing network cabling, depending on the current cable used. The proposed solution does not produce the optional result of lowering or maintaining cost. Finally, by limiting logon hours and forcibly disconnecting users, the solution may produce the requirement of improved overall security but fails to produce the optional result of improving end user satisfaction. In planning network security, ensuring that security measures are commensurate with the risks helps maintain end user satisfaction.

13. ☑ **B** and **C** are correct. Most users are solely concerned with how easily they can connect to the remote resources and how fast the connection is. User dissatisfaction rises dramatically when connection speeds are slow.

☒ **A** is not correct. Most users assume network administrators will take appropriate measures to secure data. **D** is not correct. Most users are not concerned with the cost of the solution as long as it is easy to use and provides reasonable response times so that they are able to accomplish their work in a timely manner.

14. ☑ **A.** Best practices involve placing users in groups and assigning permissions to groups. Therefore, placing the employees who will require remote access into a security group (as opposed to a distribution group) is the preferred method of providing these permissions. From the information provided, it appears that all employees are local to the one location. Therefore, it is likely that providing direct dial-in access for employees may be more cost effective than providing ISP accounts. Setting the account to call back the employee at a specified number will ensure that the user is an authorized user. Since calls are local, there is no difference in the cost. Strong passwords will reduce the likelihood of an intruder guessing or hacking their way into the network, as will using the callback feature. Finally, IPSec can be implemented from end to end so that all data is secure from the client machine back to the application server.

☒ **B** is not correct. Providing ISP accounts may be more costly than local phone access. Also, using EFS (Encrypting File System) encrypts the files on the hard drive, which makes them inaccessible to anyone but the owner of the file. It does not address secure communications. **C** is not correct. MS-CHAP is an authentication protocol, not a secure communications protocol. **D** is not correct. Logging on locally provides local access to the RRAS server, not something you want or need to provide to remote access users. EAP (Extensible Authentication Protocol) can be used in conjunction with another authentication method such as smart cards or token cards. By itself, it is not a viable solution.

15. ☑ **B.** Employees are now remotely connecting to network resources. Ensuring that they understand the risks involved with external access, including viruses, is an important part of implementing remote access for these users.

☒ **A** is not correct. A denial of service attack is feasible but is not the greatest threat to the company in this instance. **C** is not correct. Strong passwords and the security inherent in Windows 2000's Active Directory prevents unauthorized users from accessing sensitive data that is properly protected by permissions. **D** is not correct. Implementing the callback feature, along with strong passwords, makes it very difficult for an unauthorized user to gain access to network resources.

16. ☑ **A.** Depending on the level of encryption implemented, network performance may suffer because it takes more processing, as well as network bandwidth, to encrypt and decrypt files.

☒   **B** is not correct. If the data is encrypted on the network, users could be given access as needed. **C** is not correct. Encryption can be implemented using smart cards, for instance, where the user only needs to remember a PIN and all other logon information is stored on the smart card itself. **D** is not correct. Encrypting sales data on the network prevents local users from hacking into the data or viewing files they have gained access to through illegitimate means.

17.   ☑   **B.** To date, viruses have not created drive partitions.

☒   **A, C,** and **D** are not correct. Each of these can be a behavior of a virus. These are behaviors that virus protection software scans for when scanning for viruses on a computer.

18.   ☑   **B** and **D** are correct. Checking network counters will determine if network traffic has increased. It is important to create a baseline prior to implementing the security changes, then compare results after implementing the changes. Monitoring processor queue length on all processors will help determine if servers are overloaded. Processors can be busy executing various threads a majority of the time, but if the queue length remains low, it means that work is being handled by the processor. Monitoring this over time will show trends such as increased queues at a certain time of day or when starting applications or services. This is important, especially when implementing additional security measures (such as encryption) or when changing configurations for servers on the Web.

☒   **A** is not correct. Unsuccessful user logons does not reflect server capacity but may indicate someone trying to gain unauthorized access to the network. **C** is not correct. % User Time will not indicate whether various security measures have impacted network performance.

LAB ANSWER

Objectives 4.01–4.02

Here are 30 items that could be part of a high-level network security checklist and design plan. It includes all factors that are related to current and existing technology.

1. Review existing locations, branches, and sites.

2. Review existing network topology and bandwidth capacity (LAN).

3. Check existing connections: site connectivity, Internet connectivity, and remote access connectivity (WAN).

4. Review existing network resources: servers (domain controllers, application servers, and member servers), workstations, laptops, handheld devices, printers, scanners, and other specialized devices.

5. Identify existing network administration organization and resources.

6. Review IT capabilities and perform gap analysis against future IT needs to determine need for hiring, consulting, or outsourcing of future needs.

7. Review user security requirements and limitations.

8. Check system security requirements and limitations.

9. Review application and line-of-business requirements (hardware, licensing, and user training).

10. Identify current security policies: end user, network, server, remote access, Web, and email.

11. Include plans to expand in terms of company, users, and locations.

12. Identify plans to expand product or service offerings that may impact Web site or e-commerce implementations.

13. Determine plans or requirements to upgrade hardware or software.

14. Consider plans or requirements to expand network capacity (LAN).

15. Consider plans or requirements to expand external connectivity (WAN).

16. Consider plans to expand business via Web (e-commerce, Web-based applications, and Terminal Services).

17. Review recent or expected network security breaches or attacks.

18. Review secure protocols: SSL or TLS for Web-based applications, L2TP with IPSec for VPN remote access, and IPSec over TCP/IP for network security of data.

19. Assess current use of various secure protocols, and determine need for greater, lesser, or same level of security.

20. Review, assess, and implement technology improvements such as Windows 2000, smart cards, or biometric hardware, as appropriate.

21. Review and apply NTFS file systems and EFS data encryption, where applicable.

22. Establish a systematic monitoring of software installed on the network to ensure that legal software is being used.

23. Establish a systematic process for updating antivirus software, and establish policies that push virus detection and virus software updates to ensure that all users are continuously current.

24. Establish remote access guidelines and procedures.

25. Establish auditing and monitoring guidelines and procedures.

26. Establish regular log review procedures.

27. Establish emergency procedures for various security breach scenarios (physical, logical, network, and Web).

28. Educate users as to the current and changing security policies.

29. Review the effectiveness and cost of all security measures implemented; assess whether to continue or discontinue security measures where cost and effectiveness do not appear to correlate.

30. Review the impact of security on user productivity and satisfaction.

5

Designing a Security Baseline for a Windows 2000 Network

This chapter focuses on Windows 2000 domain controllers, operation masters, and group policy scenarios so you can develop a baseline for designing a Windows 2000 security plan. Earlier versions of Windows NT used a primary domain controller (PDC) and backup domain controller (BDC) model to manage domain information such as permissions and trust relationships. Windows 2000 uses domain controllers that use multimaster operations. Rather than having PDCs and BDCs, all domain controllers in Windows 2000 replicate domain information. Flexible Single-Master Operations (FSMO) are servers that manage one or more domain operations such as domain-naming master or PDC emulator master. Finally, using group policy scenarios, a network administrator can configure and control server and non-server computers on the network including desktops, laptops, and kiosks. Using group policy templates, various security scenarios can be created to establish a security baseline for your network.

TEST YOURSELF OBJECTIVE 5.01

Understanding Domain Controllers

Domain controllers are servers that share a common namespace (domain) and perform domain functions such as name resolution, user authentication, and access control. Every domain controller maintains a current copy of the Active Directory database and can make changes to that database. Since any domain controller can update the Active Directory database, Windows 2000 has a reliable method of conflict resolution. Active Directory ensures consistency by attaching a unique stamp to each replicated attribute value during an originating update. Only the data with the highest stamp value will replicate, ensuring that only the most up-to-date information is replicated.

- Domain controllers run network services such as DHCP (Dynamic Host Control Protocol), DNS (Domain Name System), and Active Directory.

- Servers can be promoted to domain controllers by running the Active Directory Installation Wizard.

- The Active Directory Installation Wizard is started by running the DCPROMO.EXE executable from the Windows 2000 command line.

■ Each domain controller holds a read/write copy of the Active Directory database.

■ The Active Directory database filename is NTDS.DIT.

■ Every Windows 2000 domain controller that participates in replication must contain a folder called SYSVOL.

■ SYSVOL can only exist on NTFS 5.0 (Windows 2000) partitions.

e x a m
🐾 a t c h

MCP exams typically highlight new features of the product. Expect to see questions that compare and contrast Windows 2000 domain controllers and Windows NT 4.0 (and lower) domain controllers. Keep in mind that Windows 2000 does not use primary domain controllers and backup domain controllers, but does provide PDC emulation for backward compatibility. Additionally, Windows NT 4.0 often utilizes multiple domains such as resource domains. Windows 2000 allows for all resources to be managed in a single domain environment, with management of resources delegated through the use of organizational units (OUs). When in doubt on the exam, choose single domain model with OUs unless there is specific data that would indicate otherwise, including different security needs, autonomous domain administration requirements, or separate domain namespace requirements.

QUESTIONS

5.01: Understanding Domain Controllers

1. As a system administrator, it's important to understand the features among all of the Windows operating systems. Which of the following is the only client that cannot operate with Active Directory in Native mode?

    A. Windows 95

    B. Windows 98

    C. Windows 2000 Professional

    D. Windows NT Workstation

2. The following diagram illustrates which of the following concepts?

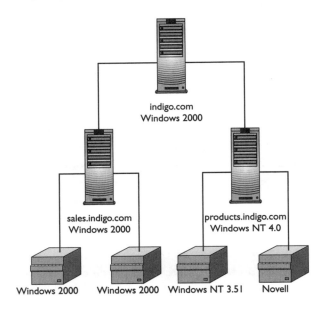

A. Multioperations, Native mode Windows 2000 domain model

B. Operations master, Mixed mode Windows 2000 domain model

C. Mixed mode Windows 2000 domain model

D. Native mode Windows 2000 domain model

3. **Current Situation:** You have a network that you would like to migrate to Window 2000. Currently, you have a Novell domain with one Novell server, a Windows domain with one Windows NT 3.51 server, and four Windows NT 4.0 servers. All are connected via Fast Ethernet and are in one location. You have one PDC running DHCP and DNS. That server is used to authenticate all network users. You have two BDCs in the network. You are running NetWare services on one of the BDCs.

Required Results: Create a plan for upgrading to Windows 2000. Ensure that all users can be authenticated, minimize network downtime, and improve security.

Optional Desired Results: Minimize costs and provide improved network services to all users.

Proposed Solution: Check the Windows 2000 HCL to ensure that all servers to be upgraded meet the minimum hardware specifications for Windows 2000. Upgrade all server hardware to Pentium 600MHz processors (or better) with 512MB RAM per server, then install Windows 2000 Server on each server. Create one domain with OUs to reflect the organization of the company. Implement Kerberos v5 user authentication and L2TP with IPSec for all network traffic.

What results are produced from the proposed solution?

A. The proposed solution produces the required results and all of the optional results.

B. The proposed solution produces the required results and some of the optional results.

C. The proposed solution produces the required results only.

D. The proposed solution does not produce the required results.

4. Your company has two sites. Each has a domain controller. Site 1 has a Global Catalog server. The connection between the two sites is impaired and running at 25 percent of its normal capacity. What impact will it have on users at Site 2?

A. Users cannot log on; each site must have a Global Catalog server.

B. Users logging on at Site 2 may experience delays.

C. Bridgehead servers at Site 2 will experience delays when using SMTP.

D. Bridgehead servers will replicate data at normal rates using all available bandwidth.

5. Your company has completed its Windows 2000 migration. However, it has become clear that more domain controllers are needed to meet some of the increasing demands on network services. What command is used to create a domain controller in Windows 2000 from a member server?

A. PROMODC.EXE

B. DCPROMO.EXE

C. DCUPGD.EXE

D. WINNT32.EXE

6. You have been asked to identify a migration plan for your Windows NT 4.0 network. In determining how many servers will be needed, you've been asked

to identify required services. Which services are required in a Windows 2000 domain? (Choose all that apply.)

A. DHCP

B. WINS

C. DNS

D. DACL

Understanding Operations Masters

There are five single-master operation roles in Active Directory: schema master, domain-naming master, relative identifier (RID) master, primary domain controller (PDC) emulator, and infrastructure master. There can be only one schema master and one domain-naming master per forest. The other operations roles are on a per-domain basis. Each domain has only one RID master, PDC emulator, and infrastructure master. In a Mixed mode domain environment, only Windows 2000 domain controllers can hold single-master operations roles.

- Domain controllers in Windows 2000 can also operate as Flexible Single-Master Operators (FSMO) by enabling one or more operator roles on the server.

- The schema master and the domain-naming master are per-forest roles and occur once in each forest.

- The RID master, PDC emulator, and infrastructure master are per-domain roles and occur once in each domain.

- The domain controller that holds a writeable copy of the schema is called the schema master. This is the only server where modifications, additions, or deletions can occur for the schema throughout the forest.

- The domain-naming master is the only domain controller in the forest that can add or remove existing domains from the directory.

- The RID master is the domain controller in charge of allocating pools of RIDs to domain controllers in common domains (every Windows 2000 domain has one).

■ The PDC emulator is the domain controller used for backward compatibility with Windows NT 3.51 and 4.0 servers. It acts as a primary domain controller for domain object updates. When used in Native mode, the PDC emulator authenticates passwords that have failed at other domain controllers. It will authenticate the user, if possible. Otherwise, user authentication will fail.

■ The infrastructure master is the domain controller responsible for updating cross-domain, group-to-user references in a multidomain model. In a single domain model, it is responsible for updating the group-to-user references whenever group memberships are changed.

exam
ⓦatch

The schema master is a per-forest role and is the only domain controller that can write to the schema. The schema is then replicated to all other domain controllers in the forest. Keep this in mind during the exam to ensure that you don't get confused on questions relating to Active Directory replication. Windows 2000 domain controllers operate in a peer mode, meaning any domain controller can make updates (write) to the Active Directory, such as a change to a user name or a change to group membership. The schema is part of Active Directory but can only be updated by the schema master via an application or an administrator with sufficient privileges.

QUESTIONS

5.02: Understanding Operations Masters

7. You are in the process of planning your Windows 2000 network and the number of servers you will need to meet the requirements of Windows 2000 and the needs of your organization. Your current network is comprised of Windows NT 4.0 servers. You've looked at the various roles your servers are currently playing and are creating a plan for the new roles in Windows 2000. Which of the following is not required for a domain?

A. Schema master

B. RID master

C. PDC emulator

D. Infrastructure master

8. Which statement is incorrect with respect to the domain shown in the following illustration?

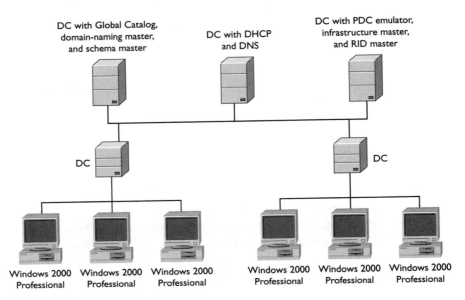

A. Global Catalog must run on the same domain controller as the DHCP server.

B. There is no WINS server present in the domain.

C. DHCP and DNS should not run on the same domain controller.

D. There is no need for PDC emulation in this domain.

9. **Current Situation:** You have upgraded most of your servers to Windows 2000. However, due to some departmental issues, you have several servers still running Windows NT 3.51 (with the latest service pack applied). Some of your users who use laptops running Windows 98 are unable to change their expired passwords.

   Required Results: Identify and resolve user logon issue and perform no upgrades to Windows NT 3.51 servers.

   Optional Desired Results: Ensure this problem does not recur. Provide two solutions to the current problem and improve network security.

Proposed Solution: Seize the PDC emulator role to the standby operations master domain controller after determining that the PDC emulator computer is offline and beyond repair. Install the Directory Services client on all user laptops.

What results are produced from the proposed solution?

A. The proposed solution produces the required results and all of the optional results.

B. The proposed solution produces the required results and some of the optional results.

C. The proposed solution produces the required results only.

D. The proposed solution does not produce the required results.

Questions 10–12   This scenario should be used to answer questions 10, 11, and 12.

You have just completed the migration of your network to Windows 2000. You set your network up as follows. Domain Controller 1 is designated as the Global Catalog server. It also was assigned the role of schema master, domain-naming master, and infrastructure master. Domain Controller 2 has the role of RID master and PDC emulator. Three other servers are configured as Windows 2000 domain controllers with no single-operations master roles assigned.

10.   What is wrong with your configuration?

A. You cannot assign single-operation roles on domain controllers running Global Catalog.

B. You do not need a PDC emulator role in a Native Windows 2000 environment.

C. Each domain controller should run no more than two single-operation roles.

D. The infrastructure master should not be on a domain controller that is also a Global Catalog server.

11.   What is right with the configuration in the scenario?

A. The domain controller hosting the Global Catalog also has the schema master and domain-naming master roles.

B.   The RID master is not on the same domain controller as the infrastructure master.

C.   Several domain controllers do not have any FSMO roles assigned.

D.   Only two of the five domain controllers are running FSMO roles.

12.   What is the impact to users on your network if Domain Controller 2 goes down for 48 hours?

A.   Users will be unable to log on to the network because they will not be authenticated.

B.   Users will be logged on using cached security credentials.

C.   Users will experience unacceptable delays in accessing network resources.

D.   Users may not notice a difference.

TEST YOURSELF OBJECTIVE 5.03

Understanding Group Policy Scenarios

Group policies are objects that contain security settings, which are applied to a domain or a computer rather than to a user. A single Group Policy Object (GPO) can be applied to all computers in a domain or organizational unit. The GPO is applied when the computer starts up and is periodically refreshed, even without restarting the computer. To access GPOs, you must have Active Directory installed and you must use the Active Directory Users and Computers snap-in in the Microsoft Management Console (MMC). Group policy can be applied to sites by using the Active Directory Sites and Services snap-in. Security templates are provided in Windows 2000 and can be edited to create customized security templates for your organization. Security templates can be imported into a GPO. The four default templates are basic, compatible, secure, and high secure.

■   A group policy scenario is a method of controlling computer settings and managing user access rights using pre-defined templates.

■   A desktop computer scenario is also known as TCO (total cost of ownership) desktop scenario. It holds settings that make the desktop easier to use and allows users to install available applications. It is the least restrictive of the scenarios.

■ A laptop scenario can be used by people who are away from the central office most of the time. These users usually log on using asynchronous means (modem), but also can log on to the corporate network at normal speeds when at the office.

■ Typically, a public workstation that runs only one application, uses one user logon account, and runs unattended is called a *kiosk*. The kiosk scenario is considered very secure for many reasons, including the fact that no data is saved to the local drive.

exam
ⓦatch

Group policy scenarios are used to create customized templates for managing the security of domain computers in various environments. Group policy is most easily used when computers are organized into OUs and policies are applied to the OUs. Group policies can also be used on a per-site basis. Both methods provide a systematic approach to standardized security settings. On the exam, do not confuse GPOs with security or distribution groups. Security groups place users (or other domain objects) in groups and assign access permissions to them. Distribution groups are used to distribute information logically throughout an organization.

QUESTIONS

5.03: Understanding Group Policy Scenarios

13. A new member of your IT staff has presented you with a plan for using Group Policy Objects in your new Windows 2000 network. However, he seems to have made an error by including several items that are not governed by group policy. Which of the following is not a use of GPOs in Windows 2000?

A. Administrative control of registry settings

B. Site replication settings

C. Application of a logon script

D. User folder redirection

14. In the following illustration, how would you access GPOs that would enable you to run a logon script for all Windows 2000 Professional workstations?

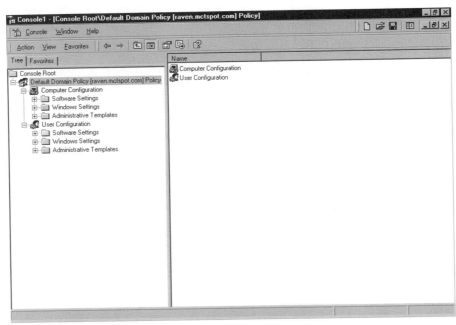

A. Local Computer Policy

B. Default Domain Policy | Computer Configuration | Windows Settings

C. Default Domain Policy | Computer Configuration | Software Settings

D. Default Domain Policy | User Configuration | Administrative Templates

15. **Current Situation:** You have a wholesale distribution company that is opening a retail outlet adjacent to the warehouse. The retail manager wants to introduce the retail operation to customers via a Microsoft PowerPoint presentation.

   Required Results: Solution must have very low security risk, must use new technologies, and must not require administrative resources after implementation.

   Optional Desired Results: Solution should be low cost, not require purchases of new hardware or software, and be user friendly.

   Proposed Solution: Create and load a Microsoft PowerPoint presentation onto four computers. Place each computer in a strategic location within the retail outlet. Set the PowerPoint presentation to run continuously, with each slide showing for 30 seconds. Create a user account called RetailInfo. Set the account so the password never expires and the user cannot change the password. Through Group Policy Objects, implement the High Security template (HISECWS.INF) to lock down all desktop features and to prevent any data from being saved to the local hard drive. Within the GPO, set the PowerPoint application to launch after the systems boot up.

What results are produced from the proposed solution?

A. The proposed solution produces the required results and all of the optional results.

B. The proposed solution produces the required results and some of the optional results.

C. The proposed solution produces the required results only.

D. The proposed solution does not produce the required results.

16. If your network does not use Active Directory, what can you use to implement security settings?

A. Configure local logon security by using the Security Policy Manager via Administrative Tools.

B. Configure security settings by using the local security policy via Administrative Tools.

C. Configure security settings by using the Local Security Manager snap-in.

D. Add the Group Policy snap-in to the Computer Configuration console.

17. You have created several OUs and delegated permission to administrate these OUs to two other members of your company's IT staff. One staff member calls, asking for assistance. He has set certain policies for his OU but the settings do not seem to be applied. What could be happening? (Choose all that apply.)

A. Account lockout settings from OUs and sites are disregarded in Windows 2000.

B. Kerberos settings can only be applied at the domain level.

C. OU password settings can only be set at the site level.

D. Site strong password settings can only be set at the domain controller.

18. You have a number of very sophisticated laptop users in your company. Many have complained about the use of group policy settings. They have stated that it interferes with their ability to get their jobs done and they would like the ability to bypass group policies, when needed. How could you address both the user concerns and network security concerns?

    A. Add these laptop users to the Domain Administrator group. This will give them the ability to define local policies for their own laptops.

    B. Give these laptop users local administrator privileges. This will give them the ability to circumvent group policy settings on their computers when needed.

    C. Give these laptop users logon locally privileges. This will give them the ability to modify group policies that are applied to HKEY_LOCAL_ MACHINE only.

    D. Create an OU and place all laptop users in the OU. Apply a group policy to the OU that allows laptop users to modify settings only when not connected to the network.

LAB QUESTION

Objectives 5.01–5.03

You currently have a network comprised of Windows NT 3.51 and Windows NT 4.0 servers. The network is divided into four domains that correlate to the four locations your company has: NT351.ONE, NT351.TWO, NT40.ONE, and NT40.TWO. Each domain has approximately 8,000 users with one PDC and four BDCs per domain. Due to budgetary and departmental constraints, one of the Windows NT4.0 servers at each location must remain (cannot be upgraded). Each user logs into their primary domain location except for the sales representatives, who travel frequently. They have been granted remote access rights. They dial into a corporate RAS server via an 800 number to access network resources.

You have been asked to provide a migration plan aimed specifically at the servers in the organization. Create a plan that addresses the following concerns:

1. Minimize downtime. The network cannot be down for any extended period of time. Users primarily work Monday through Friday, 6:00A.M. to 8:00P.M. (offices located on both coasts required extended network availability). How will you ensure that the network stays up and functional through this transition?

2. Rollback plan. If the migration runs into trouble, how will you roll back to ensure continuous network operations?

3. What domain structure will you create and why?

4. What domain controllers will you create and why?

5. What domain roles will be required and where will they be placed?

6. What other considerations should you have in the design plan?

QUICK ANSWER KEY

Objective 5.01	
1.	D
2.	C
3.	D
4.	B
5.	B
6.	C

Objective 5.02	
7.	A
8.	D
9.	B
10.	D
11.	A
12.	D

Objective 5.03	
13.	B
14.	B
15.	A
16.	B
17.	A and B
18.	B

IN-DEPTH ANSWERS

5.01: Understanding Domain Controllers

1. ☑ **D.** There is no redirector currently for Windows NT; therefore, once 2000 is in Native mode, support for Windows NT is gone.

    ☒ **A, B,** and **C** are not correct because each of these systems can operate in a Windows 2000 Native mode environment, either by default or by adding a redirector written by Microsoft.

2. ☑ **C.** There are two domain controllers running Windows 2000 and one running Windows NT 4.0. When the network contains servers other than Windows 2000 servers, the network runs in Mixed mode. Windows 2000 runs in Mixed mode by default and can be migrated to Native mode. This is a one-time action that cannot be reversed.

    ☒ **A** is not correct. There is no mode called multi-operations. The diagram shows non–Windows 2000 servers, which indicates the domain is running in Mixed mode. **B** is not correct. There are no operation masters shown in the diagram. **D** is not correct. There are no operation masters shown in the illustration and the network is not running in Native mode.

3. ☑ **D.** Required results are as follows: create upgrade plan, ensure that all users can be authenticated, minimize downtime, and improve security. The proposed solution does not produce these requirements. The plan does not specifically address users who may currently be logging onto the Novell server for authentication. Windows 2000 provides client services for NetWare, gateway services for NetWare, and file and print services for NetWare. Using clients services for NetWare, a Windows client can connect directly to a NetWare server. Using gateway services on a Windows 2000–based server, Windows clients can connect to NetWare servers. This eliminates the need to use NWLink (IPX/SPX) on the client. Finally, a Windows 2000–based server can provide file and print services directly to a NetWare server and compatible clients. The proposed solution also does not minimize downtime. By simply

upgrading all servers, you run the risk of taking the network down. Setting up a test lab, upgrading in stages, and devising fallback plans are three methods of minimizing network downtime. Finally, the solution does not improve security since L2TP with IPSec is used for VPN connections, not local LAN connections. Although Kerberos v5 may provide improved security over previous authentication methods, the solution still does not produce the minimum requirements.

☒ **A**, **B**, and **C** are not correct because the solution does not produce the required results.

4. ☑ **B.** The Global Catalog performs user authentication. If a Global Catalog server is not present on a site, user authentication is performed by the remote Global Catalog server. Going via a WAN connection, user authentication may be dramatically slower. It is recommended that each site have a domain controller running Global Catalog Service.

☒ **A** is not correct. A site does not need to have a Global Catalog server, but it is recommended for improved system performance. **C** is not correct. The bridgehead server is a single server at each site designated to perform site-to-site replication. The domain controllers at Site 1 and at Site 2 also act as bridgehead servers. This is not directly impacted by a degraded WAN connection, other than slowing replication activity. **D** is not correct. Replication traffic is treated just as any other network traffic. To improve replication and user response, replication can be set during intervals of low network usage or the interval can be increased to decrease replication traffic. Both solutions can create problems if there are frequent changes to the Active Directory data.

5. ☑ **B.** DCPROMO.EXE (short for domain controller promotion) is the command used to promote a member server to a domain controller. It is run at the command line on the server you want to promote.

☒ **A** and **C** are not correct; there are no .EXE commands with these names. **D** is not correct. WINNT32.EXE is used to upgrade existing installations of Windows NT or Windows 2000.

6. ☑ **C.** Domain Name System (DNS) is a required service in a Windows 2000 domain.

☒ **A** is not correct. Although you must employ some method of managing IP addresses for the network, Dynamic Host Control Protocol (DHCP) is not required. Most companies choose to employ DHCP because it automatically manages and monitors IP address assignments. It is highly recommended that it be implemented, but it is not actually required to run Windows 2000. **B** is not correct. Windows Internet Naming Service (WINS) is used to support NetBIOS name resolution for legacy systems, but is not required in Windows 2000. WINS is supported with enhanced functionality in Windows 2000 for networks running in Mixed mode and requiring NetBIOS name resolution. Name resolution is managed by DNS in a native Windows 2000 domain. **D** is not correct. Discretionary Access Control List (DACL) is part of an object's security descriptor that grants or denies access to the object based on user and group permissions. It is not a service that runs on a domain controller.

5.02: Understanding Operations Masters

7. ☑ **A.** The schema master, as well as the domain-naming master, is a per-forest role.

☒ **B** is not correct. The relative identifier master is a per-domain role. **C** is not correct. The primary domain controller emulator is a per-domain role. **D** is not correct. The infrastructure master is a per-domain role.

8. ☑ **D.** There is no need for PDC emulation. PDC emulation is used in a Mixed mode environment to support non–Windows 2000 servers, which require the presence of a PDC in a domain. In Native mode, the PDC emulator master receives preferential password replication. If a password change is rejected by another domain controller, it is passed to the PDC emulator for authentication prior to being rejected.

☒ **B** is not correct. WINS is not required in a Native Windows 2000 environment. It is only required for computers that require NetBIOS name resolution, such as computers running older versions of Windows. **C** is not correct. DHCP and DNS can run on the same domain controller on smaller networks. If the network increases in size and the server response slows, these two services can be placed on separate domain controllers.

9. ☑ **B.** Required results are as follows: identify and resolve user logon issue, perform no upgrades. Optional results are to ensure problem does not re-occur, provide at least two solutions to problem, and improve network security. Failure of the server running the PDC emulator role will cause users whose passwords have expired to be unable to change them. Therefore, they would not be able to logon. By seizing PDC emulation from the FSMO to the

standby operations master domain controller, you have resolved the issue, thereby producing the required results. To ensure the problem does not reoccur, you can install the Directory Services client. Directory Services client can run on Windows 95, 98, or NT 4.0. It allows users to use the fault-tolerant Distributed File System (Dfs), search Active Directory, and change passwords on any domain controllers. The PDC emulation role is still required but can be used to authenticate users whose authentication failed at other domain controllers. By seizing operations (to provide the PDC emulation role for the domain), and by installing the Directory Services client, you have provided two solutions, thereby producing two of the three optional results. Network security is not changed by this solution; therefore, it does not produce all of the optional results.

☒ **A, C,** and **D** are not correct because the solution produces the required results and two of the three of the optional results.

10. ☑ **D.** The infrastructure master is responsible for updating cross-domain, group-to-user references. If the infrastructure master and the Global Catalog are on the same domain controller, cross-domain object references in that domain will not be updated.

☒ **A** is not correct. A domain controller can run other services such as single-master operations roles. These roles can be moved if server performance is degraded by high demand. **B** is not correct. PDC emulation is used for backward compatibility, but it is also required in the Windows 2000 environment for user password authentication when authentication fails on other domain controllers. **C** is not correct. A domain controller can run multiple operations master roles, assuming the server can handle the load.

11. ☑ **A.** The domain controller that is the Global Catalog server also has the schema master and domain-naming master roles. The schema master and domain-naming master should always be on the same domain controller. This domain controller must be a Global Catalog server because the domain-naming master role requires it.

☒ **B** is not correct. The RID master role can be on the same domain controller as other operations master roles. **C** is not correct. There is no specific need to have domain controllers not running in FSMO roles. **D** is not correct. FSMO roles are not limited to a certain number of domain controllers, but they must adhere to the per-forest and per-domain requirements.

12. ☑ **D.** Users may not be impacted by the RID master and PDC emulator going down temporarily. If the domain controller's RID pool is empty and the RID master is unavailable, you cannot create new security principal objects on that domain controller. When the RID master becomes available, the domain controller will replenish its pool and regain its ability to create new security principal objects. This is transparent to the user. In a Native Windows 2000 mode, the PDC emulator receives preferential replication of password changes. The users may not have trouble changing their password. If the process fails and the PDC emulator is down, users may experience problems until the password change is replicated normally.

☒ **A** and **B** are not correct. User authentication is performed by the domain controller containing the Global Catalog. **C** is not correct. Temporary loss of the RID master or PDC emulator will not impact the user's network response time (once the user is authenticated). Temporary loss of any of the operations master roles is usually transparent to users.

5.03: Understanding Group Policy Scenarios

13. ☑ **B.** Site replication settings are managed through Active Directory Sites and Services.

☒ **A, C**, and **D** are not correct because each is a legitimate use of Windows 2000 Group Policy Objects.

14. ☑ **B.** To run a logon script automatically for computers in the domain, the correct path is Default Domain Policy | Computer Configuration | Windows Settings.

☒ **A, C**, and **D** are not correct. They do not provide the correct path to set group policy for logon scripts.

15. ☑ **A.** The required results are as follows: ensure very low security risk, use new technologies, and don't require administrative resources after implementation. This kiosk solution implements the HISECWS.INF security template to allow network administrators to lock down the computer. Settings on the computer are enforced at start up and are refreshed every 90 minutes by default. This prevents someone from circumventing the security template. One user account

is used and that account is the only account allowed to log on to the computer. The user cannot modify the password and the password does not expire. Through the group policy high security template, the administration can set these computers to run only one application—in this case, a continuous PowerPoint slide show. Through the security template, there is a very low security risk. Using group policy security templates takes advantage of the latest technology available in Windows 2000. Once the group policy is implemented and the slide show is loaded onto the computers, there is very little administrative work involved in maintaining this type of scenario. This solution produces all of the required results. The optional results are that the plan is low cost, doesn't require new purchases, and is user friendly. This solution can be run on any computer running Windows 2000; therefore it can be implemented at no additional cost, with no new purchases of equipment. (This solution does assume, however, that the computers used meet the minimum requirements of Windows 2000 and that their hardware is listed in the HCL.) Finally, this solution is very user friendly because retail customers can view the PowerPoint presentation without having to know how to use computers. It is easy on retail staff because the configuration is protected from intentional or unintentional modification.

☒   **B**, **C**, and **D** are not correct because the proposed solution produces the required results and all of the optional results.

16.   ☑   **B.** If your network does not use Active Directory, you can configure security settings by using local security policy. This is found on the Administrative Tools menu on computers running Windows 2000 Server.

☒   **A** is not correct. Security Policy Manager is not a valid option in Administrative Tools. **C** is not correct. Local Security Manager is not a valid option. **D** is not correct. Although security settings could be enabled via the Group Policy snap-in, the Computer Configuration console is not a valid option. If the computer is running Windows 2000 Professional, you must add the Group Policy snap-in to a new console by using the Microsoft Management Console (MMC).

17.   ☑   **A** and **B** are correct. Account Lockout, Kerberos, and password settings can only be set at the domain level. Windows 2000 does not process any changes that you make to these settings (i.e., password, account lockout, and Kerberos) at the OU or site level.

☒   **C** and **D** are not correct because these settings can only be applied at the domain level and will be disregarded at the site or OU level.

18.   ☑   **B.** Laptop users often need to install software or make modifications to their systems while away from the office. Granting local administrator privileges will enable them to make needed changes. However, granting this privilege also allows them to override group policy settings set by domain administrators.

☒   **A** is not correct. Adding laptop users to the Domain Administrators group grants them far more network access than needed and would create a significant security risk. **C** is not correct. Laptop users can log onto their laptops locally. This will not enable them to change group policy settings of any kind. **D** is not correct. Laptop users could be placed in an OU and group policy could be applied to the OU. However, a policy cannot be set to enable modifications only when not connected to the network.

LAB ANSWER

Objectives 5.01–5.03

There are many ways you could create this plan. Below is one plan, based on Windows 2000 best practices.

1. **Minimize downtime**   By setting up a lab for testing upgrades, servers can be upgraded and tested offline, if desired. When the configuration is tested and confirmed, the upgraded server can be added to the live network with less risk. Upgrades should be scheduled during off-peak hours. In this case, all upgrades could be started at 8:30P.M. and completed no later than 3:00A.M. If the upgrade is not successful by 3:00A.M., the server will be brought back online in its original configuration for users by 6:00A.M. Performing full backups of servers to be upgraded makes a restore fairly simple, if needed.

2. **Rollback plan**   Preserve one BDC with the current directory database and synchronize it with the PDC. Take the BDC offline and preserve it until you are sure the upgrade has been successful. If problems do occur with the upgrade, you can place the BDC in service and promote it to a PDC. Have tested computers in a lab to alleviate the need for rolling back to an earlier configuration. Have complete backups and rollback scenarios planned for the possible failure of each server upgrade. Ask and answer questions such as: who are the users?; who will be impacted?; can the server stay offline without dramatically impacting network resource availability?; and how long can the server be down before it degrades the network?

3. **Domain structure**   The four locations are currently each a domain. You don't have information on the communications links between the domains at this time. Windows 2000 allows for a single domain structure. If you created this, you would have about 32,000 users in one domain, which is feasible. Without other information, you would likely create a single domain. Within the domain, you would create four sites that map to the four locations. You would also create OUs that map to the various resource management structures in your

organization. However, these two activities are outside the scope of the plan you were asked to develop.

4. **Domain controllers**   With four sites in one domain, you would place at least one domain controller at each site running Global Catalog Services. This enables users to be authenticated via a local DC rather than spanning the WAN to be authenticated. This provides faster authentication. In the event that the Global Catalog server goes down, user authentication could be accomplished remotely since the servers will replicate Active Directory data among the four sites.

5. **Domain controller roles**   As mentioned, you will need Global Catalog servers at each site. Implement FSMO roles on domain controllers following the per-forest and per-domain requirements for the five FSMO roles. You could also install the Directory Service client on any workstation computers running Windows 4.0 or below to improve the authentication and resource location process for these. The domain-naming master and the schema master must be on a DC running Global Catalog Services. Do not place the infrastructure master on the same DC as the domain-naming master.

   Other considerations   The PDC in each domain must be upgraded first. Then BDCs can be upgraded. This ensures that user authentication is not disrupted. Group policies can be implemented by creating OUs corresponding to different user needs. For instance, laptop users can be placed in an OU and given local administrative rights to their laptops in addition to the group policies that may be implemented for laptop users. For instance, the group policy may run a logon script that launches a line-of-business application on the laptop or implements EFS on the laptop's My Documents folder. As a local administrator, the laptop user could change that to disable the line-of-business logon script if they are not using that application regularly or override the requirement to use EFS on the laptop.

MCSE
MICROSOFT CERTIFIED SYSTEMS ENGINEER

6

Analyzing Security Requirements

TEST YOURSELF OBJECTIVES

T his chapter focuses on understanding how various resources are secured and how this security is implemented in Active Directory. Resources include computers such as servers, desktops and laptops; hard drives, folders, and files on those computers; printers, scanners, and other peripheral devices on the network; and user accounts including administrator accounts.

Active Directory is tightly integrated into security in a Windows 2000 network. This chapter will review Active Directory concepts including schema, replication, and Access Control Lists (ACLs). It will also test your skills relating to planning considerations in Active Directory and how to secure Active Directory components.

TEST YOURSELF OBJECTIVE 6.01

Identifying the Required Level of Security for Each Resource

Resources include computers, data, and user accounts. Resources must be secured on the network to ensure that only authorized users are accessing network resources and that those users are accessing resources in accordance with security guidelines. For example, an engineer typically would not have access to a company-wide salary database, even though the engineer is an authorized user. Well-planned security guards against internal and external unauthorized users as well as internal unauthorized use by legitimate users.

- Unauthorized access can occur through masquerading, impostors, or identity interception.

- A denial of service (DOS) attack overloads the computer causing normal users to be denied service.

- Trojan horses and viruses attack data on networks, but typically can be avoided by educating users and employing virus-scanning software.

- Shares that are not secure can expose your entire network to an intruder.

■ Files and folders are resources that can be secured via ACLs in Active Directory.

■ Laptops can be secured using the New Technology File System (NTFS) and the Encrypting File System (EFS) file encryption.

exam
ⓦatch

The focus of the MCP exam on security, as it relates to securing resources, is how to provide access to legitimate users and deny access to unauthorized users through local and remote connections. For instance, you'll likely see a scenario question related to information input to a Web site by members of the general public and how that data can be secured. Internal, authorized users would need read/write/change access to that database, but not all internal users would require access to the database. External users, such as the general public, should have the ability to input their data and review their data, but not to see other data. The concepts reviewed below will assist you in these types of scenario questions.

QUESTIONS

6.01: Identifying the Required Level of Security for Each Resource

1. Your company has experienced several security breaches recently. Which of these would safeguard against impostors on the network? (Choose all that apply.)

   A. Certificates

   B. Kerberos authentication

   C. Windows NT LAN Manager (NTLM) authentication

   D. EFS

2. The following window depicts an example of what?

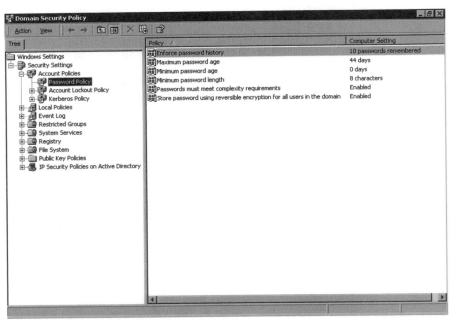

A. Strong domain security policy

B. Strong password policy

C. Stringent security policy

D. Stringent password authentication policy

3. **Current Situation:** The company you work for has recently been the object of Internet hackers trying to gain access to the network via the company's Web site.

   Required Result: Ensure Web site is secure against intruders.

   Optional Desired Results: Track the source and nature of these attacks and identify the attackers.

   Proposed Solution: Enable Transmission Control Protocol (TCP) and User Datagram Protocol (UDP) ports 135 to139 on the Web server. Disable TCP ports 80 and 443. Provide users with dial-in access until the source of the attacks is discovered and addressed. Enable event logging for successful and unsuccessful logon attempts.

What results are produced from the proposed solution?

A. The proposed solution produces the required result and all of the optional results.

B. The proposed solution produces the required result and some of the optional results.

C. The proposed solution produces the required result only.

D. The proposed solution does not produce the required result.

4. You are assigned the job of determining when to implement various security measures. When should EFS not be used?

A. When files are stored on servers in other countries

B. When files are stored on servers utilizing Active Directory

C. When files are shared with other users

D. When files are not shared with other users

5. You have been reading up on Windows 2000 and have come upon the RUNAS command. Why would you use the RUNAS command in Windows 2000?

A. To run or execute a command as an administrator while logged on as a normal user

B. To run or execute a command as an administrator while logged off

C. To run or execute a command as a user while logged on as an administrator

D. To run or execute a command as a user while logged on as another user

6. Your webmaster emailed you today to alert you that the Web site experienced a denial of service (DOS) attack over the weekend. Why is a DOS attack a security risk for an organization? (Choose all that apply.)

A. A DOS attack prevents the network from processing user authentication.

B. A DOS attack prevents legitimate users from accessing Web-based resources.

C. A DOS attack prevents users from receiving customer service from Web-based companies that use Java applets on their Web servers.

D. A DOS attack prevents Web-based servers from processing requests for service.

Understanding Active Directory Concepts

In this section, we'll review Active Directory concepts including Directory Service, schema, Global Catalog, trust relationships, namespace, sites, organizational units, replication, and group policies. These are all components of Active Directory and each plays a part in overall network security.

Sites are based on the physical topology of the network. Branch offices, campus-type locations, and individual offices are examples of various configurations that would relate directly to sites. Organizational units (OUs) are based on the logical configuration of the company. Typically, OUs are created to reflect how the company is organized: by department, unit function, or other logical grouping.

- Active Directory is used to authenticate domain users based on user account information.

- Each object in Active Directory has a Discretionary Access Control List (DACL) sometimes called an Access Control List (ACL) that is comprised of Access Control Entries (ACEs).

- The Global Catalog authenticates users during logon in a Native, multidomain model.

- Trust relationships can be one- or two-way, transitive or non-transitive.

- In a native Windows 2000–based environment, all trusts are two-way, transitive by default.

- There are five forms of trust relationships: tree-root, parent-child, shortcut, external, and non-Windows Kerberos Realm.

- Sites are local area networks (LANs) or LANs connected by high-speed links.

- OUs are logical groupings used for delegation of administration.

- Replication is the process of keeping the Active Directory information current on all domain controllers.

■ Group Policy Objects (GPOs) can be used to manage network resources in a secure, consistent manner.

■ Universal groups are only used in large, multidomain environments.

e x a m
ⓦatch

Understanding the relationship of authentication protocols and Active Directory is very important on the exam. Kerberos v5 is supported in Windows 2000. Kerberos is used in many Unix environments and using Kerberos v5 on Windows 2000 allows Windows 2000 and Unix machines to interact. However, down-level Windows NT servers do not support Kerberos. Therefore, Microsoft NT LAN Manager (NTLM) is used in mixed environments when Kerberos is not supported. If a Windows 2000 client attempts access on a Windows NT 4.0 server, Kerberos fails and NTLM is then used to authenticate the user. This is important to remember on the exam for all mixed-environment questions.

QUESTIONS

6.02: Understanding Active Directory Concepts

7. You know that Active Directory is a significant new feature in Windows 2000 and provides a number of enhanced capabilities. Which is not a feature of Windows 2000 Active Directory?

    A. IntelliMirror

    B. Multimaster replication

    C. Nonrepudiation

    D. Quality of Service (QoS) features

8. Based on the following illustration, when will replication occur if no other values have been changed?

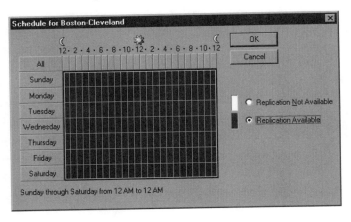

A. Every 180 minutes

B. Every 12 hours

C. Continuously

D. As often as needed

9. **Current Situation:** Your company is migrating to Windows 2000. Some servers will not be upgraded from Windows NT 4.0 for two years, due to certain business constraints. Your domains are as follows: Windows 2000 domains are WIN2K.ONE and WIN2K.TWO; Windows NT domains are NT.ONE and NT.TWO; within the NT.ONE domain, you have three child domains, SALES.NT.ONE, PRODUCT.NT.ONE, and FINANCE.NT.ONE. Your company also wants to provide access to members of your trusted partner's staff via their domain called TRUSTEDPARTNER.BIZ.

   Required Results: Create trust relationships between domains to ensure that the highest level of security is maintained.

   Optional Desired Results: Improve network management and improve logon efficiency for users.

   Proposed Solution: Create one-way, non-transitive trusts between WIN2K.ONE and TRUSTEDPARTNER.BIZ. Create two-way, transitive trusts among

NT.ONE, NT.TWO, WIN2K.ONE, and WIN2K.TWO. Create a shortcut trust among SALES.NT.ONE, PRODUCT.NT.ONE, FINANCE.NT.ONE, and WIN2K.ONE and WIN2K.TWO.

What results are produced from the proposed solution?

A. The proposed solution produces the required results and all of the optional results.

B. The proposed solution produces the required results and some of the optional results.

C. The proposed solution produces the required results only.

D. The proposed solution does not produce the required results.

10. You have migrated your network to Windows 2000, and you have promoted several servers to domain controllers. You then installed Active Directory Services. How can you verify that the installation of AD was successful? (Choose all that apply.)

A. Use the NSLOOKUP command-line utility.

B. Use the Lightweight Directory Access Protocol (LDAP) and run the VERIFY command.

C. Use DNS in the Microsoft Management Console to verify the Service Locator (SRV) resource records if you have the DNS Server.

D. View the NETLOGON.DNS file on each AD domain controller.

11. You know that the schema is part of Active Directory and that portions of Active Directory are replicated in different ways. How is the schema replicated?

A. The schema is not replicated; it is updated by enterprise schema administrators or applications with sufficient permissions.

B. A partial copy of the schema is contained on each Global Catalog server. Incremental changes to the schema are replicated according to the replication schedule for the Global Catalog server.

C. A full copy of the schema is contained on the Master Global Catalog server. Full and incremental changes are replicated on a pull basis.

D. A full copy of the schema is contained on each Global Catalog server and is replicated according to the replication configuration for each site.

Active Directory Planning Considerations

Active Directory is a new feature of Windows 2000. As such, it requires planning to be implemented in the most effective manner. Although Windows 2000 can run in a single domain model, companies often find running multiple domains to be desirable. Planning how the network will be physically and logically organized determines some of the key configuration values for Active Directory. Forests, domains, sites, site links, replication, and organizational units are the major factors that must be thoroughly planned and are reviewed in this section.

- Windows 2000 is designed to run in a single domain environment, regardless of the size of the organization.

- Multiple domains should be considered when existing Windows NT 4.0 domains are to be preserved, when administration of domains requires different policies (such as more or less security for a group of resources), if domain administration must remain autonomous, or to physically partition the network to optimize replication traffic.

- Sites are used for replication by the Windows 2000 Knowledge Consistency Checker (KCC).

- Intrasite replication uses remote procedure call (RPC) over TCP/IP as the replication method; intersite replication uses RPC, or Simple Mail Transfer Protocol (SMTP) if two systems or sites cannot communicate using RPC.

- Site links are used for replication and have four components: schedule, interval, transport, and cost.

- Group policy security templates provide standard security settings and can be modified to provide custom security templates for an organization.

exam
⚥atch

In Windows 2000, Active Directory is involved with many aspects of the distributed security model. For the exam, remember that Global Catalog servers provide user authentication and that the Global Catalog is one component of Active Directory. Each site should, ideally, have a Global Catalog server for user authentication. In addition, if Active Directory is not installed in a Windows 2000 domain, user authentication will be accomplished using NTLM since Kerberos authentication is dependent upon Active Directory.

QUESTIONS

6.03: Active Directory Planning Considerations

12. Refer to the following illustration. Site 1 has a replication window set from 1800 hours to 0600 hours (6:00P.M. to 6:00A.M.). Site 2 has a replication window set from 2200 hours to 0400 hours. Site 3 has a replication window set from 2000 hours to 0500 hours. What is the replication window for Site 4?

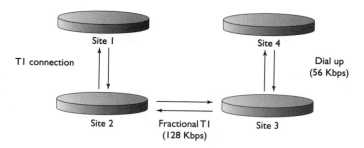

A. The replication window for Site 4 is between 1800 and 0600.

B. The replication window for Site 4 is between 2200 to 0400.

C. The replication window for Site 4 is between 2400 and 0400.

D. The replication window for Site 4 is between 2000 and 0500.

13. **Current Situation:** Your company is migrating to Windows 2000. Your company has four locations, one in the United States and three in Asia.

Required Results: Create an efficient domain plan that minimizes network administration, reflects the needs of the company, and reduces network traffic wherever possible.

Optional Desired Results: Accommodate the increased security requirements in the Research Department and minimize costs for network equipment upgrades.

Proposed Solution: Create one domain for the United States and one domain for each of the three Asian locations. Upgrade all Windows NT domains to

Windows 2000. Set replication to be only between the United States and one Asian domain and allow the two other Asian domains to pull replication data from the one Asian domain receiving updates.

What results are produced from the proposed solution?

A. The proposed solution produces the required results and all of the optional results.

B. The proposed solution produces the required results and some of the optional results.

C. The proposed solution produces the required results only.

D. The proposed solution does not produce the required results.

Questions 14–16   This scenario should be used to answer questions 14, 15, and 16.

Your company has three locations; two are connected by a high-speed link. One location, has no direct network connectivity and is reachable only via email. It does not have a domain controller although one third of the company's users are located here. Each of these three sites is running Windows 2000 on all computers. The sites are named as follows: Site 1 (corporate), Site 2 (branch-1), and Site 3 (branch-2). Site 1 (corporate) has three networks that are linked internally. Each hour (on the hour), those links are so heavily utilized that network traffic slows dramatically. Based on this information, answer the three questions that follow.

14. Why is there a problem with the site names in the current configuration?

A. Names are not unique.

B. Names do not comply with DNS naming standards.

C. Names do not comply with WINS naming standards.

D. Names are alphanumeric.

15. How can your current site plan be optimized? (Choose all that apply.)

A. Improve network connectivity between Site 2 and Site 3.

B. Improve network connectivity for Site 3 and add a domain controller.

C. Improve network connectivity for Site 3 and merge with Site 2.

D. Improve network security for Site 3 by using public key infrastructure (PKI) with SMTP.

16.   How can the hourly network slowing at Site 1 (corporate) be remedied?

    A.   Create three separate sites based on the three networks.

    B.   Create a screened subnet to protect the links from excessive traffic.

    C.   Install high-end routers among the networks to filter packets.

    D.   Create three separate domains to reduce traffic among the three networks.

TEST YOURSELF OBJECTIVE 6.04

Securing the Active Directory

Windows 2000 uses Active Directory to manage distributed security. Windows 2000 can be run without installing Active Directory, but there are many benefits to implementing AD.

Objects (such as computers, printers, and files) are protected via properties stored in Active Directory. Access to objects is allowed or denied based on the user's combined permissions. Permissions on an object can be inherited from the parent object or they can be customized to provide very granular control of objects.

Administration of many network objects can be delegated through the use of organizational units. Delegating control of a subset of network resources reduces network administration overhead and provides for more control of local resources.

- Permissions can be inherited, inheritable, or explicit.

- Inheritable permissions pass from the parent to the child object.

- Explicit permissions are permissions that are placed on the object in addition to inherited permissions.

- Permissions propagate according to settings. Typically, permissions propagate to the child objects.

- Objects created by users in the administrative group, when logged on as administrators, are owned by the group. This feature cannot be changed.

- An administrator can take ownership of an object.

- The Delegation of Control Wizard allows for standard delegation to OUs.

- Customized delegation can be done through modifying the permissions on the particular objects.

exam
ⓦatch

For the MCP exam, be sure you fully understand how permissions are managed in Windows 2000. Permissions can be inheritable from parent to child objects, but you must select the check box that enables this feature. You can also choose to reset permissions on all child objects and enable propagation of inheritable permissions. This feature is useful if there are many child objects that have had customized permissions set. Viewing permissions has changed in Windows 2000. You must enable Advanced Features in order to view permissions. Don't get caught on this one on the exam.

QUESTIONS

6.04: Securing the Active Directory

17. You want to adjust permissions for a set of files that require strong security. Which feature controls permissions in Windows 2000?

A. Access Control Entity

B. Access Control List

C. Access Control Element

D. Access Control Line

18. How can security be accessed for the computer in the following illustration?

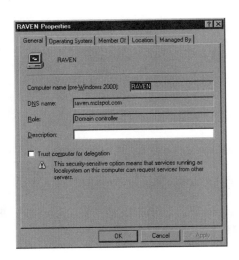

A. Go to Start | Run | Runas | security.exe.

B. Go to Start | Programs | Administrative Tools | Runas | security.exe.

C. Go to Start | Programs | Administrative Tools | Active Directory Users and Computers | View | Advanced Features.

D. Go to Start | Programs | Administrative Tools | Active Directory Users and Computers | Properties | Enable Advanced Features.

19. **Current Situation:** Your company has three domains and 14 sites. Replication of Active Directory has become a problem at two sites, in two different domains, it appears replication never completed. This has caused numerous problems since individual user accounts and group membership changes frequently. Access to network resources has been unreliable as a result. Users are complaining. The CIO has tasked you with resolving this issue quickly.

Required Results: Improve user logon, improve access to network resources, and resolve replication issue.

Optional Desired Results: Improve security across the network and improve network response time.

Proposed Solution: Place users in groups associated with their project or department. Create a universal group called WholeCompany. Copy the members of each group into the WholeCompany group so that all employees are members of the universal group to minimize replication traffic across the WAN. Set WAN replication to defaults and ensure that the links between sites are fully functional.

What results are produced from the proposed solution?

A. The proposed solution produces the required results and all of the optional results.

B. The proposed solution produces the required results and some of the optional results.

C. The proposed solution produces the required results only.

D. The proposed solution does not produce the required results.

20. A high-level executive of your company has resigned. Two weeks after his departure, the vice president of sales comes to you and asks for permission to

access the former executive's network folders on your Windows 2000 network because some important documents are there. How can this be accomplished?

A. Log on as the former executive and choose Transfer Ownership.

B. Log on as Administrator and choose Grant Ownership.

C. Log on as the vice president of sales and choose Take Ownership.

D. Log on as Administrator and choose Modify Owner.

21. When an administrator creates a network object, who is the owner?

A. The administrator

B. The Everyone group

C. The Administrator group

D. The administrator and his/her related user account

LAB QUESTION

Objectives 6.01–6.04

You have just started your new job with a company as IT director. You have been tasked with creating a network plan for migrating to Windows 2000 for your company. You have gathered the following information.

The company currently uses Windows NT 4.0 servers. There are three Unix servers and two Novell NetWare servers in your network as well. The company has three United States locations (Seattle, Boise, and Chicago), is acquiring a firm (within the next 90 days) that has two United States locations (New York and Boston), and a network consisting of four Windows 2000 servers. In Seattle and New York, the locations consist of two to five buildings located within a 35-mile radius of each other, which are connected via fractional T1 lines. The other locations are single buildings with 100MB LANs connected to the Internet via T1 lines.

Your company has a top-secret product in development in the R&D Department. In addition, you have a strong Web presence but your firm wants to extend some of its knowledge to trusted partners via an extranet. The company you are acquiring has a well-established Web presence, which is one of the reasons your firm is acquiring it. The new firm also has implemented additional security measures, including smart cards and certificates.

Your company has six departments: Corporate, HR, R&D, Sales, Support, and Finance. Each one has unique computing and access requirements. Members of the Corporate, HR, Sales, and Support groups travel regularly within the United States.

A QUICK ANSWER KEY

Objective 6.01

1. **A, B**, and **C**
2. **B**
3. **D**
4. **C**
5. **A**
6. **B** and **D**

Objective 6.02

7. **C**
8. **A**
9. **A**
10. **A, C**, and **D**
11. **D**

Objective 6.03

12. **C**
13. **B**
14. **B**
15. **B** and **C**
16. **A**

Objective 6.04

17. **B**
18. **C**
19. **D**
20. **D**
21. **C**

IN-DEPTH ANSWERS

6.01: Identifying the Required Level of Security for Each Resource

1. ☑ **A, B**, and **C** are correct. Certificates are granted either by internal Certificate Servers based on Active Directory credentials or by third-party organizations. Certificates are a secure method of user authentication. Kerberos authentication is the default authentication used in Windows 2000. Microsoft NT LAN Manager (NTLM) authentication is the default authentication used by Windows NT 4.0 and lower and is supported in Windows 2000 for backward compatibility.

   ☒ **D** is not correct. EFS encrypts files.

2. ☑ **B.** Strong password policies, enforced at the domain level, include longer passwords that contain a mixture of alphanumeric and special characters (complexity requirement), passwords that cannot be repeated often, and other characteristics of strong passwords.

   ☒ **A** is not correct. Strong domain security would include strong password policies, as well as other security measures. **C** is not correct. In Windows 2000, security is characterized as normal or strong, not stringent. **D** is not correct. Again, security is not characterized as stringent and the correct term is password policy or authentication, not both.

3. ☑ **D.** The proposed solution is just the opposite of what you should do to secure the Web site. Ports 135 to 139 are used for NetBIOS support and would enable access via these ports that should be disabled for a secure Web server. Disabling ports 80 (HTTP) and 443 (HTTPS) would effectively disable access to your Web site since most access is via HTTP (Hypertext Transport Protocol or Hypertext Transport Protocol Secure). Enabling event logging would not assist you in determining the source of the attacks since the attackers are probably not trying to log on to the network via the Web site. In some cases, enabling unsuccessful logon attempts could help pinpoint attempts at intrusion. Therefore, the solution does not produce even the required results.

    ☒ **A**, **B**, and **C** are not correct because the solution does not produce the required results.

4. ☑ **C.** EFS (Encrypting File System) encrypts files. Only the owner of the file (or a recovery agent) can decrypt the file. Therefore, files that are shared with other users should not be encrypted.

    ☒ **A** is not correct. EFS can be used on files located anywhere. EFS uses X.509 standards for encryption. Remember, however, encrypted files are transmitted across the network in an unencrypted state, so storing sensitive files on a remote server will also require a secure connection such as L2TP with IPSec. **B** is not correct. Active Directory does not use EFS, but there is no limitation regarding files stored on servers that may also be running Active Directory. **D** is not correct. When files are not shared, EFS can be used to secure sensitive data.

5. ☑ **A.** The RUNAS command is used to allow a user who is a member of the administrator's group to run a command without logging on as an administrator. In general, it is safer to run a command rather than log onto the administrator's account and inadvertently expose the network to security risks. For instance, if you are logged on as an administrator and you go out to Internet sites, you could inadvertently expose your entire network to risk.

    ☒ **B** is not correct. You cannot run any commands unless you are logged onto the network. **C** is not correct. The RUNAS command is used to avoid logging on to the administrator account, not the opposite. **D** is not correct. Typically, you would not perform actions as another user on a network and this is not how the RUNAS command is used.

6. ☑ **B** and **D** are correct. A denial of service attack overloads a Web-based server with requests for service (data). A computer can only process so many requests in a given period of time. A DOS attack intentionally overloads the processing capabilities of the server to deny service to legitimate users.

    ☒ **A** is not correct. User authentication is not specifically prevented on the network, although legitimate users can be prevented from gaining authentication via a Web site if a DOS attack is underway. **C** is not correct. A DOS attack is not directly related to the applications (or applets) a server is running.

6.02: Understanding Active Directory Concepts

7. ☑ **C.** Nonrepudiation is a basic security function of cryptography. It provides the assurance that one party in a communication cannot falsely deny that part of the communication occurred. This is not a feature of Active Directory.

☒ **A, B**, and **D** are not correct. IntelliMirror, multimaster replication, and Quality of Service features are all part of Windows 2000 Active Directory.

8. ☑ **A.** The illustration depicts the standard schedule grid for replication. It can be modified to schedule replication. However, if no other default values have been changed, replication will occur every 180 minutes, as shown in the following illustration (the screen from which the schedule grid can be accessed).

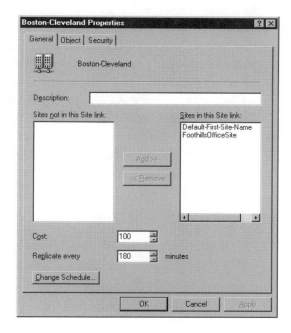

☒ **B, C**, and **D** are incorrect because the default time value for replication is 180 minutes.

9. ☑ **A.** The required results are to create trusts to maintain the highest level of security. The optional results are to improve network management and

improve logon efficiency for users. Creating a one-way, non-transitive trust between your company's domain and a trusted partner's domain will allow those members of the trusted partner's domain to use network resources. This provides high security while improving network administration related to the trusted partner. Creating shortcut trusts shortens the path for logons between any two domains in the same forest. By shortening the logon path for users from the sales, product, and finance domains of NT.ONE, logon efficiency is gained, producing the second optional result.

10. ☑ **A, C,** and **D** are correct. After the installation of Active Directory, each DNS database file will contain SRV resource records, which are pointers to DNS hosts running Active Directory Services. Using the NSLOOKUP command-line utility, you can verify that the domain controller registered its SRV resource records in the DNS database. You can also verify the SRV resources records have been created by using DNS in MMC to verify SRV resources records if you are using a server running DNS Server. If you are using a DNS Server that does not support dynamic updates, you must register the SRV resource records manually. Note that if you install the DNS Server during the Active Directory installation, you must also manually create a reverse lookup zone and set the zone attribute to Allow Dynamic Updates after the installation is complete. Finally, you can view NETLOGON.DNS, located in SYSTEMROOT\ SYSTEM32\CONFIG on each AD domain controller. You will see the Lightweight Directory Access Protocol (LDAP) SRV record. If Active Directory is properly installed, the LDAP SRV record will look similar to this:

> *ldap.tcp.Active_Directory_domain_name* IN SRV 0 150 276
> *domain_controller_name*

   ☒ **B** is not correct. LDAP does not contain a VERIFY command.

11. ☑ **D.** The schema is the universe of objects that can be stored in the Active Directory. The schema defines what attributes objects must have as well as optional attributes an object can have.

   ■ A full copy of both the schema and the configuration directory partitions are stored on each Global Catalog server.

   ■ A full replica of the domain directory partition for which the domain controller is authoritative is also stored on the Global Catalog server.

- Partial replicas of all other domain directory partitions are stored on the Global Catalog server.

- Replication occurs based on configurations for sites, site links, and replication. The schema does not change frequently. Although replication will occur according the set schedules (for instance, every 180 minutes by default), schema data will only replicate when changes occur.

☒ **A** is not correct. Although administrators or applications with proper permissions can update the schema, those updates and other changes are replicated. **B** is not correct. A full copy of the schema is kept on each Global Catalog server. **C** is not correct. The Global Catalog server does not have a Master Global Catalog server role.

6.03: Active Directory Planning Considerations

12. ☑ **C.** If replication goes through multiple site links, there must be a common window, otherwise the connection is treated as not available. For instance, if one window was from 0600 to 0800 and the second site's window was from 0900 to 1100, there would be no connection available. In this case, the common replication window is from 2400 to 0400.

☒ **A** is not correct. This is the window of replication for Site 1, but it is not the common window size. **B** is not correct. This is the replication window for Site 2, but is not the common window size. **D** is not correct. This is the replication window for Site 3, but is not the common window size.

13. ☑ **B.** Required results are to create a domain plan that reduces network administration, reflects the needs of the company, and minimizes network traffic. The optional results are to provide for the unique requirements of the Research Department and minimize costs for upgrades. The proposed solution produces the required results and only one of the two optional results. Creating these four domains would likely meet the needs of the company, since the locations of the three Asian sites are not specified. Each domain would replicate traffic within its area, although forest-wide replication would occur among the domains. User authentication traffic would be greatly reduced by creating these domains and sites. Although additional domains typically increase network

administration, in this case the reasons for multiple domains make sense and will likely ease administration. The solution does not accommodate the needs of the Research Department; an additional domain for Research would address their specific security needs. Finally, the solution does not specifically reduce costs, but it does not add any costs, thereby minimizing costs.

☒ **A**, **C**, and **D** are not correct because the proposed solution produces the required results but only one of the two optional results.

14. ☑ **B.** DNS uses site names. Therefore, site names must comply with DNS naming conventions: alphanumeric characters and hyphens only (no spaces or special characters are allowed).

☒ **A** is not correct. The names are unique. **C** is not correct. WINS is supported for backward capability to resolve NetBIOS names, but is not otherwise needed in Windows 2000. In Native Windows 2000 mode, DNS provides name resolution for the network. **D** is not correct. The names can be alphanumeric, but cannot contain spaces or special characters.

15. ☑ **B** and **C** are not correct. Site 3 poses a problem. Normally, a location reachable only via SMTP (email connectivity) would be a separate site. However, sites should each have at least one domain controller for user authentication. Since Site 3 is not connected to the network, it cannot easily be merged into another site. Therefore, the optimal solution would be to improve network connectivity for Site 3 and merge it with another site, or add a domain controller to Site 3.

☒ **A** is not correct. The network connectivity for Site 3 is at issue, not the connection between any two sites. **D** is not correct. SMTP cannot implement PKI technologies.

16. ☑ **A.** Anytime a site has network links that are very heavily utilized, you should consider creating separate sites. This will reduce network traffic by reducing or eliminating user authentication traffic as well as other site-related traffic.

☒ **B** is not correct. A screened subnet is used with Internet firewalls for network security. **C** is not correct. Routers can filter data, but creating separate sites is a more efficient and cost-effective method of reducing traffic over network links. **D** is not correct. It is not necessary to create separate domains in Windows 2000. This is exactly what sites are used for in this operating system.

6.04: Securing the Active Directory

17. ☑ **B.** The Access Control List (ACL) consists of Access Control Entries (ACEs) that determine the access levels for a particular object. These ACLs are part of the Active Directory structure.

    ☒ **A** is not correct. The correct term is Access Control Entry, not Entity. **C** and **D** are not correct. The correct term is Access Control List.

18. ☑ **C.** The Security tab can only be accessed after Advanced Features are enabled. This is to prevent unintentional modification of security access settings in Windows 2000. Advanced Features is accessed from the View menu in Active Directory Users and Computers window.

    ☒ **A, B**, and **D** are not correct because they do not reflect the correct method of accessing Advanced Features in Windows 2000.

19. ☑ **D.** The required results are as follows: improve user logon, improve network access, and resolve replication issues. Universal groups are used in Native mode, multidomain models. Remember that replication among domains occurs for forest-level information such as changes in membership to a group with universal scope. By placing all users in the universal WholeCompany group, changes to this group will be frequent. These changes must be replicated across the WAN and can be the cause of network performance degradation. If replication is not currently completing between one or more sites, this solution will exacerbate the problem. Therefore, this solution could worsen the situation and does not produce the required results. If all users were placed in groups reflecting their project or department membership and those groups were placed in the universal group, WAN replication would be minimized. This would improve the user logon experience as well as reduce network traffic. This would likely cause an improvement in access to network resources as well as overall network response time.

    ☒ **A, B**, and **D** are not correct because the proposed solution doesn't produce the required results.

20. ☑ **D.** If the former executive had the folders secured, the only way to gain access to them is to Modify Owner. This is similar to the Take Ownership permission in previous versions of Windows NT. Once you have taken ownership, you can modify the permissions on the folder(s) to grant access to others.

☒ **A** is not correct. You cannot give or transfer ownership of an object in Windows 2000. This prevents someone from making unauthorized changes and then falsely assigning ownership of the object. **B** is not correct. There is a permission called Modify Owner but not Grant Ownership in Windows 2000. **C** is not correct. The vice president of sales would have to be given permission to Modify Owner. This permission is typically only granted to network administrators. However, the permission would not be called Take Ownership because that permission was used in Windows NT 4.0 and earlier.

21. ☑ **C.** By default, when an administrator creates an object, that object is owned by the Administrator group. This is a built-in feature of Windows 2000 and cannot be modified. All members of that group have permission to modify the object. This is one reason why it is important not to log on and use the administrator account as you would a normal user account.

☒ **A** is not correct. The administrator is one of many owners of the object. **B** is not correct. The Everyone group is not the default owner of the object, although by default the Everyone group has access to the object. **D** is not correct. The individual's user account is not an owner of the object.

LAB ANSWER

Objectives 6.01–6.04

Your network plan should include information on the forest, domain, and OU structure. Next, you should define the site topology and site links. Finally, servers should be configured and placed at the sites. Here's an example of a network plan that factors in these elements and the information given:

Forest The forest will contain several domains.

Domain Domain1 for current structure and possibly part of new company. Domain2 for R&D because they need very strong security. Domain3 for at least part of the newly acquired company because they have a strong Internet presence and will likely need to keep their domain name active on the Internet.

Organizational units Five OUs will organize the company by department. Additional OUs may be created if departments want or need to further delegate administration. Since R&D is in a separate domain, that domain could be managed separately, or a sixth OU could be created to manage R&D resources across domains.

Site topology Each location is a separate site. In locations where there are multiple buildings, the connection between these buildings is slower than the Internet connection. Thus, each of these buildings would likely be considered to be a site. If you wanted to avoid this, you could increase the connectivity between the buildings. Each site would require a site link to be established to optimize replication traffic. In addition, the site bridge should be determined. The current networks are running 100MB LANs with an unspecified number of servers.

Place servers Each site should have a server running Windows 2000 with Active Directory and Global Catalog for user authentication. Each site should have other servers running the various FSMO roles (per forest and domain requirements).

Security and group policies   Users should be placed in groups based on their security and access needs. Group policies should be established for the computers on the network, to establish baseline security for all computers. The HISEC template should be used for computers in the R&D group to provide the highest level of security in that domain. Two-way transitive trusts should be established between all the domains except the R&D domain. That domain should have a one-way, non-transitive trust in place with all other domains to ensure that trusted users from the R&D domain have access to needed corporate resources, but that trusted users from all other domains do not have automatic access to the R&D domain.

MICROSOFT CERTIFIED SYSTEMS ENGINEER

7

Designing a Windows 2000 Security Solution

TEST YOURSELF OBJECTIVES

T his chapter covers designing a security solution in Windows 2000. Designing a security solution encompasses several key components: security policies, authentication strategies, public key infrastructure (PKI), and securing network services.

Security policies can be implemented at the forest, domain, site, and OU levels. Authentication strategies include authenticating local and remote users, authentication protocols, and interoperability considerations. This chapter also reviews and tests you on key concepts in designing a public key infrastructure using the new and enhanced features in Windows 2000, including certificate-based security. It is important to understand how to design a solution for securing network services, which can include Web protocols, network protocols, and TCP/IP ports.

TEST YOURSELF OBJECTIVE 7.01

Designing the Placement and Inheritance of Security Policies

In this chapter, we'll review security policies and how these policies are both applied and inherited in a network. Security policies include how users log on and use the network, as well as how computers and services on computers are secured. In Windows 2000, the most efficient way to implement security policies is by using Group Policy Objects (GPOs) in Active Directory (AD).

In Native mode, user authentication is performed using the Kerberos v5 protocol. However, Microsoft NT LAN Manager (NTLM) and remote access authentications such as MS-CHAP can be used in Windows 2000. Public key infrastructure, a framework for different types of secure authentication, involves a number of new technologies including certificates, smart cards, and various encryption technologies. Finally, this chapter will review the important features of securing network services including DNS, Remote Installation Service (RIS), SNMP, and DHCP.

- Security administrators can use digital certificates in Active Directory to control administration with greater levels of detail.

- The Active Directory can exist in small networks with only a few computers, users, and other objects or in larger networks with thousands of objects.

- WANs are commonly divided into smaller segments beginning with sites, expanding to domains, and ending in organizational units.

- Domains work as security boundaries by blocking users without explicit access privileges from gaining access.

- Conflicting policies are resolved in a hierarchical model, where sites are overruled by domains, and domains are overruled by OUs.

e x a m

ⓦatch

Remember that there are security groups and Group Policy Objects (GPOs) in Windows 2000. Both are used to administer security, but each has a very different function. Security groups are groups created for security settings. Users are placed in groups and permissions are assigned to groups. Access Control Lists (ACLs) contain the group(s) with permission to an object and individual users should be added or removed from the group. GPOs, on the other hand, are used to enforce various levels of security on computers within the domain. It is essential that you understand how these work in order to successfully navigate the MCP exam.

QUESTIONS

7.01: Designing the Placement and Inheritance of Security Policies

1. You have migrated your network from a Windows NT 4.0 network to Windows 2000 network. Some of the domain controllers are still running Windows NT 4.0 for business reasons. You want to assign certain permissions to staff for managing the domain controllers in Windows 2000. You understand that domain local groups are a new feature in Windows 2000 designed for just this purpose. However, you can't seem to create any domain local groups. What could be the problem?

    A. In a mixed environment, you must use global groups instead; domain local groups are only available in Native mode.

B. In a mixed environment, you must use local groups; domain local groups are only available in Native mode.

C. You must enable domain local groups via the Active Directory Domain Policy snap-in.

D. You must create local groups on the domain controllers, and then promote them to domain local groups.

2. What type of hierarchy is depicted in the following illustration?

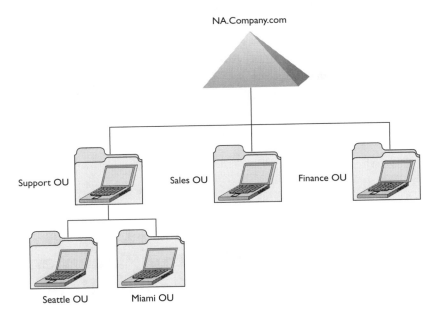

A. Two-tiered delegation model.

B. Multitiered OU model.

C. Multilevel functional OU model.

D. The diagram does not depict a legitimate hierarchy.

3. **Current Situation:** Your company is expanding dramatically. You have been asked to define a set of security policies that will work for your current company size, as well as handle any expansion that occurs in the next two years. The Western region is home to the Research group that works on top-secret

projects for the government. This group will double in size over the next 12 months.

Required Results: The security policy must provide fast network services to all users, ease of administration, and secure user authentication.

Optional Desired Results: The security policy should also utilize the latest technologies and lower total cost of ownership.

Proposed Solution: Create domains for each geographic region and install domain controllers with Active Directory in each domain. Create transitive two-way trusts between all domains except for the Western domain, which is home to the Research group. Create OUs that span the domains for each unit: Finance, Engineering, Research, HR, and Support. Implement the highest security group policy for all domains.

What results are produced from the proposed solution?

A. The proposed solution produces the required results and all of the optional results.

B. The proposed solution produces the required results and some of the optional results.

C. The proposed solution produces the required results only.

D. The proposed solution does not produce the required results.

4. George manages the Services OU, which is the parent OU of both the Installation OU and the Support OU. George has delegated Full Control of the child OUs to Lorraine. Lorraine configured a number of security policies for the Support OU, but she also left a number of default settings. However, when she inspects which policies are in effect, she finds that some of the default settings have changed. What could have caused this?

A. A child OU must have all settings configured. If settings are left in their default state, they will be overwritten by the domain values.

B. The settings Lorraine implemented were in conflict with the settings George implemented.

C. The parent OU's settings were applied.

D. Lorraine neglected to click the No Override check box.

5. If you had computers in a manufacturing plant that were rarely rebooted and you wanted to change their security configuration, how could you do this without manually rebooting each machine?

   A. Use the CMD.EXE command with the /configure switch.

   B. Use the SECEDIT.EXE command with the /configure switch.

   C. Use the SECEDIT.EXE command with the /refreshpolicy switch.

   D. Use the SECCMD.EXE command with the /refreshpolicy switch.

TEST YOURSELF OBJECTIVE 7.02

Designing an Authentication Strategy

In this section, we'll review authentication in Windows 2000. By default, Kerberos v5 provides single logon user authentication. NTLM is supported for backward compatibility. Smart cards provide strong authentication using the public key infrastructure (PKI) in Windows 2000. Windows 2000 supports Point-to-Point Protocols (PPPs) for remote authentication (MS-CHAP) and Extensible Authentication Protocol (EAP) with Transport Layer Security (TLS) for stronger security using token cards, smart cards, and other third-party methods. Access Control Lists (ACLs) are used to manage access to network resources based on user authentication.

Domains provide user authentication services to domain users. Trust relationships can be established so users from one domain can gain access to resources in another domain.

- Default user authentication occurs through Active Directory using the Kerberos v5 protocol.

- NTLM is supported for authentication on down level computers such as Windows NT 4.0 (and below) clients and servers, and non-Windows clients.

- Remote access users are authenticated using standard PPPs or more secure EAP methods, including smart cards, token cards, or one-time passwords.

- Users are authenticated by domain controllers within their domain or via domain controllers in other domains with whom there is a trust relationship.

- Computers and services can be authenticated when making network connections to other servers. Computers can also be "trusted for delegation," which means the services can make network connections on behalf of a user.

- Digital certificates are electronic documents that computer systems use to identify and authenticate users participating in an application, such as Web browsing, email, and file transfer.

- Encryption is the process of scrambling data to make it unreadable to an unprivileged user. Decryption is the process of unscrambling the data to make it readable.

- EFS allows users to protect files and folders by encrypting them with a public/private key scheme that utilizes their user profile for convenience.

exam
ⓦatch

Microsoft MCP exams typically focus on the newest technologies within the exam topic. In this case, the use of smart card technology as a secure authentication method will likely be highlighted. Keep the following information in mind. Smart cards rely upon the PKI of Windows 2000. In addition to PKI and the smart cards themselves, each computer requires a smart card reader. Also keep in mind that you need an enterprise certificate authority rather than a stand-alone or third-party certificate authority to support smart card logon in Windows 2000.

QUESTIONS

7.02: Designing an Authentication Strategy

6. Your network is running both Windows 2000 and Windows NT domain controllers. In this case, which authentication protocol will be used?

   A. Kerberos v5 for all clients.

   B. NTLM for all clients.

   C. Kerberos v5 for all Windows 2000 clients.

   D. The network administrator should set it to NTLM manually to support Mixed mode.

7. The following graphic illustrates what type of trust relationship between SupportDomain and Finance.RootDomain?

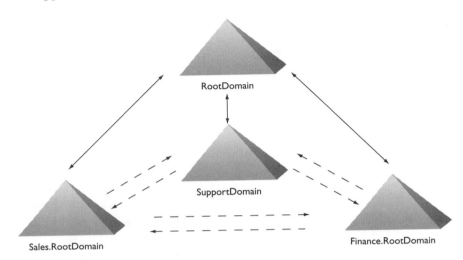

RootDomain

SupportDomain

Sales.RootDomain

Finance.RootDomain

   A. Parent-child

   B. Complete

   C. Crisscross

   D. Shortcut

8. **Current Situation:** You have four locations. Each location has users that dial into the network using Windows NT 4.0 RAS services. Network servers have all been upgraded to Windows 2000. All user laptops are running Windows NT 4.0. Some will not be upgraded to Windows 2000 for another 12 months.

   Required Results: Ensure that the laptops use highest level of security possible and improve connection security.

   Optional Desired Results: Lower connection costs and improve user authentication processes for all users.

   Proposed Solution: Place all laptops running Windows 2000 in one OU. Place all laptops running Windows NT 4.0 in a second OU. Implement a Windows 2000 Certificate Authority server and use certificates for authentication of all users running Windows 2000 laptops. Have Windows 2000 users connect via VPN connections rather than dialing into the network. Configure VPN to use L2TP with IPSec. Implement EFS on these same laptops. For all laptops running Windows NT 4.0, use MS-CHAP for strong authentication. Have NT users connect via VPN connections utilizing PPP. Implement NTFS on these laptops and EFS on all Windows 2000 laptops.

What results are produced from the proposed solution?

A. The proposed solution produces the required results and all of the optional results.

B. The proposed solution produces the required results and some of the optional results.

C. The proposed solution produces the required results only.

D. The proposed solution does not produce the required results.

9. You want to implement the most secure solution for your company's network. You have heard that a new method of authentication called Digest Authentication is included in Windows 2000. In what situation would you implement Digest Authentication?

A. To provide secure authentication of audit logs on the network

B. To provide secure authentication of Internet users via a Web browser

C. To provide secure authentication of schema changes initiated by Web-based applications

D. To provide secure authentication across ATM connections

10. You have a friend who's arguing that Kerberos authentication is faster than NTLM authentication. Which of the following statements should he use to validate his claim?

A. The structure of a Kerberos authentication packet is smaller than NTLM.

B. Kerberos authentication occurs at the Network layer in Windows 2000.

C. Users authenticated with Kerberos are issued a ticket that can be used to access network resources unlimited times.

D. Users authenticated with NTLM require access tokens that must be generated each time a user accesses a resource.

Designing a Public Key Infrastructure

Public key infrastructure (PKI) in Windows 2000 is based on certificates. Certificates are issued by certificate authorities (CAs), which can be trusted third-party organizations for public certificates or internal Certificate Servers for company employees and trusted partners. Certificate Servers can be enterprise CAs, which require Active Directory services and utilize user credentials stored in Active Directory to generate the certificate. Certificate Servers can be stand-alone CAs, which do not require Active Directory and can be used to issue certificates to users not part of the domain, such as trusted partners. Certificate Servers can also be implemented in one of three roles: root, intermediate, or issuing.

- The public key infrastructure in Windows 2000 can be used to secure email, Web sites, and applications. It can also be used for strong user authentication.

- A certification authority is a trusted entity responsible for issuing digital certificates to individuals or systems based on verification of applicants' identities.

- Using Certificate Servers, an organization has full control over the policies associated with the issuance, management, and revocation of certificates.

- Certificate authorities can be root, intermediate, or issuing. They can be installed as enterprise CAs or stand-alone CAs.

- Companies using certificates for their Web servers and browsers from a third-party vendor (third-party CAs) need to consider confidentiality, cost of ownership, and quality of service issues.

exam
ⓦatch

Certificates and certificate authorities (CAs) are new security features in Windows 2000. The use of certificates greatly reduces various security risks. For the exam, make sure you understand the relationship between root, intermediate, and issuing CAs. These are hierarchical and you must establish the root CA first. Also understand the difference between enterprise and stand-alone CAs. The enterprise CA relies upon Active Directory and therefore is for internal users only. Stand-alone CAs can be used for external users such as trusted partners or Web site users. If you're unclear about any of these items, do additional reading. It will pay off when you sit for the exam.

QUESTIONS

7.03: Designing a Public Key Infrastructure

11. **Current Situation:** You work for a company that is experiencing a serious labor dispute. As a result, the computers on the shop floor have been subject to people attempting to gain improper access during off-shift hours.

    Required Results: Ensure the computers on the shop floor are secure. Improve security for the entire network.

    Optional Desired Results: Provide improved methods for authenticating all shop floor users. Provide information about all attempts at unauthorized use.

    Proposed Solution: Install video cameras to monitor computers during off-shift hours. Place all computers on the shop floor in an OU. Create a group policy for these computers that disables all changes to the desktop. Implement smart cards for user authentication. Enable auditing successful logon events.

    What results are produced from the proposed solution?

    A. The proposed solution produces the required results and all of the optional results.

    B. The proposed solution produces the required results and some of the optional results.

    C. The proposed solution produces the required results only.

    D. The proposed solution does not produce the required results.

12. Based on the following illustration, what type of policy is in place?

A. Certificate policy

B. Administrator certificate policy

C. Stand-alone policy

D. Enterprise policy

Questions 13–15   This scenario should be used to answer questions 13, 14, and 15.

You are responsible for implementing PKI in your organization. Your company has just developed a new software application that works via the application service provider (ASP) model over the Internet. Your company believes it is about six months ahead of its competitors in the development of certain features. In order to gain funding for your company, you want to give access to the product to prospective clients and venture capitalists. Your job is to design and implement all aspects of online authentication. Users must apply for and gain approval to use the Web site to ensure that none of your competitors is trying to get a preview of your product. You must also provide a secure way for customers to pay for the use of the product via your Web site should they choose to sign up for use of the application.

13. What type of renewal policy will you establish for your certificates?

A. Automatic

B. Short

C. Long

D. None

14. What type of CA policy would you use for distributing certificates to users?

A. Stand-alone CA

B. Enterprise CA

C. Group policy CA

D. Commercial CA

15. What type of certificate mapping would you use, if any?

A. Many-to-one

B. One-to-one

C. Many-to-many

D. Grid

TEST YOURSELF OBJECTIVE 7.04

Designing Windows 2000 Network Services Security

There are risks involved with providing network services. If services are not properly configured and secured, intruders could cause network disruptions, including completely disabling a network. Some of these services are required, while others are not. Therefore, whether to provide these services as well as how to secure them is an integral part of Windows 2000 security. Services include DHCP, DNS, SNMP, RIS, Web services, LDAP, and mail services. This section will review securing these network services.

- There are no security options for DHCP because it supports broadcast-based initial requests.

- The DHCP server should not be a member of the DNSUpdateProxy group. This will give any user or computer full control of the DNS records corresponding to the domain controllers.

- DNS servers have every IP address of every host on your network; this sort of information can be valuable to anyone who may want to intrude.

- Windows 2000 uses DNS as the primary name service. It supports dynamic DNS and hosting DNS zone files within AD.

- Secured dynamic updates are a supported only in Active Directory integrated DNS zones.

- Remote Installation Service (RIS) lets you place images of built systems onto a central server and download those images to a computer with an empty hard disk.

- RIS uses Dynamic Host Configuration Protocol (DHCP) and Trivial File Transfer Protocol (TFTP) as pre-boot protocols. Neither supports user authentication. Failure to properly configure RIS exposes the network to security risks.

- Simple Network Management Protocol (SNMP) agents monitor devices and provide information to the management console or server.

- SNMP community names should be set with read-only access to MIBs to secure against intruders.

- SNMP uses UDP port 161 (general SNMP messages) and UDP port 162 (SNMP trap messages).

- The Terminal Server model is based on a company's business applications residing in one location and users accessing those applications through Windows-based terminals.

Terminal Services was introduced in Windows NT but is greatly enhanced in Windows 2000. With many companies pushing for Web-based applications, Terminal Services will be widely implemented. Expect to see one or more questions on the security exam related to Terminal Services. Remember that using Terminal Services provides added security not only because of the stronger security inherent in Windows 2000, but because the data transmitted back and forth between the server and the client are very small packets of screen-related data. This provides an extremely fast, secure solution for remote access of a wide variety of applications via the Internet. Terminal Services can also extend the life of a legacy application and allow users with older computers to utilize applications without meeting minimum hardware or software requirements.

QUESTIONS

7.04: Designing Windows 2000 Network Services Security

16. With secure dynamic update in Windows 2000, which domain members have only the Create permission for DNS?

    A. Domain Administrator group

    B. Authenticated User group

    C. DNS Zone Administrator group

    D. Everyone group

17. Based on the following illustration, how has Terminal Services been deployed
     in this organization?

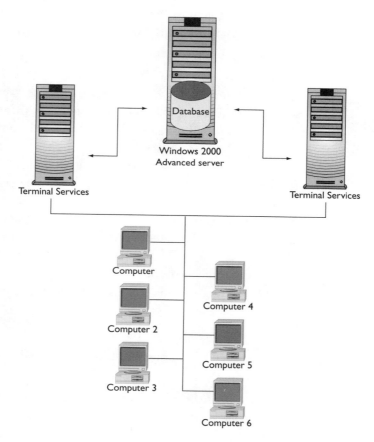

A. Remote administration

B. Line-of-business application

C. Central desktop deployment

D. Remote access

18. **Current Situation:** Your CIO wants to begin automating and standardizing
     software configuration and installation on all new computers. She would like to
     standardize on Windows 2000 Professional. She believes this will save the
     company over $480,000 annually. You have been asked to create a plan for
     implementing this.

Required Results: Install a set of applications configured in a standard and automated manner to new computers on the network. Implement using the highest levels of security possible, and prevent unauthorized use of disk resources.

Optional Desired Results: Minimize subnet traffic and create a secure method of using this solution via the WAN.

Proposed Solution: Use RIS to standardize the installation of Windows 2000 Professional on new network computers. Use the Windows Installer Service to standardize the way applications are installed on these computers. Minimize the number of administrators allowed to install or configure RIS servers on your network. Set up the distribution folder and name it i386. Copy the contents of the i386 folder on the Windows 2000 Professional CD to this folder. Assign Read & Execute permissions to the Authenticated User group for this folder. Create an answer file so you can run unattended installations of Windows 2000 Professional. Use the SYSPREP command along with a third-party disk-imaging application to duplicate the disk of a master computer configuration. Configure directories containing TFTP downloads as read-only. Use multihomed DHCP/ RIS servers. Implement router-to-router VPN for the WAN implementation of this plan. Configure RIS servers to respond only to previously installed clients or those already created in AD.

What results are produced from the proposed solution?

A. The proposed solution produces the required results and all of the optional results.

B. The proposed solution produces the required results and some of the optional results.

C. The proposed solution produces the required results only.

D. The proposed solution does not produce the required results.

19. Which is an authentication method supported by IIS for Web services in Windows 2000? (Choose all that apply.)

A. Anonymous

B. Basic

C. Clear

D. Digest

20. You've read a lot about Simple Network Management Protocol, and you know that it's a widely used network management standard used with TCP/IP networks. You'd like to implement it on your network but are concerned about security risks. Which element of SNMP poses the greatest network security risk?

   A. Read access to NMS

   B. Write access to MIB

   C. Read & Execute access to UDP ports 161 and 162

   D. Unencrypted trap events

LAB QUESTION

Objectives 7.01–7.04

Using the concepts reviewed in this chapter, design a security solution for the following company.

You work for an insurance company that is designing a new, Web-based insurance solution. The plan is that potential customers would browse your Web site for information about your company's products and services. If users sign up, they could receive a free, no-obligation quote for health, home, auto, and life insurance. They could also opt to receive regular insurance-related email updates.

Your company's agents currently work from one of hundreds of small branch offices across the United States. Each office has dial-up access to a corporate RRAS server. Agents typically work 10 to 25 hours per week from home. Agents need to enter, change, and delete data related to their set of clients. They also need access to the latest quote information that is available on the Web site. The line-of-business application they use is installed on each desktop and laptop. The application is updated every quarter.

Your company would like to deploy insurance kiosks in airports and supermarkets around the country. In airports, customers could purchase travel insurance online via these kiosks. Additionally, existing customers could change or update their information at any of these kiosks. Your company would also like to install these kiosks in hospitals so people could check or change their benefits prior to being admitted for care.

Your network is a 100MB Ethernet LAN and the dial-up connections from the branches are the only WAN connections. You have implemented several servers for your Web site including one running IIS, one with the actual Web database on it, and others that comprise your firewall.

A contract has been negotiated with a national ISP to provide Internet connectivity to all kiosks. This ISP provides local access numbers throughout the United States. Kiosks would have a live Internet connection 24/7. The ISP has cut your firm a very competitive deal because your firm agreed to allow the ISP to post their logo and contact information on your kiosks in strategic positions.

Based on this information, what security concerns do you have? How would you address these? What technologies in Windows 2000 would enable you to provide a comprehensive plan to address each of the concerns and initiatives listed? Include authentication strategies, PKI technologies, and securing network services in your answer.

QUICK ANSWER KEY

Objective 7.01

1. B
2. A
3. D
4. C
5. C

Objective 7.02

6. C
7. D
8. B
9. B
10. C

Objective 7.03

11. B
12. C
13. B
14. A
15. B

Objective 7.04

16. B
17. B
18. A
19. A, B, and D
20. B

IN-DEPTH ANSWERS

7.01: Designing the Placement and Inheritance of Security Policies

1. ☑ **B.** One of the reasons to migrate your network to a native Windows 2000 environment (all Windows 2000 domain controllers) is to take advantage of new features in Windows 2000 not available in Mixed mode. There are several new group types available, including the domain local group. Instead, you would use local groups, which serve the same purpose in Windows NT 4.0 and in Mixed mode environments. They are used to grant specific access to resources on the local computer. In Window NT environments, local groups created on the PDC are shared among the PDC and BDCs.

   ☒ **A** is not correct. Global groups are effectively the same as global groups in Windows NT. They can only contain members from within the domain in which they exist. They can be granted permissions to resources in any domain in the forest or in trusted forests. They are not specifically involved with local domain controller permissions. **C** is not correct. There is no Domain Policy snap-in, Group Policy Objects are accessed via Active Directory Users and Computers from the Administrative Tools menu. Domain local groups will not be available until the network is running in Native mode. Then, all local groups on domain controllers will become domain local groups. **D** is not correct. You cannot promote local groups. Local groups in a mixed environment will become domain local groups when the network is transitioned to Native mode.

2. ☑ **A.** The illustration shows Seattle and Miami OUs being subordinate to the Support OU. This is an example of a two-tiered delegation model.

   ☒ **B** and **C** are not correct. The proper term is two-tiered delegation. **D** is not correct because the diagram does depict a legitimate hierarchy.

3. ☑ **D.** The required results are as follows: fast network services to all users, ease of administration, and secure user authentication. The proposed solution

appears to produce all of these results until the last part of the policy—implement the highest security group policy for all domains. The HISEC template requires the use of IPSec for end-to-end data encryption. This will slow the network down significantly. This does not meet the requirement to provide fast network services to all users. Since the only apparent need for very strong security is in the Western region, implementing the HISEC template on just that domain would solve the problem and produce the required results.

☒ **A**, **B**, and **C** are not correct because the proposed solution does not produce the required results. Also, the proposed solution does not address either of the optional results.

4. ☑ **C.** When a group policy setting is configured for a parent OU and the same group policy setting is not configured for a child OU, the objects in the child OU will inherit the group policy setting from the parent OU. If the group policy setting was configured for the child OU and the configuration values for the parent and child OUs were in conflict, the child OU values would be implemented.

☒ **A** is not correct. Default values can remain if the parent OU does not have configured values for those objects. If values are not configured, they will only be overwritten if the parent OU contains values for those objects. **B** is not correct. If child OU group policy settings are in conflict with the parent OU, the child OU settings will be applied. In this case, Lorraine did not set certain values and those were replaced with settings from the parent OU. **D** is not correct. The No Override feature is used to prevent child containers from overriding a group policy object set at a higher GPO level. If Lorraine wanted to preserve her settings, she could have used the Block Inheritance setting, though this should be used sparingly.

5. ☑ **C.** At the Windows 2000 command line, using the SECEDIT.EXE command will provide certain security configuration options not available through the user interface. If a security policy is changed, a refresh can be forced using the /refreshpolicy switch. This propagates the group policy every 60 to 90 minutes and when local security policy settings are modified.

☒ **A**, **B**, and **D** are not correct because the correct command-line executable is SECEDIT.EXE with the option switch of /refreshpolicy.

7.02: Designing an Authentication Strategy

6. ☑ **C.** Kerberos v5 is used for all Windows 2000 clients, even in Mixed mode. NTLM is used for all non–Windows 2000 clients (except for Unix clients that implement v5 of Kerberos).

   ☒ **A** is not correct. Kerberos v5 does not support down level clients. **B** is not correct. Even in Mixed mode, NTLM will only be used when Kerberos cannot be used. **D** is not correct. The operating system will perform authentication based on the needs of the client, using either Kerberos v5 or NTLM. It does not need to be manually configured.

7. ☑ **D.** A shortcut trust relationship minimizes the number of domains that must be crossed before a user can be authenticated. When there are multiple domains, creating shortcut trusts can greatly enhance domain user authentication without compromising security.

   ☒ **A** is not correct. A parent-child trust relationship is hierarchical and must share a common namespace such as Sales.RootDomain, Finance.RootDomain (both child domains), and RootDomain (parent domain). **B** is not correct. A complete trust is not a trust type in Windows 2000. **C** is not correct. A crisscross trust is not a legitimate trust type.

8. ☑ **B.** The required results are to ensure the use of the highest level of security possible and to improve connection security. The proposed solution uses the highest level of security possible. Windows 2000 laptops are using certificates and Windows NT 4.0 laptops are using MS-CHAP. This is the highest level of security possible in this environment. By implementing certificates, L2TP with IPSec in VPN connections, connection security has been improved. For Windows NT 4.0 laptops, using VPN connections with PPTP also improves existing security measures. Therefore, the solution produces the required results. The optional results are to lower connection costs and improve the user authentication process. Using VPN, users can connect to local ISPs rather than incurring long distance charges. In this scenario, we don't know if users are local or remote. However, maintaining modem banks and phone lines for dial-in access is generally more expensive than local ISP charges. Therefore, the solution also provides a lower cost. Implementing certificates and VPN, the solution improves user authentication for Windows 2000 users. VPN with PPTP improves security for NT users. However, the user authentication

process has not been improved. Therefore, this solution does not produce all of the optional results.

☒ **A**, **C**, and **D** are not correct because the solution produces the required results and some of the optional results.

9. ☑ **B.** Digest Authentication (DA) is part of Windows 2000 and provides increased security for Internet users on the network. The DA prompts a user of a browser for an ID and password. These are protected by a hash created from the user ID and password and the server's public ID. The browser must support HTTP 1.1 or higher in order to implement DA.

☒ **A** is not correct. There is no authentication protocol involved with audit logs in Windows 2000. **C** is not correct. Schema changes must be made by authorized administrators or applications, but Digest Authentication is not involved in this process. **D** is not correct. Secure authentication across WAN connections in Windows 2000 is provided by one of several methods including PPP, EAP-TLS, or MS-CHAP.

10. ☑ **C.** Kerberos issues a session ticket to users when they are authenticated. During that session, users can access network resources by using the session ticket. Rather than continually requesting authentication, Kerberos-authenticated users gain more rapid access through this session-based authentication scheme.

☒ **A** is not correct. The speed of Kerberos is not based on the size of the authentication data traveling on the network. **B** is not correct. Kerberos authentication occurs at the Application layer, as does NTLM authentication. **D** is not correct. The access token is created once when the user is authenticated and is used during that logon session. Unlike Kerberos, however, access privileges must be checked each time a user wants to access a resource when authenticated using NTLM.

7.03: Designing a Public Key Infrastructure

11. ☑ **B.** The required results are as follows: ensure the computers on the shop floor are secure and improve security for the entire network. By installing video cameras, the computers are likely to be physically safe during off-shift hours. By implementing group policies that lock down the desktops of computers on the shop floor, the required result of ensuring that the computers on the shop floor

are secure is met. Security for the entire network is improved by managing the security of this group of computers via an OU with group policies applied, as well as by implementing smart cards for user authentication. It is far more difficult to gain unauthorized network access with smart card technology in place. Therefore, the required results are produced. The optional results are as follows: provide improved methods for authenticating all users and provide information about all attempts at unauthorized use. Smart card technology improves user authentication for shop floor users by adding a layer of security. However, the solution does not provide information about all attempts at unauthorized use. Auditing only successful logons will not help you assess who might be trying to gain unauthorized access. Auditing both successful and unsuccessful attempts or unsuccessful attempts only would yield that information. Therefore, the solution produces only one of the two optional results.

☒ **A, C,** and **D** are not correct because the solutions produce the required results and one of the two optional results.

12. ☑ **C.** The illustration shows a certificate being issued by a certificate server with a network administrator involved. This is the typical scenario for a stand-alone certificate authority. It can work independent of Active Directory. All CA requests are set to pending until an administrator of the CA verifies the identity of the requestor and allows the request.

☒ **A** is not correct. Certificate policies would encompass a larger issue such as how you would choose to implement certificates. Stand-alone certificate authorities would be one aspect of an overall policy. **B** is not correct. Administrator certificate policy is not a legitimate option in Windows 2000. **D** is not correct. An enterprise CA requires Active Directory to be installed. Requests for certificates are based on user information stored in AD.

13. ☑ **B.** Certificates should be configured with short renewal cycles to prevent compromise of security. Short renewal cycles discourage interception and compromise of the key.

14. ☑ **A.** A stand-alone CA provides a CA that functions independently of Active Directory. Users must be approved by an administrator of the stand-alone CA. This will enable your company to review and approve each user to ensure that your competitor does not get a sneak preview of the product.

☒ **B** is not correct. Since users are external, they would not be part of Active Directory. Enterprise CAs depend on AD services. **C** is not correct. There is no group policy CA in Windows 2000. **D** is not correct. A commercial CA could be used in some cases, but your requirement is to closely monitor all requests to use the Web site. Using a commercial CA would not meet this need.

15. ☑ **B.** One-to-one mapping is appropriate in this scenario. You have relatively few prospective clients and venture capital partners that would require access to the application at this time. Maintaining strict control over this portion of your Web site would require an administrator to review and approve or reject all requests.

☒ **A** is not correct. Many-to-one associates all certificates from a specific certification authority to a single Windows 2000 user account. This is useful if you have a large number of clients and are using an external CA. **C** is not correct. Many-to-many is not a legitimate certificate mapping type in Windows 2000. **D** is not correct. Grid is not a legitimate certificate mapping type in Windows 2000.

7.04: Designing Windows 2000 Network Services Security

16. ☑ **B.** When you create an Active Directory integrated zone, the zone is configured to allow only secure dynamic updates by default. Only the computers, groups, and users specified in the DACL can create or modify dnsNode objects within the zone. By default, all members of the Authenticated User group will have Create permission. The Authenticated User group includes all authenticated computers and users in an Active Directory forest.

☒ **A, C,** and **D** are not correct. By default the Authenticated User group is the only group with the Create permission. This secures the network from computers attempting to impersonate other computers or secure network resources.

17. ☑ **B.** The Application Server mode of Terminal Services is well suited to deploying line-of-business applications. In the illustration shown, data is entered into and retrieved from the database server. The data is maintained separate from the Terminal Services servers to provide redundancy and failover control.

☒ **A** is not correct. Remote administration enables network administrators with appropriate permissions to remotely administer Windows 2000 servers over TCP/IP connections. The illustration does not show a TCP/IP connection or any external connection. **C** is not correct. Central Desktop deployment is achieved by loading desktop applications onto a Windows 2000 server with Terminal Services enabled in Application Server mode. Applications run on the server and each client computer runs a small, single application that emulates each user's Windows-based desktop. **D** is not correct. Remote access extends the capabilities of Terminal Services server over an external TCP/IP connection. The illustration does not show an external connection.

18. ☑ **A.** The required results are as follows: install a set of applications configured in a standard and automated manner, use the highest levels of security, and prevent unauthorized use of disk resources. Using RIS allows for a standardized and automated installation of Windows 2000 Professional. You can configure it for a clean install (new computers) or an upgrade. In this case, you would choose a clean install. The Windows Installer Services is a Windows 2000 component that standardizes the manner in which applications are installed on multiple computers. By minimizing the number of RIS server administrators, setting the TFTP download directories to read-only, setting the i386 folder permissions, and configuring RIS servers to respond only to previously installed clients or those already created in AD, you have implemented strong security. TFTP download directories being read-only and the i386 folder allowing only Read & Execute permissions also prevents unauthorized use of disk resources.

The optional results are as follows: minimize subnet traffic and create a secure method of using this solution via the WAN. By using multi-homed DHCP/RIS servers, client/server data transactions are minimized and kept to the local subnet. Implementing router-to-router VPN for the WAN connections provides a high degree of security in a WAN setting. An alternative to router-to-router VPN would be to establish an end-to-end tunnel with L2TP and IPSec.

☒ **B, C,** and **D** are not correct because the solution produces the required results as well as all of the optional results.

19. ☑ **A, B,** and **D** are correct. Anonymous authentication uses the IUSR_ *computername* account for resource access. Basic authentication is implemented via a browser prompting for *username* and *password* before access is allowed. This is encoded using Base64 encoding, which is not particularly secure and is easily unencoded. Digest authentication is employed when the browser prompts for *username* and *password* and uses a one-way hashing scheme to

protect this user authentication data. The hashing scheme is based on Message Digest 5 (MD5), used to encrypt the credentials. Digest Authentication will work through a proxy server.

☒ **C** is not correct. Clear is not a legitimate authentication method in Windows 2000. Clear text is how *username* and *password* are passed using anonymous authentication.

20. ☑ **B.** There is the risk that attackers may gain useful information from reading data in the Management Information Database (MIB). However, the bigger risk is that a server, service, or network operation could be disrupted if an attacker gains Write access to the MIB.

☒ **A** is not correct. Read access may give an attacker useful information but does not pose the greatest risk. **C** is not correct. Read & Execute access is not a permission associated with a UDP port. UDP ports 161 and 162 are used for SNMP services in Windows 2000. **D** is not correct. Trap events are events that occur and generate alerts to notify network administrators of a potential problem. Trap events occur at a system level and are not encrypted.

LAB ANSWER

Objectives 7.01–7.04

There are many possible solutions to this question. The following answer is based on Windows 2000 technologies and best practices. The issues that need to be reviewed and addressed are listed, along with possible solutions for each. Yours may be organized differently.

Web browsing   Customers need to be able to browse your Web site for product and service information. This should not require any type of strong user authentication. Therefore, anonymous access to the site will suffice. Your company has implemented IIS with a firewall. One improvement would be to install additional Web servers with your product database for redundancy and failover support. However, in terms of security, this solution appears to be acceptable.

Secure Web site access   The goal is to allow the general public a secure method of providing personal data to the company in order to give an accurate insurance quote. One solution would be to implement SSL so the data and the authentication would be secure. This meets the security needs of the public for secure Web site access.

Agents dial-up access   Currently, agents dial up to corporate to access applications and other needed data. Due to the deal with the national ISP, a better solution would be to provide Internet access at all branch offices through this national ISP. Agents working from home could use this ISP account or they could use their own personal ISP account to access corporate data via the Web. Implement VPN servers to accommodate the agents connecting to corporate. Implement L2TP with IPSec for all data transmitted between the agents and corporate. For greater security, certificates could be implemented. In this case, an Enterprise CA would be implemented to issue certificates based on user credentials in AD.

Company line-of-business application   Agents need to utilize a line-of-business application. One solution would be to implement this via Terminal Services Application Server. This would make the application available to all agents via the Internet. It could be secured via group policy as well as via security groups. This would also ease administration of the application and make application upgrades easier. Rather than deploying the upgrade to each computer, the application can be upgraded centrally one time and all users will simultaneously have access to the upgrade. If computers need to be upgraded or have clean installations of Windows 2000 and applications (such as Terminal Services client software), RIS could be used to automate and standardize these configurations. Applying group policies to these computers would also provide for control and standardization of all network computers.

New and existing user authentication   User authentication is being performed either by Kerberos v5 if users are connecting via Windows 2000 clients and services, or by NTLM if they are not. In order to utilize Enterprise certificates, computers would have to be upgraded to Windows 2000. Servers would have to run Active Directory. Third-party certificates could be used to authenticate users who have signed up for services.

Secure network services   On the network, the following services should be enabled. DHCP should be enabled, but it cannot be secured. Ensure that only Authenticated Users can create DNS records to secure the network and the use (and registration) of IP addresses. Active Directory provides tight control over object access. A detailed plan of access rights and permissions should be developed and reviewed regularly to ensure that sensitive data is protected. Create OUs for each of the functional areas and use group policies to protect the configuration of computers on the network. Restrict administrators who have access to RIS services.

Kiosk security   The kiosks are going to be placed in public locations with 24/7 access to your company's Web servers via the Internet. This is a potentially risky situation. Place all kiosks in an OU and implement the HISECWS.INF template on them. Lock down the desktop, allow only one username to log onto the kiosk and have that password never expire. The kiosk can be set so it can only connect to your company's Web site. SSL can be used to protect user data being transmitted back and forth. It is assumed that these public locations have enough security to prevent the kiosks themselves from being stolen, unplugged, or otherwise tampered with physically.

Kiosk user authentication   One solution that could be implemented is to issue smart cards to all users who purchase insurance from your company. Using EAP-TLS, these cards could be used to authenticate users and allow them access to certain additional services via the kiosks at the hospitals. The smart cards would store the user's certificate and public/private keys. Access via a PIN number would make it fairly easy for users but would employ very strong security for sensitive medical or insurance data the user may access. For general kiosk authentication, digest authentication could be used to protect *username* and *password* data being transmitted.

MICROSOFT CERTIFIED SYSTEMS ENGINEER

8

Understanding Policies

T he focus of this chapter is to develop an understanding of policies in Windows 2000. Group policy is a set of configuration options that can be applied to an Active Directory object to define the behavior of the object and its child objects. Group policy can serve many purposes, from application and file deployment to global configuration of user profile settings and security deployment. The setting of audit policies, the assignment of user rights, and the management of account policies (governing user passwords) are all accomplished through the group policy console.

Auditing is the practice of capturing network events and reviewing them. Auditing policies provides the opportunity to regularly monitor and review network security and to fine-tune security policies as needed. Auditing can consume network resources, especially processor time and disk space, so implementing a well designed auditing strategy is critical.

We'll review these concepts and practice scenarios designed to strengthen your understanding of Windows 2000 policies.

TEST YOURSELF OBJECTIVE 8.01

Understanding Group Policy and the MMC

This section focuses on understanding group policy and the use of the Microsoft Management Console (MMC). Group policy is managed through a custom MMC (which you must create and to which you add the group policy snap-in) that can be accessed from the command line or from a dialog box available in other tools such as Active Directory Users and Computers and Active Directory Sites and Services. The management applications that are contained in an MMC are called snap-ins, and custom MMCs hold the snap-ins required to perform specific tasks. Custom consoles can be saved as files with the .MSC file extension.

- Group policy allows you to set configuration settings on machines in an OU, domain, or site.

- Group policy is managed through an MMC, which can be customized according to the administrator's needs by adding snap-ins.

- Group Policy Objects (GPOs) can be broken down into two major categories: local and nonlocal.

- A GPO consists of a Group Policy Template and a Group Policy Container.

- Local group policy is the only way to apply group policy in a workgroup environment.

e x a m
ⓦa t c h

Windows 2000 uses the Microsoft Management Console to manage policies. This replaces the System Policy Editor found in Windows NT 4.0 or Windows 95/98 systems. The REGISTRY.POL files in Windows 2000 are not compatible with the NTCONFIG.POL and CONFIG.POL files created by system policy. System policies created with System Policy Editor cannot be applied to Windows 2000 computers. However, you can use System Policy Editor to apply system policy to down-level clients in a Windows 2000 Domain. You must use the Policy Editor specific to the client operating system receiving the system policy.

QUESTIONS

8.01: Understanding Group Policy and the MMC

1. You are responsible for your company's network administration. A new IT employee is trying to understand group policy concepts. Where would you tell him to look for policies?

    A. Group Policy Container (GPC)

    B. Group Policy Template (GPT)

    C. Group Policy Object (GPO)

    D. Group Policy Folder (GPF)

2. In the following screen shot, the Audit logon events policy's Local Setting is set to Success, Failure. This would cause all successful and failed logon attempts to be logged. Why is the Effective Setting for Audit logon events set to No auditing? (Choose all that apply.)

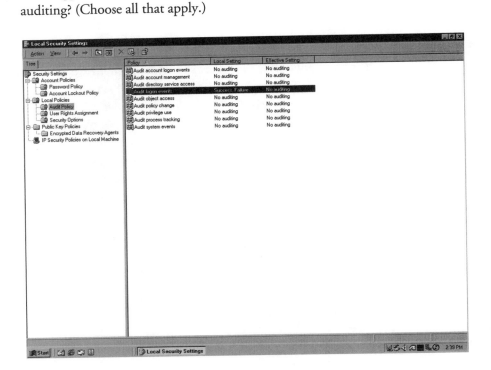

A. The policy was not applied globally.

B. The domain policy is set to No Auditing.

C. Auditing will occur for local computer logon only.

D. The computer has not been restarted since the policy was set.

3. **Current Situation:** You are migrating to a native Windows 2000 network with a multidomain model. You have been tasked with setting up group policies for your child domain. The Product Group OU has three child OUs: Finance, Customer Service, and Development.

   Required Results: Product Group users should be able to modify sound events on their systems. Finance Department users should not be able to run commands from the Start menu or change settings in Control Panel.

Optional Desired Results: Users in the Customer Service Department should not be able to change their passwords or map a network drive.

Proposed Solution: Create a GPO at the Product Group OU level that restricts the use of the Start menu and Control Panel. Create an additional GPO for the Customer Service Department that contains the change password restriction.

What results are produced from the proposed solution?

A. The proposed solution produces the required results and all of the optional results.

B. The proposed solution produces the required results and some of the optional results.

C. The proposed solution produces the required results only.

D. The proposed solution does not produce the required results.

4. You are explaining Microsoft Management Console to a colleague. Which of these are legitimate console modes in the MMC? (Choose all that apply.)

A. Author

B. User mode (full access, multiple window)

C. User mode (limited access, single window)

D. User mode (full access, single window)

TEST YOURSELF OBJECTIVE 8.02

Applying Group Policy

Group policies are applied to two types of Active Directory objects: users and computers. Security groups can be used to filter policies, but the policies are not applied to groups directly. Computer policies are applied at the time the machine boots into Windows 2000, and user policies are applied at the time that the user logs on. Policies are applied in a set order. If there are multiple GPOs for a site, a domain, or an organizational unit, the administrator can specify the order of application using a prioritized list of GPOs. The policy entries applied first are overwritten by those applied later when there are conflicts. If there is no conflict, the effective policy will be an accumulation of all applied policies. The following list highlights the important information for this section.

- Group policy is applied to computers and users.

- No Override prevents policy settings from being overwritten by other policy settings applied later in the application process.

- No Inheritance prevents group policy from being inherited from higher-level objects. No Override takes precedence over No Inheritance.

- Group policy cannot be directly applied to groups. However, you can work around this problem by using policy filtering.

- You can disable a group policy link so that you do not have to delete it. This is very helpful during group policy troubleshooting.

exam
ⓌatchWatch

Local group policy is the only way to apply group policy in a workgroup environment. In addition, for computers operating in a domain environment, Local group policy supercedes any other policy if there is a conflict in policies. Keep these facts in mind on the exam. First determine if the computer is operating in a domain or workgroup environment. Next, determine if policies are in conflict. Remember that with policies, "the last one there wins." It's an easy way to determine which policies will be applied to any given computer in scenarios on the exam.

QUESTIONS

8.02: Applying Group Policy

5. Your company is a multinational organization. In implementing Windows 2000, you chose a multidomain model to reflect the security needs of the organization. What is one possible result from applying site GPOs in a multidomain model?

   A. Increased network traffic.

   B. Site GPOs in the multidomain model are applied in reverse order, causing unpredictable results.

    C. Unable to use logon scripts.

    D. User authentication will occur at the root domain.

6. In the following illustration, GPOs are being applied to the server in the order indicated. Which GPO is being applied incorrectly? (Choose all that apply.)

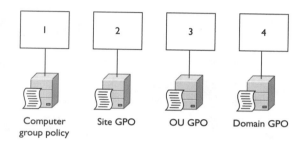

Server

    A. Computer group policy (1)

    B. Site GPO (2)

    C. OU GPO (3)

    D. Domain GPO (4)

7. You would like to apply GPOs that support your company's business practices. Which policy option is useful for enforcing company-wide business rules?

    A. Block Override

    B. No Override

    C. No Inheritance

    D. Block Inheritance

8. **Current Situation:** Your company has permanent and temporary employees. You have been asked to define and apply group policies that meet the different needs of these groups. Both permanent and temporary user accounts are contained in an OU in the domain.

   Required Results: All permanent employees should have Full Control permissions over the Product Design folder. They should also be allowed to change their desktop settings but should not be allowed to install any applications. All temporary employees should have Read-Only access. All temporary employees should also be prevented from making any changes to any computer they log on to.

   Optional Desired Results: Ease network administration, maintain or improve security, and identify all misuse of permissions by temporary employees.

   Proposed Solution: Create one GPO to prevent permanent users from installing applications (GPO1). Create a second GPO to restrict changes to desktop settings and to audit logon events for temporary employees (GPO2). Create a security group for permanent employees and assign the Full Control permission to the Product Design folder. Create a separate security group for temporary employees and assign the Read-only permission for the Product Design folder. For the permanent user security group, assign the Apply group policy and Read permissions to GPO1. For the temporary user security group, assign the Apply group policy and Read permissions to GPO2.

   What results are produced from the proposed solution?

   A. The proposed solution produces the required results and all of the optional results.

   B. The proposed solution produces the required results and some of the optional results.

   C. The proposed solution produces the required results only.

   D. The proposed solution does not produce the required results.

Configuring Group Policy

This section focuses on configuring group policy. The use of Group Policy Objects (GPOs) provides an extremely granular level of control over permissions on the network. However, applying excessive or poorly organized GPOs can reduce network response time, increase network traffic, or cause security conflicts. Certain features, such as the Block Policy Inheritance, or No Override features, should be used with caution and used sparingly. Although user-based group policy can be overridden by computer-based group policy, it should be avoided if possible. Also avoid using cross-domain GPO assignments. This section will review these configurations and the implications of ignoring these recommendations.

- Use group policy rather than Windows NT 4.0 system style policy whenever possible.

- Use the Block Policy Inheritance feature sparingly and use the No Override feature sparingly.

- Minimize the number of GPOs associated with users in domains or organizational units.

- Filter policy based on security group membership.

- Override user-based group policy with computer-based group policy only when absolutely necessary.

- Avoid using cross-domain GPO assignments.

exam
ⓦatch

Windows 2000 group policies contain tremendous capabilities to manage the network to a very fine degree. With that flexibility comes a level of complexity. Remembering some of the things not to do can be helpful in scenario-based questions. Remember that you want to avoid applying site GPOs when there is more than one domain, avoid using Windows NT 4.0 policies, avoid overusing the Block Policy Inheritance and No Override features, and avoid using cross-domain GPOs. One or more of these is likely to appear on the exam and knowing what to avoid can point you toward the right answer or help eliminate a few wrong answers.

QUESTIONS

8.03: Configuring Group Policy

9. You are creating a plan to implement GPOs in your organization. You want the policies to be easy to administer as well as transparent to the user. Why is it important to minimize the number of GPOs associated with users in the domain?

   A. The domain can only issue 256 GPOs.

   B. User accounts can only handle 256 GPOs being applied to them.

   C. Each GPO is applied in sequence, which can delay user authentication.

   D. The attributes of each GPO must be unique.

10. You have one domain with two OUs. Each has different security needs. In OU1, you have low security risks and have set the password policy so that no passwords are remembered and there is no minimum length or age of a password. In OU2, you have set the policy so that ten passwords are remembered, the maximum age of a password is ten days, and the minimum length is eight characters. The administrator of OU1 emails you to ask your advice. Apparently, the password settings for OU1 differ from what he specified. Based on the screen shot on the following page, what could be wrong?

    A. Domain password policies are applied only to users and computers that are not members of an OU.

    B. You must first disable the default domain policy.

    C. OU-level policies related to passwords are ignored. Domain settings conflict with OU1 settings.

    D. Since OU1 settings differ from domain settings, you must first set the refresh interval and offset so that they equal seven.

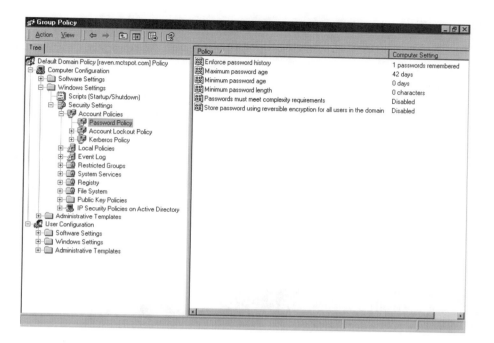

11. **Current Situation:** Your organization uses Windows 2000 domains and organizational units. You also run several kiosk-like computers in the lobby of your building for public access.

Required Results: Make sure that only the policy for the computer takes effect, regardless of which users log on. Maintain very high security for the kiosks.

Optional Desired Results: Enable auditing to ensure the kiosks are not compromised. Minimize network administration of the kiosks.

Proposed Solution: Attach a loopback serial adapter to the kiosk machines. Apply a GPO that locks down desktop features on the kiosks and enables auditing of certain events. Reboot the machines daily to refresh policies.

What results are produced from the proposed solution?

A. The proposed solution produces the required results and all of the optional results.

B. The proposed solution produces the required results and some of the optional results.

C. The proposed solution produces the required results only.

D. The proposed solution does not produce the required results.

12. You are managing a group of ten IT technicians. One of them is a new hire who is having difficulty troubleshooting a group policy problem. Which of the following recommendations will reduce the difficulty of troubleshooting this problem? (Choose all that apply.)

A. Disabling Windows NT 4.0 Policy settings

B. Using the No Override option sparingly

C. Using the Block Inheritance option sparingly

D. Using the System Policy Editor to create a troubleshooting policy for Windows 2000 domains

TEST YOURSELF OBJECTIVE 8.04

Designing an Audit Policy

This section reviews security auditing policies in Windows 2000. Auditing is the practice of tracking security-related events on your network. Auditing policies are specific to each company and its unique set of needs. Understanding what can be audited and what risks can be identified are the two fundamental components of an auditing policy. Auditing is disabled by default in Windows 2000. When auditing of an event is selected, entries are made to the security log. Auditing can track the success, failure, or both of a selected event. Carefully selecting events to audit is important because event logging can degrade system performance and create a large log file that must be reviewed regularly.

■ Audit policy should be carefully planned, and the plan should include the level of auditing required for the security necessary to the networking environment.

■ The results of the auditing process will appear in the Event Monitor, in the security log.

■ Auditing can have a large impact on processor utilization, disk access, and memory. Be judicious about the level of auditing you implement.

■ Pay close attention to how the security log in the Event Viewer is handled. Important events can be overwritten if you have not configured it correctly.

exam ⓦatch   *When creating an audit policy, it is vital to understand the difference between successful and failed events. For instance, a successful logon will capture all regular logons by users. Why would this information be useful? Perhaps your company reviews employee work hours based on logon/logoff events. Failed logon auditing would capture events such as any employee who had trouble remembering or typing their password, for instance, as well as attempts at intrusion on the network. Understanding why you would review the success, failure or both events for a particular system incident will help you on scenario questions on the MCP exam.*

QUESTIONS

8.04: Designing an Audit Policy

13. You have created an audit policy to audit all successful and unsuccessful access to files and folders on your server. After configuring the audit policy, you get complaints from users telling you that it takes longer to access files from the network server than it used to. What might be the problem in this situation? (Choose all that apply.)

  A. Auditing all files on a server consumes an excessive amount of processor time.

  B. Auditing all files on the server requires an excessive amount of disk access time.

  C. Auditing all files requires excessive network traffic.

  D. Auditing all files requires excessive time to study the security log.

14. Based on the following screen shot, what could have caused this event? (Choose all that apply.)

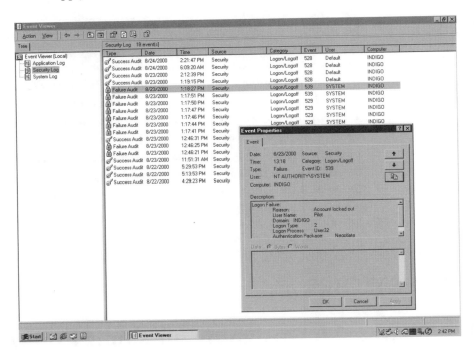

A. User Pilot exceeded maximum password expiration parameters.

B. Local computer locked out, causing user account Pilot to lockout.

C. User account Pilot was locked out by the domain controller for exceeding logon attempts.

D. Another user attempted to logon at username Pilot.

15. **Current Situation:** You are the network administrator for a small law firm. The company employs about 60 people in one location. The firm specializes in environmental protection cases and as such, has several contentious, high-profile cases ongoing at any given time. The outcome of these cases can be multimillion dollar settlements.

Required Results: Implement an audit policy that provides the highest level of security. Develop a plan to address any issues raised through the audit policy.

Optional Desired Results: Minimize impact to network performance and minimize impact to end users.

Proposed Solution: In your audit policy, enable the following auditing: successful logon, unsuccessful logon, policy changes, and object access. Review the audit log each morning at 8:00A.M. and resolve any issues raised by 10:00A.M. daily. Report serious violations to the president. Prepare an action plan for resolution for all serious violations.

What results are produced from the proposed solution?

A. The proposed solution produces the required results and all of the optional results.

B. The proposed solution produces the required results and some of the optional results.

C. The proposed solution produces the required results only.

D. The proposed solution does not produce the required results.

16. You suspect that someone is trying to hack into the network using a brute force or dictionary attack. What single auditing function would you implement to ascertain which user account may have been compromised?

A. Successful logoffs

B. Server shutdown

C. Unsuccessful logoffs

D. Unsuccessful logons

TEST YOURSELF OBJECTIVE 8.05

Utilizing Security Templates

In this section, we'll review the use of security templates in Windows 2000. Microsoft provides a full set of templates that conform to a number of common security scenarios. The default or basic templates are applied by the operating system when a clean install has been performed. They are not applied if an upgrade installation has been done. However, they can be applied after the upgrade has been completed. The incremental templates can be applied after the basic security templates have been applied. The four types of incremental templates are compatible, secure, highly secure, and dedicated domain controller.

Templates can be configured to set parameters for the following: account policies, local policies, event log, restricted groups, system services, registry, and file system.

- Security templates provided with the Windows 2000 operating system come in two types: basic and incremental.

- Basic templates are applied during the installation of the operating system. Incremental templates should be applied after the basic template settings have been implemented.

- Basic security template information is not applied on machines that have been upgraded, or on those that use the FAT file systems for the boot partition.

- The security templates allow you to configure security for the following nodes in group policy: account policies, local policies, event log, restricted groups, system services, registry, and file system.

- You cannot apply different account policies in a single domain. Account policies set at the site or OU level will be ignored.

- Always apply new security policies through templates. In this way, you can easily revert to your previous policy by reapplying the template that was in use.

- There is no Undo button to allow you to undo the changes you make when you apply new security settings when importing templates.

exam
⚠ atch *Recall that there are three security settings that can only be applied at the domain level: Account Lockout, Kerberos, and password settings. They are disregarded by the domain if set differently at other levels (site, OU, and so on). Remembering this will help you in troubleshooting scenarios on the exam. You're likely to see at least one question that tests your knowledge of this rule. On the exam, if settings are not working, determine if one of these three settings is involved and how it is configured at the domain level. This should help you navigate these kinds of questions.*

QUESTIONS

8.05: Utilizing Security Templates

17. You would like to reverse the changes you make to an organizational unit's security policy after you imported a security template's settings to the OU. How would you go about doing this?

    A. Use the Undo button in the group policy editor.

    B. Export the changes you made to the group policy in the Group Policy editor.

    C. Import the basic template OU template.

    D. You cannot undo the changes directly.

18. Refer to the following screen shot from Windows 2000. As a network administrator, what are you likely doing in this screen?

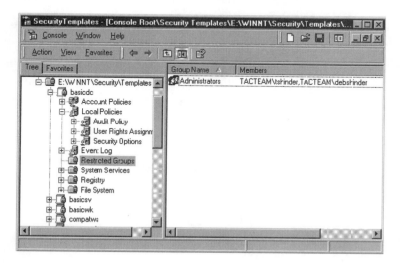

    A. Adding a user who temporarily needs full Administrative privileges

    B. Reviewing restricted group policy to determine why a member that was added is missing from the group

    C. Modifying alerts generated by members of the restricted group attempting unauthorized access to restricted resources

    D. Deleting restricted groups node from the HISEC security template

19. You want to restrict certain functions on all computers via a security template for kiosks. You are concerned that if you miss one setting, the computer will not be secure. What Windows 2000 tool could you use to assist you?

    A. Windows 2000 Default Security Policy | Registry node

    B. Windows 2000 Default Security Policy | HKey node

    C. Windows 2000 Domain Security Template | Registry node

    D. Windows 2000 Domain Security Template | Registry mode

20. You've had several instances recently where rogue DHCP servers have appeared on the network. You've also noticed a few rogue RRAS servers showing up. What step could you take to prevent this from occurring again? (Choose all that apply.)

    A. Restrict access to the DHCP server object in Active Directory.

    B. Place all computers that are assigned to run DHCP services in separate OUs.

    C. Place all computers that are assigned to run DHCP services in a separate OU. Place restrictions on all other computers via the System Services node.

    D. Place all computers in the network into one of three OUs: DHCP, RRAS, and All Others. If a server attempts to come online as a DHCP or RRAS server and is not a member of one of those first two OUs, disable it.

LAB QUESTION

Objectives 8.01–8.05

You are the administrator of a large network. You oversee the company Help Desk where you field user questions daily. You are reviewing the log of the prior week's issues and you see the following problems that were addressed by your staff.

Case Number 1234   Employee cannot install application.

Case Number 1235   Administrator of OU reports policies are not as she had set them.

Case Number 1236   New OU Administrator having trouble managing users and computers in OU.

Case Number 1237   Site policy problem reported.

Case Number 1238   Employee cannot open a file with .MSC extension.

Case Number 1239   Logon script failed.

Based on these problems, what observations could you make about group policy in your network and what solutions would you propose for each problem?

A QUICK ANSWER KEY

Objective 8.01

1. C
2. **B, C,** and **D**
3. **D**
4. **A** and **C**

Objective 8.02

5. **A**
6. **C** and **D**
7. **B**
8. **B**

Objective 8.03

9. **C**
10. **C**
11. **D**
12. **A, B,** and **C**

Objective 8.04

13. **A** and **B**
14. **C** and **D**
15. **C**
16. **D**

Objective 8.05

17. **D**
18. **A** and **B**
19. **C**
20. **A** and **C**

IN-DEPTH ANSWERS

8.01: Understanding Group Policy and the MMC

1. ☑ **C.** Policies are stored in group policy Objects. An individual GPO is analogous to individual document files, each of which contains information separate and distinct from other documents.

   ☒ **A** is not correct. A Group Policy Container (GPC) is a directory service object, which includes subobjects for machine and user group policy information. The GPC contains version and status information, a list of components and the class store. **B** is not correct. The group policy Template (GPT) is a node structure consisting of the GPT folder and a set of subnodes, which together contain all the group policy configuration settings for that particular GPO. The GPT is located in the system volume folder on the Windows 2000 domain controllers. **D** is not correct. There is a Group Policy Template folder, but not a group policy Folder.

2. ☑ **B, C,** and **D** are correct. Domain policies are applied after local policies. Therefore, if the domain policy is set to No Auditing, the local policy settings of Success, Failure will be overridden. If the computer is a member of a workgroup, the local policy will apply. Finally, if settings are changed on the local computer, it must be restarted for the settings to take effect.

   ☒ **A** is not correct. Group policies can be applied to a wide range of computers and users, but the reason no auditing is set is because the local and domain policies are in conflict and the domain policy will prevail.

3. ☑ **D.** The required results are as follows: Product Group users should be able to map a network drive, and Finance Department users should not be able to run commands from the Start menu or change settings in Control Panel. By applying a GPO at the Product Group OU level that restricts the use of the Start menu and Control Panel, you have prevented all users in child containers from using these features. This would prevent these users from modifying

sound events (accessed through Control Panel). Therefore, the proposed solution does not produce the required results. One alternative would be to remove the Read permission from the policy for the groups you want to have those abilities. The optional result of preventing Customer Service users from changing their passwords is met but the optional result of preventing mapped network drives is not met. However, since the required results are not produced, the optional results are not considered.

☒ **A**, **B**, and **C** are not correct because the proposed solution does not produce the required results.

4. ☑ **A** and **C** are correct. The four legitimate console modes in Windows 2000 are as follows: Author, User mode (full access), User mode (limited access, multiple window), and User mode (limited access, single window).

☒ **B** and **D** are incorrect because they are not legitimate console modes.

8.02: Applying Group Policy

5. ☑ **A.** A GPO that is linked to a site is inherited by all of the accounts in every domain contained in the site. The GPO is stored in one domain. Therefore, every account in the site must contact the domain controller that contains the GPO. This can dramatically increase network traffic.

☒ **B** is not correct. GPOs are not applied in reverse order. **C** is not correct. Logon scripts can be utilized. **D** is not correct. User authentication will occur at domain controllers at each site, or via remote domain controllers if the site does not contain any DCs.

6. ☑ **C** and **D** are correct. The order in which GPOs are applied is as follows: computer group policy, Windows NT 4.0 style policies, local group policies, site GPOs, domain GPOs, and OU GPOs. The policy entries applied first are overwritten by those applied later when there are conflicts. If there is no conflict, the effective policy will be an accumulation of all applied policies.

☒ **A** and **B** are not correct. They are in the correct order.

7. ☑ **B.** The No Override option prevents child containers from overriding a GPO set in a higher-level GPO. The No Override option is set on a per-GPO basis. The No Override option always takes precedence over the Block Inheritance option.

☒   **A** is not correct. Block Override is not a legitimate option in Windows 2000. The correct term is Block Inheritance. **C** is not correct. No Inheritance is not a legitimate option in Windows 2000. The correct term is No Override. **D** is not correct. The Block Inheritance option is used by child containers to block policy inheritance of parent container policies. This is useful when an OU requires unique group policy settings.

8.   ☑   **B.** The required results are as follows: to permit permanent employees Full Control over the Product Design folder, to restrict their ability to install applications, to restrict temporary employees to Read-Only access to the Product Design folder, and to restrict their ability to modify the computer they log on to. By creating separate security groups, the folder permissions requirements are met. Using the Apply group policy and Read permissions to GPO1 restricts permanent employees from installing applications and does not prevent them from modifying their computers. Using Apply group policy and Read permissions to GPO2 restricts temporary employees from modifying their computers. The proposed solution produces the required results.

The optional results are as follows: ease network administration, maintain or improve security, and identify all misuse of permissions by temporary employees. By applying GPOs and using security groups, network administration is both consistent and simplified. Security is maintained (or perhaps improved) through the use of these GPOs to restrict settings based on security group membership. However, the optional result of identifying all misuse of permissions by temporary employees was not produced. Although temporary users' permissions are extremely limited, no steps were taken to monitor misuse of existing privileges.

☒   **A, C,** and **D** are not correct. The proposed solution produces the required results and some of the optional results.

8.03: Configuring Group Policy

9.   ☑   **C.** Each GPO applied to a user account in a domain is applied in sequential order. The more GPOs that are applied to a user, the longer it takes for the user to log on.

☒   **A** and **B** are not correct. A domain can manage a virtually unlimited number of GPOs. However, if more than 1,000 GPOs are applied to a user, the group policy application will fail. **D** is not correct. If GPO settings conflict with one another, the settings nearest the user or computer will prevail. However, there is no uniqueness requirement.

10. ☑ **C.** Domain password policies override OU password policies. Only one password policy can exist per domain. Domain controllers ignore password, Account Lockout, and Kerberos Policies defined at any other level.

    ☒ **A** is not correct. Domain password policies are applied to all objects in the domain. **B** is not correct. You cannot disable domain policy settings related to password, lockout, and Kerberos. **D** is not correct. The refresh interval makes no difference. The default refresh interval for group policy is 90 minutes, with a default offset of 30 minutes.

11. ☑ **D.** The required results are to ensure that only computer policies are implemented, regardless of the user logging on, and to maintain secure kiosks. Attaching a loopback serial connector, locking down the desktop, and enabling auditing does not produce these results. To ensure the computer always implements the computer policy regardless of user, you would enable loopback processing through the Administrative templates. Normally, when a user logs on, policy linked to the user account will be applied, and if there are conflicts between user settings for the computer account and the user account, then the user account policies overwrite the computer account linked policies. You can change this default behavior by enabling loopback processing. Loopback can be enabled to be in either a replace or a Merge mode. In Replace mode, the user policies defined in the Computer Accounts Group Policy Objects replace the User Account's Group Policy Object settings. In Merge mode, the Computer Account's User settings are merged with the User Account's User settings, and if there is a conflict, the Computer Account's User settings are applied.

    ☒ **A**, **B**, and **C** are not correct. The proposed solution does not produce the required results.

12. ☑ **A**, **B**, and **C** are correct. You avoid many problems by disabling Windows NT style policies. You can reduce troubleshooting problems when you use the No Override options infrequently and you can simplify troubleshooting group policy behavior by using the Block Inheritance attribute sparingly.

    ☒ **D** is incorrect. You cannot use the System Policy Editor to create any policy for Windows 2000 network clients. Also, there is no troubleshooting feature in group policies.

8.04: Designing an Audit Policy

13. ☑ **A** and **B** are correct. When you audit all files for successful and unsuccessful access, you create an excessive workload on the processor and disk subsystems of the server. This can have a significantly negative effect on server performance. You should audit only specific files of interest, and for a short period of time, in order to reduce the negative impact such auditing behavior might exert.

    ☒ **C** is not correct. Auditing does not typically increase the amount of network traffic. **D** is not correct. Although it might take a lot of time on your part to sift through the security log, this is not a factor in why the users have noticed decreased performance.

14. ☑ **C** and **D** are correct. The user account, Pilot, is locked out due to failed logons. Lockout occurs after the number of unsuccessful attempts exceeds the policy settings. The Event Viewer indicates that these are events on the local computer. Account lockout occurs for a number of reasons including user Pilot having trouble remembering his/her password or someone attempting to log on as Pilot and guess the correct password. Auditing this type of event provides information about attempts at intrusion.

    ☒ **A** is not correct. If the user's password had expired, the system would not allow the user to log on until the password was changed. The account would only lockout if the current password used was incorrect and the number of attempts exceeded policy. **B** is not correct. A computer locking up would not lockout the user account.

15. ☑ **C.** The required results are as follows: implement an audit policy that provides the highest level of security, and develop a plan to address any issues raised through the audit policy. The plan to audit the four events specified provides very comprehensive auditing for a secure environment. The risk of an illegal break-in and the compromise of data is very high. This setting should be treated as a high-risk setting that requires a very high level of security. Monitoring all logon events, all policy changes, and all object access will create a burden for the network, but this level of security is not excessive. Object access auditing for all files that may represent proprietary information or information that may give an advantage to a courtroom opponent should be audited for successful and unsuccessful access.

The desired optional results are to minimize network impact and minimize end user impact. Your solution does not address this. Event auditing will always impact the network and end user. However, the impact can be mitigated through increasing processors or processor speed, increasing RAM, and increasing disk capacity.

☒ **A**, **B**, and **D** are not correct. The proposed solution produces the required results but fails to address the optional results.

16. ☑ **D.** When a hacker uses a brute force or dictionary attack, it is likely that he will suffer many failed logons before the correct character sequence is entered. If you audit unsuccessful logons, you will see that a specific account, or several user's accounts are reported to have unsuccessful logons, and perhaps at times of the day when those users would not be available to attempt a logon.

☒ **A** is not correct. A successful log off would give you no useful information regarding a dictionary attack. **B** is not correct. A hacker attack of this type would not be characterized by a server shutdown. **C** is not correct. Like successful logoffs (choice A), unsuccessful logoffs would not provide helpful information when such a hacker attacker is taking place.

8.05: Utilizing Security Templates

17. ☑ **D.** There is no direct mechanism, such as an Undo button, that will allow you to reverse the change. Before you enact any changes to a security policy, back up the present configuration by exporting the current settings to an .INF file. Then you can restore the system to its previous state by importing the .INF file into the database, and reapplying the changes.

☒ **A** is not correct. There is no Undo button that would allow you to reverse the changes made to group policy. **B** is not correct. There is no facility that tracks the changes you made form the previous group policy. **C** is not correct. There is no basic OU template.

18. ☑ **A** and **B** are correct. The Restricted Groups node represents a new security option that was not available in Windows NT 4.0. You can predefine, through policy, members of a particular group. There are times when the administrator needs to temporarily add users to groups with a higher classification than the users' typical group membership. This might be the case when an administrator

goes on vacation and another member of the team is assigned full administrative rights. By defining Restricted Group membership rules, you can return group membership to that defined by security policy. The administrator could have been adding a member (by double-clicking the desired group in the results pane) or setting Restricted group policy. By default, temporary membership is lost when group policy is refreshed.

☒ **C** is not correct. Restricted Groups relates to restricted membership in a group. Access to restricted resources would still be accomplished via the ACL for the object. Alerts are not generated in this manner. **D** is not correct. The template is the basic domain controller (BASICDC) template, not the HISEC template.

19. ☑ **C.** In Windows 2000, the various security templates have a node called registry. This node provides the ability to control registry settings to a very detailed level. You can define a security policy for a registry key or a value in the database, and then customize the propagation of the setting through the key.

☒ **A** and **B** are not correct. Although these can be considered security policies for the domain, they are set through the templates. **D** is not correct. The registry is a *node*, not mode, in Windows 2000.

20. ☑ **A** and **C** are correct. The DHCP server object in Active Directory lists the IP addresses of servers that are authorized to provide DHCP services to the network. When a DHCP server attempts to start on the network, Active Directory is queried to determine if the server is authorized to run the service. If it is not, DHCP service is automatically shut down. Placing all computers authorized to run DHCP (and other system services) into an OU and restricting all other computers from running system services is another viable option, especially as it relates to services other than DHCP. This is an appropriate use of the System Services node of the security templates in Windows 2000.

☒ **B** is not correct. Placing each computer in a separate OU defeats the purpose of OUs. This would create a very difficult administrative environment. **D** is not correct. You cannot disable a computer by simply placing it in an OU. Using the security template nodes to control the actions of computers in various OUs is viable, but disable is not an option.

LAB ANSWER

Objectives 8.01–8.05

Certainly the observations you could make are more subjective than the solutions to these problems. However, it can be said that there appears to be confusion about how group policy is and should be implemented in the network. Group policy is a new Windows 2000 feature that may cause confusion for users and administrators who are not familiar with it. However, if the explanation is broken down into segments, it may be more understandable. A training session for your network administrators is in order!

As for specific solutions, we'll take them on a case-by-case basis. The answers are brief and are intended to point you in the right direction for further reading if the subject is still unclear to you.

Case Number 1234: Employee cannot install application

If an employee is trying to install an application and cannot, it would indicate that either the user doesn't know how to perform an installation or, more likely, there is a group policy in place that specifically denies this user (or computer) this ability. Security templates have a registry node that can be set to restrict changes within the registry; applications write values to the registry.

Case Number 1235: Administrator of OU reports policies are not as she had set them

If an OU administrator has full permission to set policies at the OU level and is finding that the policy settings she has implemented are not being implemented, one of two things is happening. First, assuming the OU administrator was fully trained and competent, you would confirm which settings are being overwritten. Three settings (password, Account Lockout, and Kerberos) are set at the domain level and will disregard OU and site level changes. Second, you would check to see how the specific settings vary from domain settings. Remember that settings are applied in a specific sequence and "the last one there wins." If higher-level settings are being applied to the specific settings, the OU settings may be overwritten.

Case Number 1236: New OU Administrator having trouble managing users and computers in OU

While this issue is clearly a training issue for the new OU, there is a tool in Windows 2000 you can use to help the new administrator come up to speed. Using the Microsoft Management Console, you can create a custom snap-in for the OU administrator. This will enable him to walk through certain tasks using a template. This can also be used if a network administrator will be away and wants to temporarily delegate administrative tasks to someone who may not be completely familiar with Windows 2000. The Microsoft Management Console allows you to create custom consoles. Once you create the console, you can set it to User mode (limited access, single window). This will restrict the user's ability to modify the settings and will provide a simple, easy-to-follow routine for the Finance OU administrator until proficiency is gained.

Case Number 1237: Site policy problem reported

The group policy Container contains information about a policy, including status information. Status information indicates whether the Group Policy Object is enabled or disabled for this site, domain, or organizational unit (SDOU). Use this to determine the status of the site policy for further troubleshooting. Also, review the order in which group policies are applied to determine if this might be part of the problem. Remember, "the last one there wins."

Case Number 1238: Employee cannot open a file with .MSC extension.

The .MSC extension indicates that the file is a console created in Microsoft Management Console. An employee would not likely have access to the MMC. This is not a tool you want your users to have access to and you should notify the employee to forward the file to your staff. Your staff should determine whether the extension was incorrect or not. If it was not, the incident should be investigated as a potential security breach, depending on the source and nature of the file.

Case Number 1239: Logon script failed

Using group policy, you can implement a logon script. The script would be placed in \USERS\SCRIPTS. This is a subfolder of the group policy Templates folder. The GPT is located in the system volume folder on the Windows 2000 domain controllers. If the script failed, there may be a problem with the script or it may be placed in the wrong folder. Verify its location and test the script itself to ensure that it accomplishes the desired result.

MICROSOFT CERTIFIED SYSTEMS ENGINEER

9

Managing
Data Security

T his chapter reviews the important concepts in managing data security. Developing a delegation of authority strategy entails reviewing the Windows 2000 elements that support delegation of authority, including domains, groups, organizational units, IT department structure, and other elements that impact the overall delegation strategy. Disaster recovery planning encompasses physical and logical planning. We'll review best practices for preparing for disaster recovery in Windows 2000, including backup and restore procedures, fault tolerance, and emergency repair procedures. Finally, we'll review the key elements for using the Encrypting File System (EFS) in Windows 2000, including best practices and recovery strategies.

TEST YOURSELF OBJECTIVE 9.01

Designing a Delegation of Authority Strategy

In previous versions of Window NT, delegation of authority was accomplished using various built-in groups such as the Account Operators group. This model has been changed significantly in Windows 2000, allowing for a finer degree of control. Designing a delegation of authority strategy for Windows 2000 encompasses implementing elements of Active Directory, including domain structure, organizational units, and the ability to grant specific administrative privileges based on these structures.

- A company's core domain/OU structure should reflect its delegation of authority strategy first and foremost, and not necessarily its business or organizational structure.

- A company with centralized IT administration means that domain administrators will typically be responsible for creating the entire OU structure and for most administrative tasks within an organization (such as user and group management).

- A company with decentralized IT administration translates into administrative tasks being delegated to the lowest-level OU possible.

- Administrators should delegate tasks within an OU to local security groups for ease of management.

■ Delegation of authority is accomplished in Active Directory Users and Computers either by using the Delegation of Control Wizard to delegate common tasks within an object or by modifying the ACL on the Active Directory object (for example, an OU) through that object's Security properties.

■ Common tasks that are often delegated to OU administrators at various levels within a domain include managing user accounts, managing groups, managing group membership, resetting user passwords, and managing group policy links.

exam
ⓦatch

On the exam, it's a good idea to draw a diagram of a structure, whether it maps to the company's functional structure or its IT structure. When answering questions related to OUs, having a diagram of the structure described in the question can help you determine the right answer more quickly. Also, remember that Windows NT 4.0 (and below) resource domains map very closely to Windows 2000 organizational units (OUs). Any migration strategy from Windows NT 4.0 resource domains will likely map directly over to the use of OUs in Windows 2000 on scenario questions.

QUESTIONS

9.01: Designing a Delegation of Authority Strategy

1. You are designing a delegation of administration model for your organization. Which element would you list as the one that has the most control over all objects?

   A. Access Control List (ACL)

   B. Domain structure

   C. Access Database (.MDB)

   D. Organizational unit

Questions 2–4   This scenario should be used to answer questions 2, 3, and 4.

You have designed a delegation strategy that includes the creation of the OUs seen in the following illustration. You delegated permissions so administrators of the Web Services, Client Services, Training, and Publishing OUs all have full control over the resources in their OU. The administrator of the Client Services OU delegated administration to two people in her department. She delegated administration of the Support OU to Jalal and administration of the Deployment OU to Fernando, with create and manage user account privileges.

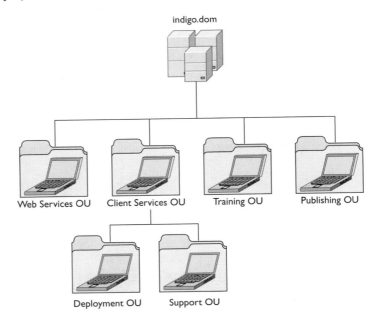

2. Jalal calls you saying he is having trouble installing a new network printer. What could be causing this problem?

   A. Jalal would have to coordinate with Fernando because they each manage a child OU under Client Services.

   B. Child OUs cannot create domain-wide resources such as network printers.

   C. The Support OU cannot create new network printers.

   D. Jalal can create a new network printer but he must use the RUNAS command to access his administrative rights.

3. What is this type of delegation called in Windows 2000? (Choose all that apply.)
   A. Multilevel
   B. Layered
   C. Nested
   D. Hierarchical

4. Fernando has several objects in his OU that he wants to move to the Publishing OU because he believes that's where they belong. What permissions would Fernando need to do this?
   A. Fernando must have permission to create an object in the destination OU, in this case, the Publishing OU.
   B. Fernando must have permission to create an object at the domain level.
   C. Fernando must have Read and Write access.
   D. Objects cannot be moved between OUs.

5. **Current Situation:** Your company is currently running a Windows NT 4.0-based network. You are designing a migration strategy for the network. Today's task is to design the migration strategy for the training division. The training division is located in two physical locations, the Northside campus and the Eastside campus. Each campus, in your current model, is a resource domain.

   Required Results: Migrate the two resource domains to Windows 2000, maintain the logical groupings of resources, and maintain network security.

   Optional Desired Results: Ensure local administration groups can add users and computers to their OUs and maintain or improve ease of administration.

   Proposed Solution: Create two OUs named Northside and Eastside. Create a local group called Northside Admins and delegate Full Control of computer objects to the Northside OU to this group. Create a local group called Eastside Admins and delegate Full Control of computer objects to the Eastside OU to this group.

   What results are produced from the proposed solution?
   A. The proposed solution produces the required results and the optional results.
   B. The proposed solution produces the required results and some of the optional results
   C. The proposed solution produces the required results only.
   D. The proposed solution does not produce the required results.

Implementing Disaster Recovery

Disaster recovery planning includes the physical and logical structures of your data. The plan should answer very high-level questions such as, "What steps would we take to repair our network if an entire building was wiped out by a hurricane?" The plan should also answer very low-level questions such as, "What level of RAID should we implement to ensure that our data is fault-tolerant?" In this section, we'll review disaster recovery as it relates to network security, including redundant array of independent disks (RAID), uninterruptible power supply (UPS), virus protection, backup procedures, and emergency repair processes.

- Supported disaster recovery and prevention mechanisms in Windows 2000 include fault-tolerant disk arrays (RAID), UPS systems, virus protection software, regular backup procedures of system and user data, and the emergency repair process.

- Windows 2000 supports RAID levels 0, 1, and 5 on dynamic disks, which are disks that are fully managed by Windows 2000 Disk Administration.

- The ability to back up the System State in Windows 2000 allows for the restoration of Active Directory and other critical system files, should there be a disaster.

- Active Directory and other replicated data sets on domain controllers can be restored in one of three modes—primary, authoritative, and non-authoritative—depending on the state of the domain at the time of the restore and whether deleted or missing data needs to be recovered.

- Emergency repair disks are created using the Backup utility in Windows 2000. The creation of an emergency repair disk also backs up the registry and system file information so that they can be restored in the event that a file or registry problem causes Windows not to load properly.

- The Recovery console in Windows 2000 allows a local administrator to access files on an NTFS, FAT, or FAT32 volume and also provides a new set of repair options when Windows 2000 will not load properly.

exam
🆆atch

While it is unlikely you'll be asked a specific question on disaster recovery on the Windows 2000 Designing Security MCP exam, disaster recovery is a critical element of designing network security. Also, you may find references to various disaster recovery methods as part of scenario questions on the exam. Even if disaster recovery doesn't directly tie into the possible answers, a clear understanding of these elements will help you sort out the right answers from the obviously (and sometimes not-so-obviously) wrong answers more quickly and easily.

QUESTIONS

9.02: Implementing Disaster Recovery

6. Your company has just hired a new CIO. He has held a meeting with every member of the IT staff. One of his main initiatives is to improve fault tolerance within the network. He has demanded that the highest level of fault tolerance be implemented but indicated that the cost of the solution will be a major factor in his decision. The department's budget has been cut by more than 30 percent due to lagging sales over the past year. You delegate the planning of this task to one of your employees, who is anxious to impress the new CIO. He recommends that you implement RAID10, mirrored stripe sets, in your Windows 2000 network. What challenges will you face?

    A. RAID10 is only supported as an add-on feature to Windows 2000.

    B. RAID10 can only be implemented on systems that are not used outside North America.

    C. RAID10 does not exist.

    D. RAID10 is not supported in Windows 2000.

7. Based on the following screen shown, which statements regarding the currently configured backup are true? (Choose all that apply.)

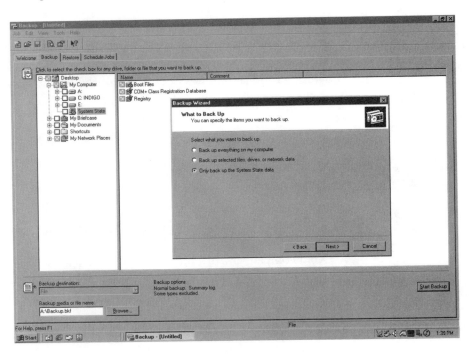

A. Only the registry, Active Directory, Sysvol (includes policies and scripts used by Active Directory), COM+ database, and boot files will be backed up.

B. Only the boot files, COM+ database, and registry will be backed up.

C. System State data can only be backed up on the local computer.

D. You must be a member of the local Administrators group in order to back up System State data.

8. **Current Situation:** Two of the four domain controllers in your Windows 2000 network have experienced complete failure due to an electrical problem in the server room. As a result, these two domain controllers must be replaced and the network must be made fully functional as quickly as possible.

Required Results: Bring the network back to full functionality. Restore the domain controller's Active Directory information.

Optional Desired Results: Minimize the number of steps taken to restore the network, ensure security is maintained, and minimize disruption to end users.

Proposed Solution: Replace the two servers with two fully functioning servers that meet or exceed the capabilities of the two former servers. Install Windows 2000 Server on both servers. Perform an authoritative restore by booting into Directory Services Restore mode by pressing F8 at Windows 2000 startup. Then perform a non-authoritative restore to force replication and synchronize all domain controllers.

What results are produced from the proposed solution?

A. The proposed solution produces the required results and the optional results.

B. The proposed solution produces the required results and some of the optional results

C. The proposed solution produces the required results only.

D. The proposed solution does not produce the required results.

9. You have a domain controller that will not boot properly. You begin your troubleshooting process by reviewing your recovery options in Windows 2000. Your manager suggests you use the Windows 2000 Recovery console. What does the Windows 2000 Recovery console allow you to do? (Choose all that apply.)

A. Have limited access to NTFS, FAT32, and FAT volumes.

B. Repair the active system partition boot sector or the master boot record (MBR).

C. Edit the Last Known Good Configuration.

D. Create and format partitions and drives.

10. You are attempting to restore a system that crashed. You choose the Fast Restore option but find that once complete, some of your system settings appear to be default Windows 2000 settings. Why did this happen and what could you do to fix this problem?

A. One or more registry key restores failed. Manually restore the System State data.

B. This is normal. For all values in the registry that are not included within one of the Hkey nodes, default values are restored.

    C. Fast Restore will not restore registry settings. You must use Manual Restore instead.

    D. The registry was not restored properly. You must choose the registry Restore method of restore.

11. It appears that one of your domain controllers has a serious problem with the boot process. However, when you were originally installing Windows 2000, you didn't have a blank diskette handy and chose not to create an emergency repair disk. What can you do now?

    A. Resign from your job before anyone finds out.

    B. Start the computer and choose the L option.

    C. Create an emergency repair disk on another domain controller and edit the ARC path in the BOOT.INI file. Restart the domain controller with this diskette.

    D. Use the RDISK.EXE command to create an emergency repair disk.

TEST YOURSELF OBJECTIVE 9.03

Designing an Encrypting File System Strategy

File encryption using the Encrypting File System (EFS) is a new tool in Windows 2000 that allows a user to encrypt data directly on volumes that use the New Technology File System (NTFS) so the data cannot be used or modified by any other user. Although NTFS permissions protect data when accessed through the operating system, data can be compromised if someone is able to bypass the operating system. This is often the case with mobile devices such as laptops. EFS encrypts files using public key encryption methods that prevent anyone but the owner or a recovery agent from accessing the file, regardless of whether or not the operating system has been compromised.

- EFS allows users to encrypt all files within an NTFS directory using a strong public key–based cryptographic scheme.

- Individual file encryption is not recommended because of the unexpected behavior of applications in opening and saving files.

■ Backup and restore of encrypted files is supported by EFS using a backup utility such as Windows 2000 Backup, thereby protecting file encryption during transport.

■ EFS prevents the leaking of key information to page files and ensures that all copies of an encrypted file, even if moved, remain encrypted on Windows 2000 NTFS partitions.

■ EFS does not provide encryption of network data if an encrypted file is copied or moved across the network.

■ EFS supports encryption of remote files accessed through file shares, by using the same key and certificate if roaming profiles exist and the server is trusted for delegation, or by using local profiles and keys on the remote server.

■ EFS recovery policy is integrated with Windows 2000 security policy and is required in order to encrypt data. Administrators can delegate recovery policy to individuals with recovery authority, and different recovery policies may be configured for different parts of the organization.

exam !
ⓦatch

Keep in mind that EFS cannot be used for files shared with others, since only the owner or a recovery agent can access that file. However, placing encrypted files on network shares and checking Trust For Delegation allows network backups to save encrypted files. This is accomplished through EFS "impersonating" the EFS user and making network connections on their behalf when encrypting and decrypting files in the backup process. This is one reason why it is critical that network servers and backup devices remain well secured.

QUESTIONS

9.03: Designing an Encrypting File System Strategy

12. There have been a few strange incidents related to the sales numbers being shared inappropriately lately, so Lisa has encrypted a file she uses to update company-wide sales data. She placed the file in a folder called DEPTSALES. She shared the folder and assigned Full Control to the members of the SALESMANAGER

group, since there was other data in the folder that she wanted to share with members of her team. Rosie is a member of the SALESMANAGER group and cannot access several files in the shared folder. The error message she gets suggests she contact the file owner or administrator. She emails Lisa and asks to be given permission. Lisa is on a four-month sabbatical trekking through Nepal and is unreachable. Rosie contacts the network administrator and confirms that Rosie is a member of the SALESMANAGER group and that the group has Full Control of the files in the DEPTSALES folder. What could be wrong and what can be done to solve the problem? (Choose all that apply.)

A. The network administrator should generate a duplicate key for Rosie so Rosie can access the file using Lisa's key.

B. Lisa probably encrypted the entire folder, not just the file she was working on.

C. The network administrator can use the data recovery agent to recover Rosie's files.

D. Lisa should have added Rosie to the encryption recovery key list (ERKL) before she left.

13. In the following illustration, if the file is moved as shown, what state will that file be in on the destination server?

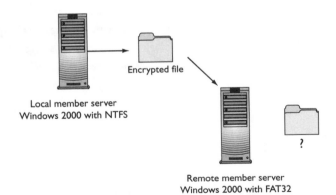

Local member server
Windows 2000 with NTFS

Encrypted file

Remote member server
Windows 2000 with FAT32

A. Encrypted

B. Unencrypted

C. Cannot transfer an encrypted file from an NTFS volume to a FAT32 volume

D. Depends on state of destination folder

14. **Current Situation:** Your company works with sensitive data on a regular basis. As a precaution, your CIO has asked that all sensitive data be encrypted on the network. You have identified the four people in the company who work with sensitive data.

    Required Results: Ensure that sensitive data is encrypted in folders, ensure that users can access their data from any network location.

    Optional Desired Results: Provide a fail-safe method of recovering the data, ensure the encryption process is user-friendly, and allow users to back up encrypted files to removable media.

    Proposed Solution: Create a network share for each user. Also create a roaming profile for each user. This will enable them to use their own credentials no matter where they are located when they attempt to encrypt or decrypt files. Set the shared folder so it uses encryption. Point all user files (for these four users only) to this share location. Use the backup and restore capabilities built into Windows 2000 as your recovery solution. Have users save encrypted files when they're not connected to the network by copying them to removable media.

    What results are produced from the proposed solution?

    A. The proposed solution produces the required results and the optional results.

    B. The proposed solution produces the required results and some of the optional results

    C. The proposed solution produces the required results only.

    D. The proposed solution does not produce the required results.

15. Jackie has a laptop connected to the network. She travels extensively and works with very sensitive data. She is currently in Malta, Montana, working on a top-secret project and wants to encrypt her files. She's used EFS before, but she's not sure if EFS will work, since she's not connected to the network at the moment. How will she get the required certificate for encrypting her files?

    A. She must use a third-party certificate authority.

    B. She must wait until she returns to the office to get a certificate from an enterprise certificate authority.

    C. She can encrypt her files without any problem.

    D. She can encrypt her files and choose the No Certificate option as a temporary workaround.

16. Your new manager is not a big fan of graphical user interfaces. In fact, he comes from a mainframe background and often grumbles about "eye candy." You're up for a big promotion and wouldn't mind making a positive impression on him. What utility could show him that would allow him to work with EFS without the Windows 2000 graphical interface?

    A. X-Windows console

    B. CIPHER command

    C. ENCRYPTION command

    D. Boot in Safe mode and choose VGA mode; then select the Encryption console

17. Your network administration tasks seem to expand continually. You'd like a way to manage file encryption that will ease administration. What feature of Windows 2000 could you use?

    A. Group policy

    B. NTFS

    C. MMC

    D. Security identifiers

LAB QUESTION

Objectives 9.01–9.03

You live in a coastal town in the southeastern part of the United States. Your town is often battered by storms during the hurricane season. Recently, you were forced to evacuate the town in preparation for Hurricane Nelly. The storm came in so quickly, you did not have time to shut your systems down in an orderly manner. Nelly ripped through your town and did extensive damage. Upon returning to your company offices, you found the building and the server room had been flooded. Windows had been broken and there was debris strewn throughout the server room and other rooms in the building.

Upon inspecting the damage, you found the power had run at 70 percent of normal power for an extended period of time. As the storm hit, the power surged and caused several of your servers' surge protection devices to kick in, causing breakers to pop and power to be disabled to servers. It appears that three domain controllers are in bad shape, other servers appear to be powered down or appear to be up and running, on initial inspection.

Based on this information, what steps would you take to inspect your network and restore full functionality to the network quickly?

QUICK ANSWER KEY

Objective 9.01

1. A
2. C
3. C and D
4. A
5. B

Objective 9.02

6. D
7. A, C, and D
8. D
9. A, B, and D
10. A
11. B

Objective 9.03

12. B and C
13. B
14. B
15. C
16. B
17. A

IN-DEPTH ANSWERS

9.01: Designing a Delegation of Authority Strategy

1. ☑ **A.** Each object in Active Directory has an Access Control List (ACL). This list is comprised of Access Control Entries that specify which users, groups, or computers have the right to access that object. This is the element that exerts the most control over objects.

    ☒ **B** is not correct. The Active Directory includes all objects in a domain, but the domain does not exert control over those objects. **C** is not correct. The correct term is Access Control List. An Access Database uses the .MDB extension. It is a file generated by the Microsoft Access program. **D** is not correct. An organizational unit is used to delegate administration, but is not the most basic component of object access.

2. ☑ **C.** The parent OU (Client Services) only delegated permission to create and manage user accounts. The ability to create new network printers was not delegated. Therefore, adding a new network printer would have to be done by the administrator of the Client Services OU.

    ☒ **A** is not correct. Administration of each OU is dependent only on the permissions given by the administrator of the parent OU to the child OU administrator. Jalal would not have to coordinate with anyone to make changes to the OU settings. **B** is also not correct. Child OUs can create resources available throughout the domain if they possess sufficient permissions to do so. **D** is not correct. The RUNAS command is used to run a command as an administrator without logging onto the administrative account. This would not impact Jalal's ability to create a new network printer.

3. ☑ **C** and **D** are correct. The ability to delegate to smaller and smaller units is called nested or hierarchical delegation. The OUs in the diagram are nested

OUs, which creates a hierarchical delegation model. Note that Microsoft uses both terms interchangeably, so be aware that you will see both on the exam.

☒ **A** and **B** are not correct. Although both terms describe the structure, they are not terms used in Windows 2000 to refer to OUs.

4. ☑ **A.** Fernando must have appropriate permissions in the Publishing OU to create objects. He must also have permission to delete objects from the current (Deployment OU) container.

☒ **B** is not correct. Fernando only needs permission to create an object in the destination OU, not at the domain level. This is why OUs exist: so the most restrictive settings can be delegated to maintain a secure network, while administering some of the routine tasks associated with managing network resources. **C** is not correct. Read and Write access are permissions associated with files and folders, not OU administration. **D** is not correct. Objects can be moved if the administrator has sufficient privileges to create objects in the destination and deleted them from the source OU.

5. ☑ **B.** The required results are as follows: migrate the two resource domains, maintain logical groupings of resources, and maintain network security. Creating two OUs that map to the resource domains meets the first requirement. Delegating Full Control of computer objects to the local administration meets the requirements of maintaining the logical groupings as well as maintaining security. The use of OUs and the ability to selectively delegate control therefore produces all three required results.

The desired results are to ensure OUs can add users, ensure OUs can add computers, and maintain or improve network administration. Only one of these results is produced by the proposed solution. The local administration were given the ability to add computers to their OUs. However, the permission to add users, which is not included in the ability to add computers to the OU, was not granted. By not delegating the ability to manage users, network administration is made more difficult. Therefore, only one of the three optional results was produced.

☒ **A**, **C**, and **D** are not correct. The proposed solution produces the required results and one of the three optional results.

9.02: Implementing Disaster Recovery

6. ☑ **D.** RAID10 is not supported in Windows 2000. This may be a feature added to subsequent releases of Windows 2000. At this time, Windows 2000 supports RAID Levels 0, 1, and 5 only. The highest level of RAID you could implement to meet your new CIO's goals is RAID5 using at least three disk drives. You could also implement disk duplexing, which is the use of two hard disk drive controllers to provide redundancy at both the controller and the disk level. Keep in mind that RAID can be implemented as a hardware or a software solution. Windows 2000 provides a software solution. Software solutions typically are less costly but also less efficient than hardware solutions. You could implement a RAID10 hardware solution, if cost was not a factor.

    ☒ **A** is not correct. RAID10 is not currently supported in Windows 2000. **B** is not correct. There are no legal geographic limitations with RAID levels as there are with encryption technologies. **C** is not correct. RAID10 exists but is not yet supported in Windows 2000.

    RAID0 is a stripe set without parity. It improves read/write performance but provides no fault tolerance. RAID1 is a mirror set, where the data on one disk is mirrored to a second disk. This does not impact the performance of the disk subsystem significantly, but it does provide an initial level of fault tolerance. RAID5 is a striped set with parity. This provides improved disk subsystem performance, because data can be written across several drives rather than waiting to sequentially read/write data to a single drive. It also provides fault tolerance. If a single disk is lost, the data can be recovered through the use of parity information written across the set.

7. ☑ **A, C,** and **D** are correct. The components of the System State data are the elements that determine the "state" of the system. This includes the registry, the Active Directory, sysvol, COM+ database, and boot files. System State data is unique to each system and can only be backed up on the local computer. System State data contains sensitive information (Active Directory and registry settings, among others). Therefore, you must be a member of the local Administrators group in order to be able to back up and restore System State data.

    ☒ **B** is not correct. Although these things are included in System State data, the list is not complete.

8. ☑ **D.** The required results are full network functionality, and restore the DC's Active Directory information. Replacing the servers and installing Windows 2000 Server is clearly the first step in any solution. The computers are ready to accept Active Directory replication data. However, you must perform a non-authoritative restore prior to performing an authoritative restore. A non-authoritative restore is used when at least one other domain controller is still available and fully functional, as is the case here. An authoritative restore is used when data has been accidentally deleted from a replicated data set. In the case of two servers that were replaced, you would perform a non-authoritative restore. You should perform an authoritative restore only if data has been lost, which is not indicated in this scenario. Therefore, the proposed solution does not produce the required results to restore Active Directory information.

   ☒ **A, B,** and **C** are not correct. The proposed solution does not produce the required results.

9. ☑ **A, B,** and **D** are correct. In Recovery console, you can access a number of features. You must have administrative rights, and the SAM database must be intact, in order for you to use this new Windows 2000 feature. Once enabled, you can gain limited access to NTFS, FAT32, and FAT volumes, create and format partitions and drives, repair the active system partition boot sector or MBR, and enable or disable services or devices when you next start Windows 2000.

   ☒ **C** is not correct. The Recovery console does not allow you to edit the Last Known Good Configuration.

10. ☑ **A.** The Fast Repair option performs all the repairs available in Manual Repair, but without prompting for choices. In addition, the Fast Repair option tries to load each Windows 2000 registry file. If it is unsuccessful, the Fast Repair option may revert parts of the operating system's registry back to the values present when Windows 2000 was first installed.

   ☒ **B** is not correct. This behavior indicates that Fast Restore had trouble restoring one or more keys. All registry values are included when restoring. **C** is not correct. Fast Restore will attempt to restore registry values. Manual mode will not restore the registry. **D** is not correct. There is no specific registry Restore mode. You can restore the System State data, which includes the registry, or use Fast Restore mode.

11. ☑ **B.** If you do not have an emergency repair disk and you would like to perform an emergency repair, you can have the emergency repair process try to locate the Windows 2000 Repair folder by choosing the L option. In fact, the Repair folder and its contents are much more important than the existence of an emergency repair disk in Windows 2000 when attempting to perform the repair process. The registry is no longer stored on the emergency repair disk because it is too large. When you create a Windows 2000 emergency repair disk, the only files that get copied to the disk are SETUP.LOG, AUTOEXEC.NT, and CONFIG.NT. Only the SETUP.LOG is used if this floppy disk is present—to find the Windows 2000 installation point where the Repair folder exists.

☒ **A** is not correct. The presence of an emergency repair disk in Windows 2000 is less important than the Repair folder. Next time, follow best practices! **C** is not correct. The information in the files written is machine-specific; you cannot use an emergency repair disk created on another controller. **D** is not correct. RDISK.EXE is a command used in Windows NT 4.0 but is not present in Windows 2000.

9.03: Designing an Encrypting File System Strategy

12. ☑ **B** and **C** are correct. Files that need to be shared should not be encrypted. Files can be placed in shared folders, but they will not be able to be accessed by anyone other than the owner or a recovery agent. The contents of the shared folder appear to be encrypted. The network administrator could check the status of the folder to determine this. If the folder is encrypted, the network administrator could use the data recovery agent to decrypt the files that Rosie needs access to, since Lisa is not reachable.

☒ **A** is not correct. Rosie may or may not have her own key, but this will not allow her to access Lisa's encrypted file. Lisa's key cannot be duplicated. This would create a major security hole. **D** is not correct. There is no encryption recovery key list in Windows 2000.

13. ☑ **B.** The file will be unencrypted. EFS does not support FAT32 or FAT volumes. You can only implement EFS on NTFS 5.0 (Windows 2000) volumes.

☒ **A** is not correct. The file will not be encrypted. It is moved in plaintext to the destination since EFS does not support FAT32. **C** is not correct. The file can be moved; it just cannot be encrypted. **D** is not correct. The destination does not support EFS, so the file will not be encrypted. If the file were to be moved on a local computer with NTFS 5.0, the system would prompt you if you moved an encrypted file to an unencrypted folder.

14. ☑ **B.** The required results are as follows: encrypt sensitive data in folders, and allow users to access data from any location. By creating shared network locations and creating roaming profiles, you have allowed users to access their data from any location. This produces the required results. The optional results are failsafe recovery method, user-friendly encryption process, and users having the ability to back up to removable media. The proposed solution of using Windows Backup utility is considered a best practice for recovering encrypted files in Windows 2000. Therefore, this optional result is produced. In addition, the process of encrypting files, especially when using roaming profiles, is very user-friendly and transparent to the user. This requirement is met. However, files saved by users to removable media are not encrypted. Therefore, this requirement is not met.

☒ **A**, **C**, and **D** are not correct. The proposed solution produces all required results and two of the three optional results.

15. ☑ **C.** Jackie can encrypt her files. When a user marks a folder or file for encryption using Windows Explorer, EFS automatically generates a public key pair and has the public key pair certified by a certificate authority (CA). If a CA is not available to issue a certificate, EFS will self-sign the certificate.

☒ **A** is not correct. She does not need to use a third-party certificate authority. EFS will self-sign the certificate. **B** is not correct. If Jackie had to wait until she returned to her office to encrypt her files, EFS would not be a very compelling security solution. Jackie can encrypt her files immediately due to the self-signing feature of EFS. **D** is not correct. Jackie cannot choose whether or not to use certificates with EFS. EFS technology is built upon PKI technology, which requires the use of certificates to function.

16. ☑ **B.** By running CIPHER from the command line in Windows 2000, you can access the encryption capabilities. Various options follow the CIPHER command and allow you to encrypt, decrypt, or view the state of files on the system.

☒　**A** is not correct because there is no X-Windows Console option in Windows 2000. **C** is not correct. The correct command is CIPHER, not ENCRYPTION. **D** is not correct. Using the Safe mode or VGA mode will not assist in using the non-graphical encryption utility, Cipher. There is no encryption console in Windows 2000.

17.　☑　**A.** Through group policy, you can manage both encryption and recovery settings for the network. EFS recovery policy is configured as part of the overall security policy for the system using Group Policy Objects at the domain, organizational unit, or computer level. EFS recovery policy is implemented in the Encrypted Data Recovery Agents (EDRA) node of the of public key policies area of the Group Policy snap-in. By integrating the EFS recovery policy within Windows 2000 group policy, the application of the recovery policy is handled by the Windows 2000 security subsystem. Therefore, enforcing, replicating, caching, and updating the recovery policy is handled automatically and enables users to use file encryption on an offline system, such as a laptop, using cached credentials.

☒　**B** is not correct. NTFS must be implemented prior to using EFS but in itself will not assist with the network management of EFS. **C** is not correct. Group policies can be accessed via the MMC but this, in itself, is not a method of managing encryption. **D** is not correct. Security identifiers are domain-unique values built when a user or group is created. This is a feature of Windows 2000 security but is not a feature that helps you manage network security directly.

LAB ANSWER

Objectives 9.01–9.03

Keep in mind there are many ways to approach this situation. These answers are based on Windows 2000 best practices. Your answer should contain all these elements. It should also have a logical, organized flow to the sequence of events.

1. Check overall network status.

Overall status of building or site   The status of the building will determine whether you can begin working to restore network functionality. Lack of power or other utilities or dangerous conditions will delay the restore.

Power to the building   If the building has power, you should check the power levels. Ensure that the power is within specifications. Low power (brown out) can burn out motors and other electronic components. High power can have the same effect, though usually more quickly.

Overall status of server room or location   If the power or air conditioning to the server room is disrupted, attend to these prior to working on servers. Remove water and debris from room prior to working on equipment.

Power to the servers   Check the level of power to the servers. Again, high or low power for extended periods of time and fluctuating power can cause additional damage to equipment.

Status of UPS devices and surge protector devices   Unless you have a generator or other longer-term power devices, a UPS will generally only provide enough power to ensure the safe shut down of the system. Depending on how they were configured, your UPS devices may have allowed the servers to shut down safely after generating a power alarm, or they may simply have provided power for a specified period and then shut down. Surge protector devices may have to be reset or replaced, depending on the nature of the device and the power fluctuations that occurred during this event. Check each device to be sure that it is reset and fully functional. Check the power output from these devices. Test the UPS devices by removing power and observing the behavior. Replace UPS batteries or allow UPS batteries to recharge and retest, if needed.

2. Check domain controller status.

    The first thing that will have to be checked after the general environment is inspected and readied for use is the status of domain controllers. Since these computers serve vital network functions, these should be the first machines inspected. If a server is not online, check the power, the UPS and any surge protection devices to help determine what caused the machine to go down. Then, attempt to bring the device back up. Monitor each stage of the boot process to make sure that each stage completes successfully. If it does not, see step 6.

3. Check member server status.

    Member servers typically store user data or run applications for the network users. These are the second most important set of servers. The same actions taken for step 2 should be taken for each member server.

4. Check disk sub-system status.

    Often servers will have associated RAID systems or sometimes servers will share devices. Inspect these devices and determine if there have been any failures. If one disk of a RAID5 set has failed, it can be replaced and the set will be restored. If more than one disk has failed, the data will have to be restored from backup.

5. Verify location and availability of backup media.

    Best practices include regularly scheduled backups and storing one full set of the backup media offsite. One recommendation would be to store your network configuration diagrams and information with your backup media offsite. In the event of a catastrophic event, having this data available with your backup media will enable you to more quickly assess the situation and requirements for repair. Determine the status of your network in relation to your backup plan. When was the last Full backup completed? Where is the backup media stored? How much data has potentially been lost? Are Incremental backups available onsite? Are they useable or will you have to restore back to your last Full backup set?

6. Go through backup and restore procedures.

   Domain controllers Use the Windows 2000 Backup utility to restore your data. Remember that if domain controllers have gone down but domain controllers remain on the network, a non-authoritative restore would be performed. If it appears that Active Directory data has been lost, you will need to perform an authoritative restore. Remember also that if you determine that data has been lost, you must perform a non-authoritative restore prior to performing an authoritative restore. If you have trouble booting the device, you can use the emergency repair disk or point the system to the Repair folder.

   Member servers Member servers do not contain data that is replicated. Therefore, they would need to be restored to their prior functionality via the Restore utility in Windows 2000. Authoritative and non-authoritative restores do not apply.

   Network devices Inspect network devices for damage and for connectivity. For instance, are all network printers online and available? Are network desktop computers damaged? Are all mobile devices accounted for? Check powered hubs, cabling, and other network components to ensure that each network component is fully functional.

7. Provide restart or help instructions to all end users to assist them with restoring their systems or receiving timely assistance, if needed.

8. Communicate the nature of the outage, the impact, and measures taken to restore the system to your management team.

9. Run tests, monitor results, and check with end users to ensure that the network is back to full functionality.

10. Review disaster recovery procedures and look for areas for improvements. Record these improved processes, store a copy of these instructions with backup media at offsite location.

MICROSOFT CERTIFIED SYSTEMS ENGINEER

10

Designing a Security Solution for Access Between Networks

TEST YOURSELF OBJECTIVES

This chapter focuses on two distinct aspects of designing a secure access solution. Providing access to the Internet *from* your company's network to public networks, like the Internet, as well as to other private networks is one aspect. Providing access *to* your company's network from the Internet (using RRAS or VPN) is the second aspect of a secure access solution. There are many protocols that you can implement to provide varying levels of security. PPTP/MPPE or L2TP/IPSec will enable you to secure VPN connections over the Internet. IPSec can also be implemented to secure all LAN traffic between two or more machines. EAP-TLS with digital certificates, MS-CHAP (version 1 or 2), SPAP, or PAP can be used to secure authentication traffic only, such as when users access a private network via a dial-up connection. We'll review these access solutions and protocols in this chapter.

TEST YOURSELF OBJECTIVE 10.01

Providing Secure Access to Public Networks from a Private Network

Providing access to the Internet from a private (corporate) network often entails securing the internal IP address ranges, DNS namespace, and client computers for heightened security. For large, corporate networks, Windows 2000 Proxy Server can be implemented for the most comprehensive and flexible solution. For medium-sized networks, network address translation (NAT) can be implemented. It provides slightly less flexibility than Proxy Server. It allows medium-sized networks to enable network and port translation, and it provides DHCP services to DHCP clients. Internet Connection Sharing (ICS) can be used for SOHO (Small Office Home Office) networks. It can be run on Windows 2000 Professional or Windows 98 Second Edition. It provides network and port address translation, as well as DHCP and name resolution services similar to NAT. Unlike NAT, ICS is not configurable.

- IP address protection is important for data packets leaving the internal network and heading out to the Internet.

- IP spoofing is defined as an attacker sending packets with source addresses from the internal network, making it appear as though the packets are internal.

■ DNS namespace protection is accomplished through implementing an internal and an external DNS server to conceal internal namespaces from the Internet. Internal data that can be misused includes resource records, Active Directory directory service–related SRV resource records, and internal addressing schemes.

■ Windows 2000 Server can be used with the Proxy Server 2.0 service. Proxy Server provides both proxy server and firewall functions.

■ In order to utilize the advanced features of Microsoft Proxy Server 2.0, client computers must have the Microsoft Proxy Server client installed and configured properly. Computers without a properly installed and configured client (such as computers on the Internet that are not clients of your Proxy Server), receive the same basic service as anonymous users. This may prevent the internal client from connecting to resources on the Internet.

■ Network address translation (NAT) is a protocol used within Windows 2000. It conceals the internal address scheme by intercepting network traffic and replacing outbound packets with a common source address.

■ Internet Connection Sharing (ICS) is a feature of Network and Dial-Up tools that permits multiple computers in a workgroup environment to share a single Internet connection. It cannot be used on a network that has Windows 2000 domain controllers, DNS, or DHCP servers.

■ Automatic Private IP Addressing (APIPA) configuration consists of allocating a unique address in the range of 169.254.0.1 through 169.254.255.254, with a subnet mask of 255.255.0.0, when a DHCP server is not present. This is used by ICS to automatically assign IP addresses in a small network environment.

exam
Ⓦatch

On the exam, you're more likely to see scenarios and questions relating to larger networks and Internet access. However, fully understanding NAT and ICS will enable you to answer questions about large networks as well. For instance, if an answer on the exam suggests using ICS with domain controllers, internal DNS, or DHCP servers, or with clients that have statically configured IP addresses, you'll know the answer is wrong. Similarly, if an answer suggests manually configuring ICS for a medium-sized network, you'll know that answer is wrong. Understanding these topics, even if they aren't directly tested on the exam, will help to eliminate wrong answers.

QUESTIONS

10.01: Providing Secure Access to Public Networks from a Private Network

1. Based on the following illustration, what configuration changes should be made to improve security? (Choose all that apply.)

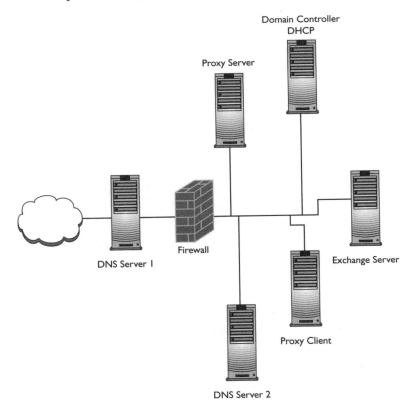

A. Move DNS Server 1 to the other side of the firewall.

B. Remove the connection between DNS Server 2 and the firewall.

    C. Move the connection from the Proxy Client so it connects directly to the Proxy Server instead of the firewall.

    D. Move the connection from the Exchange Server so it connects directly to the Proxy Server instead of the firewall.

    E. Remove the connection between the Domain Controller and the firewall.

2. **Current Situation:** You are reviewing Internet access for your company. You require a high level of security, but you do not want the policies to be overly restrictive. Recently, it's become clear that some employees are misusing Internet access and you have been asked to design a solution that will curtail some of this activity.

    Required Results: Block inappropriate Internet access, allow only specified users access to various Internet services such as NetMeeting, and require user authentication to access the Internet.

    Optional Desired Results: Restrict protocols used to access the Internet, provide a method of monitoring Internet access, and restrict Internet content that is inappropriate for your company.

    Proposed Solution: Implement Proxy Server. Configure Proxy Server to deny access to specific domain names by using domain filters. Create security groups and place users in appropriate groups. Then, configure Proxy Server to allow only specific groups access to defined protocols. Implement dynamic packet filtering. Configure IIS to use Integrated Windows Authentication. Customize security zone settings for Internet Explorer via the IEAK Profile Manager and Customization Wizard to prevent users from accessing specific Internet content.

    What results are produced from the proposed solution?

    A. The proposed solution produces the required results and all of the optional results.

    B. The proposed solution produces the required results and some of the optional results.

    C. The proposed solution produces the required results only.

    D. The proposed solution does not produce the required results.

3. You work for a startup company. You have limited funds and cannot afford a large-scale network solution for Internet security. However, you also recognize the need for strong security. Your network consists of ten computers running Windows 2000 Professional or Windows 98 Second Edition in a workgroup environment. You have recently installed broadband Internet service to your company location, but it is directly connected to one computer. Recently, the computer had a destructive VBScript loaded into the Startup group via an Internet intruder. How can you provide access to the Internet to the whole company and maintain a secure network?

A. Use ICS. Enable ICS on the connection to the local ISP. Manually configure the static IP address to 169.254.1.1. Manually configure the other IP addresses from a range of APIPA addresses. Configure ICS to use DNS for name resolution.

B. Use NAT. Implement Routing and Remote Access Server. Manually configure NAT with desired IP addresses and subnet masks. Use IPSec to secure communications. Configure NAT to use DNS for name resolution.

C. Use ICS. Configure all workgroup computers as DHCP clients. Configure ICS using the check box that enables connection sharing. Allow ICS to automatically assign IP addresses from the range 192.168.0.1 to 192.168.254.254.

D. Promote one computer on the network to a domain controller. Implement Proxy Server on this computer. Then, implement NAT and manually configure the IP address ranges desired. Configure NAT to use DNS for name resolution.

TEST YOURSELF OBJECTIVE 10.02

Providing External Users with Secure Access to Private Network Resources

This section focuses on users connecting to corporate resources from remote locations. Access can be through direct dial-up access into a Routing and Remote Access Server via the computer's modem. Access can also be via the computer's modem to a local Internet service provider (ISP) account through the Internet to the company's Internet server. Access in this manner can be to a secure corporate Web site or to a company's virtual private network (VPN) server. The risks associated with this primarily revolve around unauthorized users gaining access to your company's network resources.

- A demilitarized zone (DMZ) is a network that is between a private network and the Internet. It permits data to flow from the Internet into a private network while maintaining a very secure environment. A DMZ contains equipment such as servers, routers, and switches, which maintain security by preventing the internal network from being exposed to the Internet.

- Virtual private networks (VPNs) make use of public networks such as the Internet to allow access to private internal network resources by encrypting the data. With VPNs, you can use modems, ISDN modems/routers, cable modems, or DSL connection devices.

- Remote Access Service (RAS) has been part of Microsoft networking products since LAN Manager. It allows users to dial directly into the network and acts as a remote node. Windows 2000 provides Routing and Remote Access Services (RRAS or RAS).

- Accessing network resources from external locations exposes the network to security risks, including social engineering, exploitation of default security configurations, IP spoofing, exploitation of excess services, and exploitation of system backdoors.

- NAT can be used to conceal internal addresses for all outbound traffic. Routing and Remote Access in Windows 2000 provides the ability to implement NAT.

- Protocols can be filtered at the firewall to prevent unused protocols from passing through the firewall to the internal network.

- Port mapping can be used to conceal the true address of the destination computer (unlike NAT, which conceals the true address of the source computer). Port mapping defines which ports will be redirected to internal servers. Connections to non-defined ports will be denied.

■ Screened subnets, also known as DMZs, consist of portions of the network that reside between the Internet and the internal network. Any resources that are made available to the Internet reside on this screened subnet. Screened subnets are implemented as three-pronged firewalls or mid-ground screened subnets.

■ Three-pronged firewalls consist of one firewall with one interface assigned to the Internet and one interface assigned to the internal network. A third interface is assigned to the screened subnet.

■ Mid-ground screened subnets consist of two firewalls with a screened subnet between them. A mid-ground screened subnet can provide additional security if the two firewalls are from different manufacturers. If security is breached on one firewall, it cannot be replicated to breach security on the second firewall.

exam **!** atch

Remote access is a major focus on the Designing Security exam. Remember that users can essentially connect remotely to corporate resources in one of two ways: dial-up or VPN. Dial-up services are managed by Routing and Remote Access servers and by RADIUS. Users create VPNs via Internet connections such as ISPs. These connections are managed by VPN servers configured to provide a secure tunnel, or virtual network, for users. Fully understanding how each of these is configured and in what circumstances you would implement each is key to successfully navigating this exam.

QUESTIONS

10.02: Providing External Users with Secure Access to Private Network Resources

4. If you wanted to provide SQL Server capabilities to remote users, how should the SQL Server in the illustration on the following page be connected to the network?

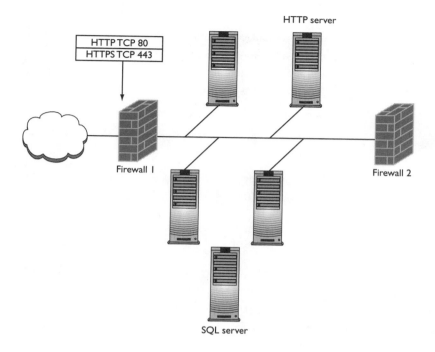

A. Between Firewall 1 and Firewall 2; enable TCP port 1433 on Firewall 2.

B. To the left of Firewall 1; enable TCP port 1433 on Firewall 1.

C. To the right of Firewall 2; enable TCP port 1433 on Firewall 2.

D. Directly to the HTTP server; enable TCP port 1433 on HTTP server.

5. **Current Situation:** Your computer has a firewall set up to protect your private network from the Internet. You've been asked to review the firewall configuration and adjust it to ensure that the network is secure.

Required Results: Only allow TCP ports 80 and 443. Configure a default value so if configuration rules do not apply, security will be maintained.

Optional Desired Results: Monitor and avoid attacks.

Proposed Solution: Configure the firewall to use packet filtering. Define a rule that specifies that only TCP port 80 (HTTP) and TCP port 443 (HTTPS) can be used. Create the last rule to be a Deny All so that if a protocol comes in for which there is no matching rule, it will be denied. Configure the firewall to alert if a packet arrives at the external interface of the firewall with a source address from the internal network. Set timeout intervals so the firewall can drop suspicious sessions.

What results are produced from the proposed solution?

A. The proposed solution produces the required results and all of the optional results.

B. The proposed solution produces the required results and some of the optional results.

C. The proposed solution produces the required results only.

D. The proposed solution does not produce the required results.

6. Your company has grown rapidly over the past couple of years. You've been providing remote access to your users via dial-up services. However, management of this service has become difficult. What solution could you implement that would improve network management of remote access?

A. IAS to act as RADIUS server to provide authentication, authorization, and accounting; Remote Access Servers to act as RADIUS clients to pass authentication requests to the RADIUS server, and remote access clients using dial-up or VPN connections

B. RADIUS server to act as IAS to provide authentication; RADIUS clients to act as Remote Access Servers to authenticate IAS requests; and remote access clients using VPN connections

C. Configure local policies on each RRAS server, implement RADIUS clients using these policies, and manage all RRAS services via the MMC

D. Configure IAS to use RADIUS servers as IAS clients. Configure local policies on each RRAS server to pass authentication through to the RADIUS servers, allow remote client access via VPN tunnels only.

Providing Secure Access Between Private Networks

Secure access between private networks occurs for two primary reasons. First, if your company has several separate networks in different geographic regions, you would have several private networks that may require secure access to one another's resources. Second, companies occasionally want to extend network resources to another company such as a trusted partner. The use of certificate authorities can provide secure authentication of a variety of users, including internal users and trusted partners. This section focuses on providing secure access between private networks.

- Remote office networks can be connected via dedicated private network connections such as T1, T3, Frame Relay, or DSL (digital subscriber line).

- Remote office networks can be connected via shared, public access network connections via the Internet.

- Dedicated lines are not completely secure and can be compromised.

- More damage is done by internal employees than by outside hackers, so securing network connections is critical, whether using dedicated private connections or shared public connections.

- Router security can include packet filtering, mutual authentication, and encryption.

- Windows 2000 Server can be configured as an IP router by installing Routing and Remote Access Server (RRAS) service. A Windows 2000 Server configured as an IP router can provide network address translation, IP packet filtering, and VPN.

- VPN provides a secure method of connecting two private networks via a private or public connection.

- Certificate authorities (CA) can be internal (enterprise or stand-alone) or external (third party). CAs manage and issue certificates used for authentication.

- Public key infrastructure (PKI) is not one single product, but the framework for providing public key security on networks. PKI in Windows 2000 relies upon the use of certificates.

e x a m

ⓦ a t c h

It's likely you'll see a number of scenario questions on the exam that focus on secure access between private networks. Remember that VPN can be used for individual clients accessing corporate resources via the Internet. VPN can also be used to connect two private networks via the Internet. This provides a secure, cost-effective solution. It also allows for strong security measures to be implemented via L2TP with IPSec. On the exam answers, select L2TP if (a) the client supports it, (b) you require machine authentication, and (c) you require stronger security than PPTP. PPTP supports NAT and down-level clients. Both PPTP and L2TP support multiple protocols.

QUESTIONS

10.03: Providing Secure Access Between Private Networks

7. Your company has four sites. Each site is connected to the others via fractional T1 lines. Data is transferred over these wires in an unsecured fashion. What solution would you recommend to improve the connectivity and security of these sites?

   A. Install third-party routers between the connection points; configure mutual authentication and encryption between these routers.

   B. Configure Windows 2000–based servers as IP routers by installing Routing and Remote Access Service. Implement NAT, IP packet filtering, and VPN for security.

   C. Configure Windows 2000–based servers as NAT servers to provide network address translation and encryption services.

   D. Install bridgehead servers that support L2TP tunnels with IPSec. Establish filtering and routing rules for higher security.

8. **Current Situation:** Your company has two locations. Each location is connected to the Internet via a DS3 line to an ISP and is configured as shown in the following diagram. Until recently, the two sites communicated and shared files by emailing them back and forth. You have been asked to provide a better solution.

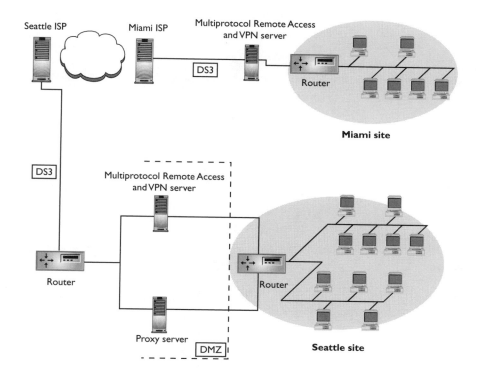

Required Results: Provide a low-cost solution for both sites to share files and data more easily, and provide a secure method of connection.

Optional Desired Results: Ensure data transmitted back and forth is secure against intrusion. Do not increase network traffic or CPU loads significantly (other than the traffic increase that will occur because users are now connected). Utilize existing infrastructure if possible.

Proposed Solution: Configure a single demand-dial interface at each router. Establish a permanent router-to-router VPN connection. Use L2TP with IPSec for encryption between routers. Use Routing and Remote Access filters (not IPSec filtering) on the Internet interface of the VPN server to set input and output permit filters for L2TP. Prohibit all traffic but L2TP over IPSec.

What results are produced from the proposed solution?

A. The proposed solution produces the required results and all of the optional results.

B. The proposed solution produces the required results and some of the optional results.

C. The proposed solution produces the required results only.

D. The proposed solution does not produce the required results.

9. Your company has just acquired another firm with one location. You and a co-worker have been assigned the task of configuring a new connection to this site. You argue that an on-demand router-to-router VPN solution is the best. What statements support your position? (Choose all that apply.)

A. A permanent WAN link is not possible because the only connection to the new site uses an ATM link.

B. The new company's router is already configured with a single demand-dial interface.

C. You can use your existing analog line to create a secure connection.

D. Your answering router is already permanently connected to the Internet.

TEST YOURSELF OBJECTIVE 10.04

Designing Windows 2000 Security for Remote Access Users

We have already reviewed the methods of providing remote access (Test Yourself Objective 10.02). In this section, we'll review designing security for remote access. We'll review the protocols and services that can be used in a design solution.

Dial-up connections primarily employ PPP protocols, including MS-CHAP and BAP. VPN connections primarily employ PPTP protocols including PPTP and L2TP with IPSec. EAP is a new protocol used in Windows 2000 that extends PPP protocols and can use a variety of authentication methods. It can be used with TLS for added security.

- Point-to-Point Tunneling Protocol (PPTP) can provide authenticated and encrypted communications between a client and a server, without requiring a PKI.

- Layer Two Tunneling Protocol (L2TP) encapsulates PPP frames to be sent over IP, X.25, Frame Relay, or ATM networks.

- Microsoft Challenge Handshake Authentication Protocol (MS-CHAP) is used in dial-up sessions for secure user authentication.

- Bandwidth Allocation Protocol (BAP), a PPP control protocol, is used on a multiprocessing connection to dynamically add and remove links.

- Bandwidth Allocation Control Protocol (BACP) negotiates the election of a favored peer for a multiprocessing connection.

- Extensible Authentication Protocol (EAP) is an infrastructure that allows the addition of arbitrary authentication methods such as certificates, one-time passwords, smart cards, and token cards.

- Transport Layer Security (TLS) is a standard protocol used to provide secure Web communications via the Internet or intranet. It can be used by clients to authenticate servers or by servers to authenticate clients. It also encrypts communications.

exam
ⓦatch

Having a strong understanding of remote access authentication protocols is critical to successfully navigating this exam. Remember that PPTP is an extension of PPP and that L2TP is an extension of PPTP. L2TP works over a wider type of connections including X.25 and Frame Relay circuits. It also works with ATM, DSL, and other connection types. PPTP does not support any connection type that does not use TCP/IP standard. L2TP does not support down-level clients. These distinctions will help you figure out right and wrong choices to find the best answer for each question on this topic.

QUESTIONS

10.04: Designing Windows 2000 Security for Remote Access Users

10. Your company is reviewing your remote access policies and procedures. Currently, authorized users dial in to corporate servers. You submit a proposal to convert all remote access to VPN access. What components would you put in your proposal to demonstrate a compelling solution? (Choose all that apply.)

A. You can use a single Windows 2000–based server, which is a domain member, to provide all remote access services. Dial-in access could be kept in place and you can enable additional ports for VPN connections, thus creating a flexible, extensible solution.

B. The number of VPN ports is not limited by physical hardware as it is with dial-up lines. When you start a VPN server the first time, 128 PPTP and 128 L2TP ports are automatically created.

C. You can use L2TP with IPSec ports for Windows 2000–based clients that require a very secure connection. However, this configuration also supports backward compatibility via PPTP support for legacy and non–Windows 2000–based clients. This also provides a secure connection method for down-level clients.

D. You can assign static IP routes for clients that required dedicated, secure lines. You can implement firewall IP packet filtering via the VPN connection to ensure that data is both authenticated and tamper-proof.

11. You are having a discussion with a colleague about the similarities and differences between PPTP and L2TP. How would you compare the two? (Choose all that apply.)

A. PPTP provides user authentication, access control, and the ability to restrict certain types of remote access on a per-user basis.

B. L2TP requires the use of IPSec to encrypt all protocols that run over IP.

C. PPTP is a TCP/IP protocol that encapsulates IP, IPX, or NetBEUI protocols.

D. L2TP uses UDP and can be used over ATM, Frame Relay, and X.25 networks. Like PPTP, it also works with IP, IPX, or NetBEUI protocols.

12. **Current Situation:** Your company currently uses X.25 circuits for dial-in access to corporate resources. Your system is configured per the following diagram. Currently, some users (Client D) are being denied access to network resources due to constraints on the hardware systems in place.

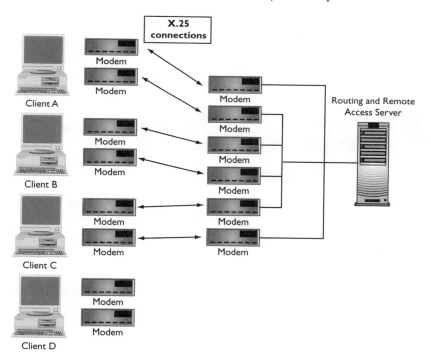

Required Results: Use existing infrastructure, and improve connectivity throughput.

Optional Desired Results: Provide more flexibility in terms of number of users that can be supported. Minimize telecommunications costs.

Proposed Solution: Enable the PPP multilink protocol over existing X.25 on each RRAS server. Do this by selecting Multilink Connections and Dynamic

Bandwidth Control (BAP/BACP) check boxes on the PPP tab of the Properties dialog box for each server. Disable callback requirements on servers using PPP multilink. Enable PPP multilink on each client using this service. Configure BAP settings through remote access policies. Specify that an extra line is dropped if link utilization drops below 40 percent.

What results are produced from the proposed solution?

A. The proposed solution produces the required results and all of the optional results.

B. The proposed solution produces the required results and some of the optional results.

C. The proposed solution produces the required results only.

D. The proposed solution does not produce the required results.

TEST YOURSELF OBJECTIVE 10.05

Designing an SMB Signing Solution

A Server Message Block (SMB) transports file data between a client and a server computer. SMB signing, also known as Common Internet File System (CIFS), mutually authenticates client and server for a communication session. A digital signature is placed in each server message block. This ensures the client is connecting to the proper server and not to a server impersonating the proper server. SMB signing is supported both in Windows 2000 and in Windows NT 4.0 (Service Pack 3 or later).

- Server Message Block (SMB) is a protocol developed by Microsoft, Intel, and IBM that defines a series of commands used to pass information between network computers.

- Common Internet File System (CIFS) is another term for Server Message Block (SMB) signing.

- SMB signing can be used with Windows 2000, Windows NT 4.0 SP3 clients, or Windows 98 clients. You cannot use SMB signing with Windows 95 clients.

- SMB provides mutual authentication to Windows NT clients as well as Windows 2000 and Windows 98 clients.

- SMB signing adds overhead to the packet building process. Resulting processing time can increase 10 to 15 percent overall. Network traffic does not increase, only processing time.

- IPSec (covered in the next section) provides the same functionality through Authentication Headers. However, this is only supported with Windows 2000 clients.

exam
ⓦatch

CIFS is a native file-sharing protocol in Windows 2000 and is an enhanced version of the Microsoft open, cross-platform SMB protocol. You may find the term CIFS in Microsoft exam scenarios. CIFS is the standard way computer users share files across the Internet and across intranets. CIFS defines a series of commands used to pass information back and forth between computers on a network. The redirector packages requests meant for other computers in a CIFS structure. Using a CIFS snap-in makes a NetWare server respond like a Windows 2000–based server to a Windows-based client. Installing a CIFS add-in to a Unix server enables the Unix server to respond like a Windows 2000–based computer to any Windows-based client.

QUESTIONS

10.05: Designing an SMB Signing Solution

13. You and a colleague are having a rather animated discussion about securing network communications. You are trying to explain to your colleague that SMB signing provides two key enhancements over standard SMB data exchanges. What are these two key features?

    A. SMB packets cannot be modified in transit.

    B. SMB packets move more quickly to destination computers.

    C. SMB packets have a digital signature from the CA that authenticates each packet.

    D. SMB packets allow the client or the server to recognize each other, preventing "man-in-the-middle" attacks.

Questions 14–16 This scenario should be used to answer questions 14, 15, and 16.

Please refer to the following illustration. Network A is a Windows 2000–based network. The server is set to always use SMB signing. Clients 1 to 4 on Network A are set to use SMB signing when possible. The server in Network B is a Window NT 4.0–based server (with Service Pack 4 installed). It is set to use SMB signing when possible. Clients 1 and 2 on Network B are set to use SMB signing always. Clients 3 and 4 are set so that Always Use SMB Signing is disabled and Use SMB Signing When Possible is disabled. Based on this diagram and the settings listed here, answer the following three questions.

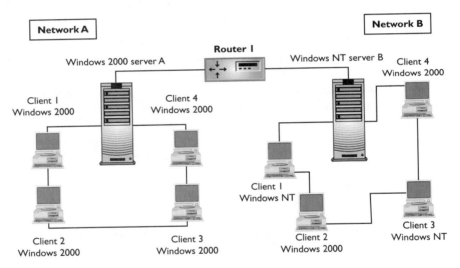

14. What is the highest (most secure) level of data communication security that will occur on Network A?

    A. Always uses SMB signing

    B. Uses SMB signing when possible

    C. Never uses SMB signing

    D. Depends on other network settings

15. What is the highest level of data communication security that will occur on Network B?

    A. Always uses SMB signing

    B. Uses SMB signing when possible

    C. Never uses SMB signing

    D. Depends on Clients 3 and 4

16. What level of data communication security will occur between Client 1 on Network A and Client 3 on Network B?

    A. Always use SMB signing.

    B. Use SMB signing when possible.

    C. Never use SMB signing.

    D. Client 1 on Network A cannot communicate with Client 3 on Network B.

17. **Current Situation:** You've had instances where network communications were compromised.

    Required Results: Implement secure communications between client and server machines on your network and do not increase network traffic.

    Optional Desired Results: Do not increase server processing requirements by more than 30 percent. Implement across the network using Windows 2000 tools.

    Proposed Solution: Implement SMB signing. On the server, go into Default Domain Policy. Select Computer Configuration | Windows Settings | Security Settings | Local Policies | Security Options. In the right side of that window, right-click Digitally Sign Server Communications (Always) and select Security. This will bring up the Security Policy Setting dialog box for this setting. Click the check box entitled Define This Policy Setting and click the radio button to the left of Enable to enable this setting. Click OK. Close the Default Domain Policy window.

    What results are produced from the proposed solution?

    A. The proposed solution produces the required results and all of the optional results.

    B. The proposed solution produces the required results and some of the optional results.

    C. The proposed solution produces the required results only.

    D. The proposed solution does not produce the required results.

Designing an IPSec Solution

This section focuses on designing an access solution using Internet Protocol Security (IPSec). IPSec is a protocol for securing IP network traffic that provides complete security between two computers using this protocol. Configuration is performed by IPSec policies that contain security rules. Each rule specifies a certain type of traffic with filters, associated filter action, and authentication method. IPSec policies can be created in Active Directory within group policy or on a local computer.

- Internet Protocol Security (IPSec) is a protocol that provides authenticity, data integrity, privacy, and anti-replay capabilities.

- With IPSec, two security negotiation phases are used. ISAKMP manages the first phase, which is the negotiation policy.

- Windows 2000 uses security policies. A security policy is an individual configuration of Windows IP security attributes.

- The negotiation policy and the security policy together are considered the security association (SA).

- IPSec can be deployed using one of two protocols, Authentication Header (AH) or Encapsulating Security Payload (ESP).

exam
ⓦatch

IPSec and SSL can both be used to protect data over the Internet. These two protocols are used very differently. IPSec is transparent to the application. Applications do not need to be specifically written to utilize the security it features since IPSec occurs between the client and server computers at the Network layer. IPSec provides protection for all IP and upper-level protocols in the TCP/IP suite. This includes IP, UDP, and ICMP among others. SSL, however, works at the Application layer. Therefore, applications must be written specifically to take advantage of the security features provided by SSL. Keep this in mind during the exam to help you choose the best answer.

QUESTIONS

10.06: Designing an IPSec Solution

18. You have configured your network to use IPSec for secure communications. You open Network Monitor to determine if IPSec is actually being used between two hosts. What would you have to do in order to make this determination in Network Monitor?

A. Local security policy must be applied.

B. Filter out all protocols except ISAKMP, AH, and ESP.

C. Filter out all protocols except IPSec, L2TP, EAP, and TLS.

D. Capture the data in Network Monitor then open it in Event Viewer to check IPSec events.

19. You and a friend are discussing methods of implementing IPSec. He strongly recommends the use of pre-shared key authentication. Which of his arguments is faulty?

A. The pre-shared key is stored unprotected in the IPSec policy.

B. The pre-shared key authentication method can be secured by restricting access to administrators only with read and write access of IPSec policies.

C. Pre-shared key authentication is part of the IPSec standards set forth by the IETF.

D. The IPSec policy using pre-shared key should be restricted to system read-only access on each computer.

20. **Current Situation:** You are the IT Manager for a financial services company. Your company recently implemented a Web site to provide financial advice to clients. This advice is tailored to each client's needs based on financial data they input. In addition, the Corporate Financial Analysis (CFA) Department

in your organization works with financial data from a number of publicly traded corporations that is highly confidential and must not be compromised.

Required Results: You must provide the highest security for the CFA data, minimize network overhead, and provide a method for non–Windows 2000 computers to participate in a secure network.

Optional Desired Results: Use the lowest reasonable security across the network, and provide a method of centralized management.

Proposed Solution: The following diagram shows the proposed solution.

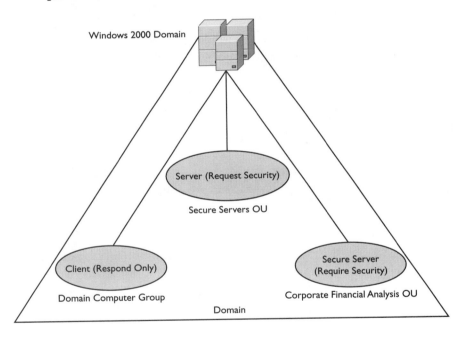

Place the Corporate Financial Analysis (CFA) servers on OU. Configure this OU to use the pre-defined policy, Secure Server (Require Security). Create a second OU called Secure Servers. Assign these computers the pre-defined policy Server (Request Security). Finally, assign the domain computers to a domain group called Domain Computer Group. Use the pre-defined policy Client (Respond Only) for all computers in this group.

What results are produced from the proposed solution?

A. The proposed solution produces the required results and all of the optional results.

B. The proposed solution produces the required results and some of the optional results.

C. The proposed solution produces the required results only.

D. The proposed solution does not produce the required results.

LAB QUESTION

Objectives 10.01–10.06

We've reviewed a number of secure access methods in this chapter. Focus on the material we've reviewed to complete the following lab.

You are the director of IT for a fast-growing consulting firm located in the United States. You have clients around the world that rely upon your firm for unique, innovative solutions. These solutions often give your clients a significant competitive advantage in their respective markets.

Lately, you have noticed a number of strange things on your network, including an increase in network traffic with protocols you didn't think were in use. In addition, you've heard a few complaints from some of your most trusted consultants. They are concerned that some of their client-sensitive data may have been compromised. While they're not sure, they feel the attack was external and came via some remote access method. They do not believe it is a company employee, but they wonder if perhaps a company employee's log-on credentials have been stolen or compromised.

Your network configuration is a 100MB Ethernet LAN running mostly Windows 2000–based servers. You have a handful of Windows NT 4.0–based servers that will be upgraded in the next fiscal year when your budget allows for the hardware upgrade that will be required to make the machines compliant with the Windows 2000 HCL.

Your firm was located in one building until recently. A strategic acquisition last month added a second and third location to your company. Each of those sites has an Internet connection; the second location (Site 2) has a fractional T1 line and the third location (Site 3) is using a Frame Relay connection. Neither site is connected to each other or to your headquarters (Site 1).

You have auditing set to monitor successful and unsuccessful logons to the network. No other auditing is currently in place.

Your firm has a number of consultants who travel worldwide. You have maintained a bank of modems for users to dial into remotely. In order to cut costs and increase security, you've instituted the callback feature of the Routing and Remote Access Server. However, as it currently stands, consultants have to email a network administrator to have the callback number configured when they change locations. This works fine except in cases where the time difference is substantial or when the consultant neglects to request the change.

Based on this information, prepare a plan for improving network access. Required elements include plans to connect the two new locations to corporate, plans to improve remote user access, and plans to improve security while maintaining or decreasing administrative work.

QUICK ANSWER KEY

Objective 10.01

1.   C and E
2.   B
3.   C

Objective 10.02

4.   C
5.   A
6.   A

Objective 10.03

7.   B
8.   A
9.   B, C, and D

Objective 10.04

10.   A, B, and C
11.   A, C, and D
12.   A

Objective 10.05

13.   A and D
14.   A
15.   A
16.   D
17.   D

Objective 10.06

18.   B
19.   A
20.   A

IN-DEPTH ANSWERS

10.01: Providing Secure Access to Public Networks from a Private Network

1. ☑ **C** and **E** are correct. The Proxy client contains configuration parameters that work in conjunction with the Proxy Server. The Proxy client should not connect directly to the firewall. In doing so, it bypasses all the protection the Proxy Server provides and relies solely on firewall settings. The connection between the domain controller and the firewall should also be removed. This direct connection exposes the network to attack. Best practices include identifying the minimum number of computers that requires a direct Internet connection to reduce security risks.

   ☒ **A** is not correct. Having an external (DNS Server 1) and internal (DNS Sevrer 2) DNS server will enable you to protect internal configuration information. **B** is not correct. The internal DNS server should be connected to the firewall for address and namespace resolution or forwarding. **D** is not correct. The Exchange Server can be configured so it only connects with other computers running SMTP. The firewall can be configured to allow the mail server to connect to other mail servers only if the destination port is TCP port 25 (SMTP).

2. ☑ **B.** The required results are as follows: block inappropriate Internet access, allow only specified users access to various Internet services, and require user authentication to access the Internet. Inappropriate Internet access is blocked through several measures. First, implementing Proxy Server and configuring it to filter by domain name will block access to specific domain names on the Internet. When this is configured, Proxy Server also resolves the URL to the IP address and stores the IP address to prevent users from circumventing security by accessing the site via its IP address rather than its Web address. By placing users in security groups and assigning Internet permissions by group, you can restrict Internet usage as well. Creating customized zone settings for Internet

Explorer will also help restrict users from accessing objectionable content that is not specifically denied by its URL or IP address. The second requirement of only allowing specified users access to certain Internet services is accomplished via security group permissions. Finally, requiring user authentication is accomplished through the use of Integrated Windows Authentication, which requires the use of Windows and Internet Explorer. It uses credentials obtained from the user's access token to provide appropriate access.

The optional results are as follows: restrict protocols used to access the Internet, provide a method of monitoring Internet access, and restrict Internet content that is inappropriate for your company. The proposed solution restricts protocols used to access the Internet by implementing dynamic packet filtering. Restricting inappropriate content is accomplished through the Internet Explorer Administration Kit (IEAK), which lets you customize the browser and zone settings to prevent users from accessing unauthorized content. However, the solution does not provide an ability to monitor Internet access. This could be accomplished through auditing proxy server usage. This file can be stored as text or stored to an Open Database Connectivity (ODBC)–compliant program, such as Microsoft SQL or Microsoft Access, to filter and review large amounts of data in an orderly manner.

☒ **A**, **C**, and **D** are not correct. The proposed solution produces the required results and two of the three optional results.

3. ☑ **C.** ICS, or Internet Connection Sharing, is specifically designed for small-to-medium-sized businesses. It is a simple package consisting of DHCP, NAT, and DNS. ICS requires that you enable connection sharing on a computer connected to the ISP. The computer must have a network interface card (NIC). ICS will be assigned an IP address used to communicate with the ISP and will automatically assign the internal address ranges to be used by the workgroup computers. Once ICS is enabled, no further configuration of services, such as DNS or IP addressing, is allowed on the network. These services are all implemented automatically by ICS.

☒ **A** is not correct. ICS cannot be manually configured. DNS is provided by ICS and does not need to be separately implemented. **B** is not correct. NAT requires Windows 2000 Server, whereas ICS can be implemented with Windows 2000 Professional or Windows 98 Second Edition. Also, NAT cannot be used with IPSec. If using domain controllers, implement Proxy

Server to provide these same services and more. **D** is not correct. Proxy Server should not run on a domain controller for security reasons. Proxy Server will perform the same functions (as well as additional services) as NAT.

10.02: Providing External Users with Secure Access to Private Network Resources

4. ☑ **C.** The SQL server, like any application server, should not be exposed directly to Internet users. Application servers can be accessed via Web-based front ends, tunnels into private networks, or Terminal Services. Therefore, the SQL server computer should be connected to the right of Firewall 2, or inside the private network. TCP port 1433, used for SQL data, should be enabled on Firewall 2. The internal firewall (Firewall 2) must be configured to only allow the Web server in the screened subnet to connect to the application server located in the private network.

   ☒ **A** is not correct. The application server should not be on the screened subnet. **B** is not correct. This placement would put the application server directly on the Internet in front of even the firewall. **D** is not correct. The application server should not be part of the Web server on the screened subnet but on the private network protected by the firewall.

5. ☑ **A.** The required results are as follows: allow only TCP 80 and 443 and configure default security. Through configuring the firewall to allow TCP ports 80 and 443 only and to deny all other protocols, the proposed solution produces the required results. The Deny All setting is used to catch any protocols for which there is not a specific Allow or Deny rule. Packet filter rules are processed in their defined order. The last rule is the Allow Any or Deny All rule. This provides the highest security setting. The optional results are as follows: monitor and avoid attacks. Firewalls can be configured to scan for well-known attacks. Preventing IP spoofing can be accomplished by denying access to any external packet that contains an internal IP address as its source address. Defining acceptable timeout intervals allows firewalls to drop suspicious sessions and prevent certain attacks. Denial of service attacks can be started by sending TCP SYN (synchronization) packets that fill the server's buffer while waiting

for a response. Recognizing and dropping these sessions is a configurable firewall option.

☒ **B**, **C**, and **D** are not correct. All optional results were produced.

6. ☑ **A.** Internet Authentication Service (IAS) is the Microsoft implementation of RADIUS (Remote Authentication Dial-in User Service). It can be used for centralizing authentication, authorization, and accounting for dial-up and VPN connections. Once IAS is implemented, the various RRAS servers become RADIUS clients. These servers pass authentication requests through to IAS. Remote access clients can access the network either via dial-up access or by using VPN tunnels via the Internet.

☒ **B** is not correct. Although IAS is the Microsoft implementation of the RADIUS server, RADIUS clients (or RRAS servers) do not authenticate IAS requests; they pass client authentication requests to IAS. **C** is not correct. you can centralize the management of remote access policies to enforce configuration of the required security settings on all RRAS servers. You can centralize remote access policies by (a) configuring a Windows 2000–based server as an IAS server, (b) creating a central set of policies on the IAS server, and (c) configuring each RRAS Server as a RADIUS client to the IAS server. Any local policies will no longer be used. Local policies can still be configured on the RRAS servers, but they will be ignored when the server is configured as a RADIUS client. **D** is not correct. IAS is the Microsoft implementation of RADIUS servers, so you would not configure IAS to be a client of itself. Local policies can be set on RRAS servers but once they are configured as RADIUS clients, those local policies will be ignored.

10.03: Providing Secure Access Between Private Networks

7. ☑ **B.** Windows 2000–based servers can be used as routers through the implementation of Routing and Remote Access Services (RAS or RRAS). It can provide network address translation (NAT), IP packet filtering to restrict the types of traffic it will route, and virtual private networking to establish secure connections via public (Internet) connections.

☒ **A** is not correct. Windows 2000 Routing and Remote Access Service provides an alternative to purchasing third-party routers. This can help keep network management and costs lower. **C** is not correct. Windows 2000–based servers do not implement NAT servers. Rather, NAT is a service or feature utilized for providing address translation to protect internal IP addressing schemes. **D** is not correct. While you could establish L2TP tunnels with IPSec for secure connections, you would not do this with a bridgehead server. A bridgehead server is used between sites to manage site replication data.

8. ☑ **A.** The required results are as follows: provide a low-cost solution for both sites to share files and data more easily, and provide a secure method of connection. By using existing infrastructure, including the ISPs, the routers, and the Internet connectivity, you have provided a low-cost solution. Establishing a router-to-router L2TP with IPSec VPN, you have provided a very secure solution. The required results are produced.

The optional results are as follows: ensure data transmitted back and forth is secure against intrusion, do not increase network traffic or CPU loads significantly, and utilize existing infrastructure if possible. Using L2TP with IPSec, the first optional result of ensuring data is secure is produced. Using L2TP with IPSec between the routers only, rather than on the entire network, you have not significantly increased network traffic or CPU loads. While it is true that network traffic will increase because users will be connected, the solution itself does not impose a significant additional burden on the network. Finally, the optional result of using existing infrastructure is produced because the solution uses existing servers, routers, and Internet connections.

☒ **B**, **C**, and **D** are not correct. The proposed solution produces all required and optional results.

9. ☑ **B, C,** and **D** are correct. When a permanent WAN link is not feasible for location or cost reasons, you can use on-demand router-to-router VPN connections as an alternative. This requires three things. First, the answering router must be configured with a single demand-dial interface (answer B), it must be permanently connected to the Internet (answer D), and you can use your existing analog line to dial into the answering router to establish this connection (answer C).

☒ **A** is not correct. Asynchronous Transfer Mode (ATM) provides a flexible, scalable, and high-speed solution for high-bandwidth connection requirements.

ATM requires special switches both at the site and at the connection point to manage this traffic. However, this is not an argument that supports the use of an on-demand VPN solution.

10.04: Designing Windows 2000 Security for Remote Access Users

10. ☑ **A**, **B**, and **C** are correct. VPN provides a number of features that can be implemented to design a secure remote access solution. The RRAS server can accommodate modems, direct connections, and VPN connections. The ability for these connection methods to be managed via RRAS is a compelling feature of VPN in Windows 2000. Removing the physical port limitation with the use of virtual VPN ports (rather than additional modem banks) provides a very cost-effective solution that scales well. In addition, the ability to support newer protocols, including L2TP with IPSec via a VPN connection, as well as older secure protocols such as PPTP with MS-CHAP, provides a solution that works well with a number of different client types.

☒ **D** is not correct. VPN is designed to use the Internet to route private communications securely. Static IP routes are used with demand-dial routing. Packet filtering would be done by the RRAS server, Proxy Server, or firewall, not by the VPN connection itself.

11. ☑ **A**, **C**, and **D** are correct. PPTP provides down-level support for clients. It is a network protocol that provides authentication and access control features. It encapsulates IP, IPX, or NetBEUI protocols over TCP/IP connections such as the Internet. It cannot be used for ATM, Frame Relay, or X.25 networks. L2TP can work on these types of networks and provides the same functionality as PPTP as well. L2TP expands the capabilities of PPTP and has the added capability of working with the IPSec protocol for securing IP traffic.

☒ **B** is not correct. IPSec does provide end-to-end security but it does not encrypt all protocols that run over IP. IPSec has built-in exemptions for certain types of traffic, including IKE negotiations, Kerberos authentication, IP broadcast, and IP multicast traffic.

12. ☑ **A.** The required results are as follows: use existing infrastructure and improve connectivity throughput. Current connectivity is via X.25 circuits.

Multilink and Bandwidth Allocation Protocol work with this type of connection. Therefore, existing infrastructure can be used. Enabling multilink protocols will enable computers to use more than one modem connected as a virtual circuit, thus increasing user throughput. The required results are produced. The optional results are as follows: solution should provide more flexibility in terms of number of users that can be supported and it should minimize telecommunications costs. BAP enhances multilink by dynamically adding or dropping lines on demand. If Client D is trying to gain access and Client A is not fully utilizing the connection, one leg of Client A's connection may be dropped to allow Client D to connect. This produces the optional result of providing a more flexible configuration for users. Configuring utilization parameters for BAP through remote access policies enables you to dynamically manage a static set of resources. BAP is useful when telecommunication charges are based on bandwidth utilization. Therefore, all optional results are produced.

☒ **B**, **C**, and **D** are not correct. The proposed solution produces all required and all optional results.

10.05: Designing an SMB Signing Solution

13. ☑ **A** and **D** are correct. The two major enhancements SMB signing provides are message authentication (answer A) and mutual authentication of client and server (answer D). With message authentication, SMB signing places a digital signature in each packet. This prevents the packet from being tampered with in transit. With mutual authentication, if data is intercepted and an attacker attempts to modify the contents, both the client and the server will recognize that the source of the data is not from either the recognized client or server. Thus, a "man-in-the-middle" attack will be prevented.

☒ **B** is not correct. The packets do not move any more quickly than normal packets. It will take more CPU cycle time to prepare the packets, which could cause a slower response. **C** is not correct. SMB signing does not use certificate authorities. The security is generated by both client and server computers digitally signing their data transmissions.

14. ☑ **A.** In this case, the server requires SMB signing and all four clients are set to use it when possible. Therefore, data communications with the server in Network A will occur with SMB signing.

☒ **B** is not correct. Although the clients will use SMB signing when possible, Server A requires it. **C** is not correct. Because the server requires SMB signing, it must be implemented in order to communicate with that particular server. **D** is not correct. The requirement for SMB signing is not dependent upon other settings.

15. ☑ **A.** Clients 1 and 2 require the use of SMB signing. Since the server is set to use SMB signing when possible, SMB signing will occur when Clients 1 and 2 communicate with Server B. Clients 3 and 4 are set so that Always Use SMB Signing and Use SMB Signing When Possible are both disabled, so they essentially are set to Never Use SMB Signing. Therefore, when Clients 3 and 4 communicate with Server B, they will not use SMB signing. Since the question asked what the highest level of data communication security would be on the network, answer A is correct.

☒ **B** is not correct. Although Server B will use SMB signing when possible, this is not the highest level that will be used. **C** is not correct. Clients 3 and 4 are set so they will not use SMB signing. **D** is not correct. Both clients are set so they will not use SMB. In this case, the highest level of security is dependent upon Clients 1 and 2 because they always require SMB signing.

16. ☑ **D.** Server A requires SMB signing. Server B will use SMB signing when possible. Therefore, any communication with clients on Network A must make use of SMB signing. Since Clients 3 and 4 on Network B are configured to not use SMB signing, they will not be able to communicate with Client 1 on Network A through Server A.

☒ **A** is not correct. Network A's server is configured to require SMB signing. Since Clients 3 and 4 on Network B are configured to never use SMB signing, they will not communicate with clients on Network A. **B** is not correct. Network B's server is configured to use SMB signing when possible. It would use SMB signing when communicating with Network A, since Server A requires it. However, Clients 3 and 4 on Network B are set to never use SMB signing. When they communicate with Server B, SMB signing will not be used. **C** is not correct. Although Clients 3 and 4 on Network B are set to never use SMB signing, Server A requires it. Therefore, all communication via Network A must use SMB signing.

17. ☑ **D.** The required result is as follows: implement secure communications between client and server machines, and do not increase network traffic.

Implementing SMB signing would meet both requirements. However, in the proposed solution, you have enabled SMB signing only on the server side and you have implemented it as always being required. Therefore, clients that do not have SMB signing configured will not be able to communicate with the server. In the proposed solution, client-side SMB signing is not implemented. Therefore, the first requirement is not met. SMB signing can be implemented using group policies in Windows 2000 to ease network administration of this security solution.

☒ **A**, **B**, and **C** are not correct. The proposed solution does not produce required results. Therefore, the optional results are not considered.

10.06: Designing an IPSec Solution

18. ☑ **B.** The following screen shots show the Network Monitor Display Filter (first illustration) and the Expression Filtering (second illustration) dialogs. Network Monitor is accessed via Start | Programs | Administrative Tools | Network Monitor. In order to filter, you must first complete a capture, stop the capture, and then view it. To filter the data, use Display | Filter, or press the F8 key. Keep in mind that filtering does not remove frames: it simply filters what you're looking at. To remove filtering, press the F7 key.

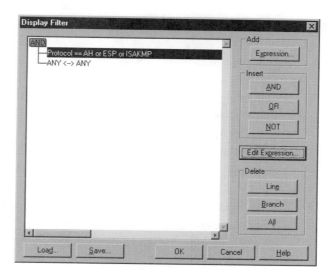

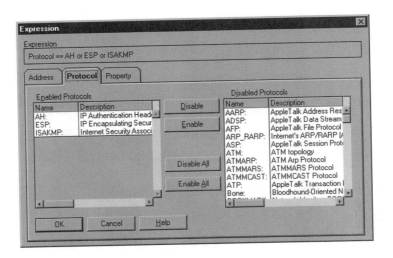

Filtering out all protocols except ISAKMP, AH and ESP will show just traffic related to IPSec. IPSec creates two separate security negotiations behind the scenes. The Internet Security Association/Key Management Protocol (ISAKMP) provides a method for two machines to establish a security association (SA). ISAKMP manages the first of two phases, which is referred to as the negotiation policy. The second negotiation phase follows the key exchange. This is referred to as the security policy. Together, these two phases form the security association. Therefore, seeing ISAKMP traffic would indicate the use of IPSec on the network.

IPSec can be deployed using one of two protocols: AH or ESP. Authentication Header (AH) provide data authenticity, data integrity, and anti-replay and anti-spoofing protection. You can configure AH to ensure that only authorized users communicate with a specific server using a predetermined protocol. With this configuration, if AH cannot be used by the client, communications do not occur. Encapsulating Security Payload (ESP) provides source authentication, data encryption, and anti-replay and anti-spoofing protection. ESP is used if the actual data flow must be encrypted between the client and server. Using IPSec filter actions to use ESP will ensure that data that matches the filter list will be encrypted when transmitted between client and server. Therefore, seeing ISAKMP, AH, or ESP traffic will confirm that IPSec is being used on the network.

☒ **A** is not correct. Applying a local policy only applies the computer you're working on, not the entire network. **C** and **D** are not correct. Network Monitor works at the Network layer. Therefore, protocols that can be monitored must work at that level. IPSec uses protocols (AH and ESP) that work at this level. L2TP is used to create a secure tunnel in conjunction with IPSec. Monitoring L2TP, EAP, or TLS would not help you assess whether IPSec had been successfully implemented.

19. ☑ **A.** The pre-shared key is stored, unprotected, in the IPSec policy. Microsoft recommends against using pre-shared key authentication for this reason. Microsoft has included this ability to provide interoperability and adherence to IETF IPSec standards.

☒ **B** is not correct. Restricting Read and Write access to IPSec policies only to administrators helps protect this method of authentication. **C** is not correct. Pre-shared key authentication is part of the IETF standard for IPSec. **D** is not correct. in order to secure the pre-shared keys, the policy should be restricted to system Read-Only access on each computer.

20. ☑ **A.** The required results are as follows: provide the highest security for the CFA data, minimize network overhead, and provide a method for non-Windows computers to participate on the network. The highest level of security has been applied using the pre-defined IPSec security policy Secure Server (Require Security). This policy will enforce IPSec security for all communications with the servers in this OU. The appropriate level of security is used by placing these computers in an OU and applying the policy to only these computers. This avoids excessive security. Requiring IPSec on all network communications would be excessive and would bog down network servers. By using the Server (Request Security) IPSec policy for network servers, IPSec is initiated when needed. This also avoids excessive security on the network. It also meets the third requirement of providing resources to non-Windows computers that are unable to use IPSec.

The optional results are as follows: use the lowest reasonable security across the network and provide a method of centralized management. Configuring the client computers in a domain group and applying the domain security policy to them ensures these computers can respond as needed to requests for secure communications. They will not initiate security but can respond to requests. This, along with the server-side settings [Servers (Request Security), Secure

Server (Require Security)] provides the lowest reasonable protection by using IPSec only as needed. By using IPSec policy and domain policy settings, management of the security for these resources is centralized and organized. Therefore, all optional requirements are produced. One additional note: IPSec should be used in conjunction with access control security. IPSec will secure the communications on the network between various computers. However, access to sensitive data on the CFA servers must still be managed through access control via security groups.

☒   **B**, **C**, and **D** are not correct. The proposed solution produces the required and all of the optional results.

A LAB ANSWER

Objectives 10.01–10.06

As with other labs, there may be several right answers. Those listed here are based on Windows 2000 best practices.

Connecting the two locations   Connecting the two sites can be accomplished in a number of ways. However, the pertinent information here is that both sites currently *can* connect to the Internet. The RRAS server, which is already in place for dial-in access, can also be configured to be a VPN server. Using the VPN server with L2TP and IPSec, a secure connection can be established with both the fractional T1 line and the Frame Relay line.

There is no indication as to whether the corporate office currently has an Internet connection. If it does not, one would have to be established. Conversely, a demand-dial connection between Sites 1, 2, and 3 could be established, if desired. Part of the solution will be determined by what each site does and the nature of the communication and data sharing needs among the three sites. Check router and server configurations to determine the best access solutions once communication needs have been clearly defined.

Remote access for consultants   A corporate Internet connection would also be useful in establishing VPN capabilities for traveling consultants. If the firm is rapidly expanding and if the two acquired firms also have staff that travel, it is likely that the modem bank will need to be significantly increased to meet demand. Although BAP with multilink could be established to make use of the existing modems and increase bandwidth, adding VPN capabilities would provide a more flexible solution. Having the ability to create a VPN connection or use dial-in access would enable consultants to use the method that best meets their needs as they travel the world.

Increasing security   VPN or dial-in access can be secured using secure authentication protocols. Kerberos provides initial user authentication. This could be strengthened through the use of certificates or smart cards relying on certificates in Windows 2000. Data security can be established via L2TP with IPSec for end-to-end security for traveling consultants.

Security administration   Additional security can be implemented via IP packet filtering and IPSec policies. By strictly controlling which protocols can be used and which protocols will be allowed through the network, security can be greatly enhanced. These can be implemented via group policies to ensure consistent application of security policies throughout the organization. In addition, implementing these measures via group policy provides a logical approach to troubleshooting access problems should they occur.

Auditing   If consultants are concerned that an employee's log-on credentials have been compromised, you could enable various kinds of auditing. If you can identify the likely employees, you could enable auditing of successful logon and logoff. You could also enable auditing for access to some of the files that the consultants are concerned about. Auditing for a specific set of resources or employee accounts for a set length of time are best practices. Review the audit logs regularly.

Practice Exam

T his practice exam is made up of two testlets. These testlets are scenarios that provide background on a specific company and that pose a unique set of circumstances. Please read and review each carefully; 20 multiple-choice questions, based on the information provided, will follow each testlet.

TESTLET 1: BLUE HOUND ENTERPRISES CASE STUDY

Company Profile and History

You have been promoted to director of information and Internet technologies at the fast-growing firm of Blue Hound Enterprises (BHE), an Internet development firm. BHE was founded in 1995 around the concept that companies would be embracing the Internet as a business tool and would require newer technologies to fully harness the power of the Internet. The president of the company is passionate about the Internet and using leading edge technologies to improve businesses. He believes that by implementing the right technology in the right setting, economies of scale as well as significant competitive advantages can be created. Blue Hound's solutions have changed over the past several years. Its current focus is a hardware and software solution for high-speed Internet access that companies can use with existing infrastructure such as computers, networks, and Internet connections.

Blue Hound began with the president, David, and two other members. Lisa met David in college on the West Coast and decided to join David's firm just after completing post-graduate studies. Lisa's PhD in electrical engineering, combined with her uncanny ability to spot technology trends, made her a logical choice for BHE's chief technology officer. The third member of this startup was Lorraine who came on board as the financial manager and took the position of CFO shortly after joining BHE. The three founders together created a vision and mission for the company that was so compelling that they attracted $50 million in venture capital in their first round of financing. A second round raised $350 million, an unprecedented sum at that time for an Internet technology startup. Well funded, Blue Hound was ready to expand its services globally.

In 1998, Blue Hound began acquiring companies around the world. Their world headquarters was established in Redwood City, California, situated between San Francisco and Silicon Valley. Their first four acquisitions were in Sweden. Three more acquisitions that year were in France, and the final five acquisitions of that year were in

India. Now a truly global company, Blue Hound was ready to expand its support services for firms that had implemented their Internet solution. Around this time, they hired a budding new technology genius (you) to oversee the integration of technology and support services for the firm. In the following two years, you built a staff of 50 to support the company as it grew. You developed a help desk solution with the assistance of Vilbig International, a company whose specialty was delivering high-quality outsourcing help desk solutions. With this strategic partnership, you were able to provide all Blue Hound clients, as well as Blue Hound employees, 24/7 access to technical assistance throughout the world.

In late 1999, the company went through an initial public offering (IPO). Through this process, employee stock options went up in value by 800 percent. Everyone who was part of this made a tremendous amount of money on paper. However, in early 2000, when the stock market cooled off in the technology sector, Blue Hound's share price dropped 80 percent in a three-week period. The fundamentals of the company had not changed; the company still had a revenue stream and a profit margin, but investors were turning a cold shoulder to technology stocks. Fortunately, Lorraine did such an excellent job managing corporate finances that the company was still well positioned for continued growth and investment in its infrastructure for the next five years.

You have been asked to prepare a comprehensive two-year technology plan for your company. It must integrate the technology of your firm with the technology implemented at the firms you've acquired. It must be cost-effective and it must address current and future company needs.

Systems and Technology Needs

As the company grew, you implemented a number of newer technologies. Currently, the company is running on Windows 2000 and Windows NT 4.0 servers. Some of the European companies you acquired are running Unix-based networks and some also have implemented Linux Web solutions. However, one of your goals for this integrated plan is to standardize the company in one platform to make network administration more manageable. In developing your plan, you conduct in-depth interviews with a number of Blue Hound staff members to ensure that your plan will meet the varying needs of the company and can accommodate future growth.

You meet with the human resources director, Foster Russell. This is what Foster had to say: "I'm kind of pressed for time, so if you don't mind, I'd like to get right down to business. As you know, we've grown to over 10,000 employees worldwide in just a few short years. This has put tremendous strain on my staff, trying to keep up with all aspects of managing an international workforce. One of the things we don't yet have in place that I'd like included in your infrastructure plan is the ability for employees to track and manage their stock options via the Web. Questions we've had to field about that have been overwhelming, especially since the stock decline back in March. Although we've sent out emails to keep people informed, the different options based on different countries' laws and regulations have been hard to manage.

"In addition, we'd really like a solution where employees could manage their own 401K and other configurable benefits such as health coverage. This, too, has consumed a lot of my staff's time. We want employees to have consistent information and a much more robust self-service function via our Web site. We've got the software that can handle it, but we'll need your department to handle the implementation of this quickly.

"I think it goes without saying that both of these projects must have the highest security associated with them. I mean, you know the rumors flying when our stock took a hit. Can you imagine what the press would do if they were able to hire some young hacker to get into our system and expose the details of our stock or benefits plans? I don't even want to think about that! So, those are really my two big project requests and my one biggest concern. If you have any questions once you get the plan roughed out, please let me know. I'm anxious to implement a solution that will really help our department deal with the more pressing issues and bring greater value to the organization.

"Oh, there is one other thing. We've noticed lately that there have been some problems with inappropriate Internet usage. Our company policy is very clear about inappropriate use, but it's getting harder and harder to manage that policy. As you're probably aware, it's not just that people should be spending their time at work on more useful and productive pursuits. It's also that viewing certain material via the Internet at work can become an issue. Some find that kind of material offensive and the argument could be made that it creates a hostile work environment. We must take strong steps to ensure that all employees are comfortable in our environment and that offensive material is not viewed at work. I don't want it to be overly restrictive, but if there's something you can do technology-wise to help us out, that would be great. Thanks and feel free to talk with my staff as well. They may have other concerns."

You talk with members of Foster's staff and hear the same concerns reiterated. Confident that you have the primary needs of the employees of Blue Hound covered, you meet with the director of marketing, Amy Blondelle. Amy was instrumental in helping you set up your strategic partnership with Vilbig International. You want Amy's take on other ideas or suggestions she might have. This is what Amy had to say:

"Hi, how are things going with Vilbig? That partnership seems to be working out very well. I read last quarter's quality report from them—the quality is through the roof! When is that new site in Ireland coming online, have you heard?

"So, I hear you're putting together a plan for better utilizing technology for our company. I think that's great. The more technology solutions we implement ourselves, the better role model we are for prospective clients when we try to convince them that they need *our* Internet solution.

"Anyway, here's what our team needs. Right now, our Web site is awesome. We've got it translated into a number of different languages, so we're getting into the markets we want. We're getting a good hit rate and our visitors seem to be rather sticky, so that's great. However, our system for responding to these visitors is a bit out of date. If you could implement a solution that allows us to sign up visitors, gain some information about them securely, and then contact them with special offers, that would really give us some added mileage.

"I hear that the Chicago research and development team is close to a break-through solution for that problem we discussed in Tuesday's meeting. I guess that will mean even higher security out there now. If our competitors got their hands on that one, we'd really have a problem. I heard they installed retinal scanners as a security measure just to get into the building. It gives new meaning to the phrase 'Don't look now!'

"That's really all we need at the moment. I'm sure that will change, but you know me. I won't hesitate to come talk with you. Thanks again."

Your third and final interview is with Vilbig International. Dibran Vilbig is the brother of the founder. Unlike many firms where family members are involved, the company does not suffer from typical family-run-business problems. In fact, Vilbig is now publicly held and Dibran and his brother, Frank, are running a very successful concern. Dibran is the executive vice president of sales and marketing and is your primary contact at Vilbig. The conversation was as follows:

"Hi, thanks for calling. Hey, did you hear we improved quality by 3 percent last month? We're sitting at 92 percent overall 'very satisfied' in our client surveys. With our new site in Ireland coming online next month, we expect to be able to do some additional staff training that we've been putting off. We think that will give quality numbers another 1 percent boost.

"Anyway, I understand you're on a fact-finding mission about technology requirements. First, I really want to thank you for including us in your plans. A lot of companies would forget that their partners should be included in these kinds of plans in order to really capitalize on the technology available to generate an even stronger, more efficient partnership.

"I've given some thought to this and I think the one thing you could do that would have a tremendous impact on our firm would be to open up your extensive internal database of technical knowledge to our staff. I know you've kept it internal for a number of reasons. However, if we had access to that data, I think we could do an even better job and at a lower cost. Don't let your CFO get a hold of *that* information. I sure don't want to have to lower my prices! But seriously, we could probably get another 1 to 2 percentage points in client satisfaction if we had access to that data. Our average time to close an issue would probably go down by 2 to 3 minutes, which would translate into a net savings for our company. We could probably look into extending your current pricing structure for another year, without any increases, if we could gain this kind of efficiency.

"Let me know if this is something you can do and I'll begin putting plans together on our end to integrate access to that data to our internal support tools."

Just before you leave for a long weekend, Lorraine calls you into her office. Here's how the conversation went:

"I know you're taking off for a long weekend, so I'll only take a few minutes of your time. As you know, our stock price has been badly hurt by the fluctuating emotions about Internet stocks in the market. While we're well capitalized, a lower stock price impacts us in a number of ways. One key way, which Foster probably didn't mention to you, is our compensation for employees. With options changing valuation so dramatically, we've decided to re-assess our stock option packages. We want to make sure we can still hire and retain top-notch employees. Although that's not what I wanted to talk with you about, these facts do play into my concern. Money is not a problem right now, but we will have to put more emphasis on higher salaries, at least until our stock price turns around. I'm concerned that with higher salary costs, we're going to have to find some efficiencies elsewhere to ensure we can meet our financial commitments. Remember, when we tell market analysts that we're going to improve our margins one percent by next quarter, we *have* to do that or our stock price will really get pummeled.

"I know you're working on a technology plan along with a budget for that plan. I want you to incorporate savings wherever possible. If we need to improve our infrastructure, that's fine. I don't want us hobbling along with a patched-together solution. But we don't need to have the shiniest new toys, either. So, wherever you can find a cost-effective solution, a way to utilize existing infrastructure, or a phased solution that could be implemented over time, I'd really appreciate it. Actually, our stockholders, industry analysts, and employees will appreciate it too! Have a great weekend."

Technical Specifications and Considerations

Your company's computer assets are distributed as follows:

Redwood City, CA United States	3 buildings in campus setting 18 Windows 2000 Advanced servers Windows 2000 Professional 35 desktops, 200 laptops 1 RRAS server 1 VPN server 1 Web email server 2 Web content servers
Chicago, IL United States	1 location 4 Windows NT 4.0 servers Windows NT 4.0 Workstation, Windows 98 125 desktops and laptops
Sweden	2 locations 2 Linux servers 2 Windows 2000 servers 2 Windows NT 4.0 servers Windows 2000 Professional, Windows NT 4.0 Workstation 200 laptops, no desktops
France	2 locations 2 Unix servers Windows NT 4.0 Workstation Combined 300 computers, about half are laptops

India	8 locations
	18 Windows 2000 Advanced servers
	Windows 2000 Professional
	450 desktops, 98 laptops
	1 RRAS server
	1 VPN server
	2 Web content servers
Trusted Partner	Technology and connections unknown
Future Acquisitions	Technology and connections unknown

The network layout is shown in the following diagram:

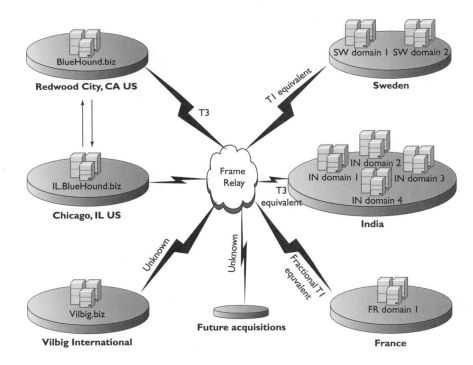

TESTLET 1: QUESTIONS

Based on the information in the case study, answer the following multiple-choice questions with the best answer.

1. What are Blue Hound's biggest security concerns? (Choose all that apply.)

   A. External attacks to Web site

   B. Unauthorized access of Chicago data

   C. External access of employees' personal data

   D. Internal access of employees' personal data

   E. Unacceptable Internet usage

2. What are the technology or company solutions that your comprehensive plan will need to address? (Choose all that apply.)

   A. Manage employees, track Internet usage, improve the Web site, implement cost-effective solutions, use new technology, and improve security.

   B. Manage employee benefits, improve Web site traffic, track Web site usage, track Internet usage, provide trusted partner access to data, use the newest technologies, and provide the highest security.

   C. Manage employee benefits, monitor and control Internet usage, ensure Chicago branch is secure, track Web visitors, provide resource access to trusted partner organization, use newest technologies, and implement cost-effective solutions.

   D. Manage employees, monitor Internet usage, ensure all communications to and from Chicago are secure, improve connectivity to European and Indian domains, use newest technologies, and enhance remote connectivity for employees.

3. Based on the network diagram, what one change could you make immediately to improve security for Chicago?

   A. Place Chicago servers between the firewall and the Internet.

   B. Create a new domain with a non-contiguous namespace for Chicago to help prevent users from guessing the naming configuration for the network.

   C. Change the trust relationship from corporate to Chicago to be a one-way, non-transitive trust.

   D. Create a shortcut trust between corporate and Chicago to hide the external trust relationship.

4. Based on the diagram of the network, how many domains will you need to create in your new model?

   A. Two (Corporate and Chicago)

   B. Four (Corporate, Chicago, Sweden, and France)

   C. Five (Corporate, Sweden, France, India, and Partner)

   D. Six (Corporate, Chicago, Sweden, France, India, and Partner)

5. If you wanted to provide a method for all employees to access personal data via the Web, what challenges would you face?

   A. Each operating system in the domain (Windows 2000, Windows NT, Unix, and Linux) would require a separate solution.

   B. Each country would require a solution based on its Web connectivity and domain structure.

   C. Each employee would require access to the Internet via a standardized Web browser.

   D. The Web browser used would have to interoperate with both your Web solution and the operating systems in place.

6. The human resources director, Foster Russell, wants to implement a secure solution allowing employees to access their stock and benefits information online. What solution best fits this need? (Choose all that apply.)

   A. Export the SQL data to a Microsoft Access database. Place that database on an external Web server. Secure the data with PPTP/MPPE connections via dial-in or VPN connections. Replicate changes in SQL or Access every ten minutes so data is always current.

B. Place SQL Server at headquarters. Provide access to the database via the Web server only. Require all employees to connect via VPN using PPP with CHAP for authentication. Integrate SQL security with Windows authentication security (Kerberos/NTLM) to ensure that each user accesses only his or her own data. Ensure that only data that should be managed by the user has Read and Write access permissions.

C. Place SQL Server at headquarters. Provide access to the database via the Web server only. Require all employees to connect via VPN using L2TP with IPSec. Integrate SQL security with Windows 2000 authentication security (Kerberos/NTLM) to ensure that each user accesses only his or her own data. Ensure that data that is not configurable is set to Read-Only access.

D. Replicate SQL database to Web server. Set the database to Read and Write access. Allow users to connect to Web server via VPN or standard ISP Internet connection. Implement SSL for secure user authentication. Set configurable fields to Read and Write access and non-configurable fields to Read-Only access.

7. What can you do about the human resources director's request to monitor and prevent inappropriate Internet usage? (Choose all that apply.)

A. Integrated Windows Authentication

B. Digest Authentication

C. Proxy Server URL and IP filtering

D. Use of zone configurations in Internet Explorer 5.0

8. Corporate resources must be available to end users around the clock. What disaster recovery methods would you likely implement at corporate headquarters?

A. Implement RAID10 via hardware.

B. Implement RAID5 via software.

C. Implement RAID10 via software.

D. Implement RAID5 with full disk duplexing and mirroring.

9. Chicago connects to the Internet via a Frame Relay connection. What could you implement to provide secure access from the Internet for users of this domain?

   A. Upgrade to Windows 2000 Server; use VPN connections using L2TP with IPSec for very secure connections with a Frame Relay connection.

   B. Keep the existing Windows NT 4.0 servers; use VPN connections using PPTP with MPPE for very secure connections with a Frame Relay connection.

   C. Keep the existing Windows NT 4.0 servers; use RRAS connections using PPTP with MPPE for very secure connections with a Frame Relay connection.

   D. Upgrade to Windows 2000 Advanced Server; use VPN connections using demand-dial callback with EAP-TLS authentication.

10. What solution could you provide to address the Marketing Department's concerns? (Choose all that apply.)

    A. Have prospective clients access a secure Web site that uses PPTP/MPPE for them to input their user information. This data gets input into the database. A customer ID and password are generated based on their certificate credentials. Mail the client timely marketing material.

    B. Have prospective clients download an ActiveX control or Java applet that gathers information for registration (user name, for example), generates customer ID and password, and adds the user to the database.

    C. Have prospective clients access a secure Web site that uses SSL for them to input their user information. This data gets put into the database. A customer ID and password are generated and emailed to the prospective client along with a timely marketing message.

    D. Have prospective clients download an encrypted ActiveX control to enable secure Web site access for client registration. Issue customer ID and password, add user to database, email timely marketing information.

11. If Vilbig International was running a Windows 2000 native network and wanted to heighten its own security as well as participate in a secure

solution for accessing your knowledge database, what solution would you recommend?

- A. Implement stand-alone CAs in your organization. Create certificates for each authorized Vilbig user. Create a user account called VilbigSupport. Create a many-to-one mapping for that account so any users with a certificate from the stand-alone CA can access the knowledge database.

- B. Have Vilbig implement CAs. Use certificates for all user authentication. Create a single-user account called VilbigSupport. Create many-to-one mapping for that account so that any users with a certificate from Vilbig will be given Read-Only access to the knowledge database.

- C. Create a two-way, transitive trust between Vilbig and your corporate domain. Add Vilbig's authorized support users to your Active Directory database. Issue certificates for all Vilbig employees via the use of a third-party CA. Require certificates for authentication to access the knowledge database.

- D. Create a one-way, non-transitive trust between Vilbig and corporate. Map all user accounts from Vilbig to a single-user account called VilbigSupport. Give Read-Only permissions to the VilbigSupport user account when accessing the knowledge database. Set No Access permissions to all other files and folders.

12. What group policy could be implemented to secure data communication across all LANs and WANs within the company?

- A. SMB signing
- B. IPSec
- C. MPPE
- D. IP encryption

13. What is the biggest network change you would notice if you implemented SMB signing?

- A. Increased disk space requirements
- B. Increased network bandwidth requirements
- C. Degraded processor performance
- D. Degraded disk drive performance

14. If you wanted to use IP security on your Chicago network, how would you implement it?

    A. Upgrade all servers in the company to Windows 2000 Server. All servers in the domain would be set to Server Secure (Request Security). All clients in that domain would be set to Client (Respond Only).

    B. Upgrade all servers in the Chicago domain to Windows 2000 Professional. All servers that require high security should be placed in an OU. All servers in that OU should have Server Secure (Require Security) enabled. All servers that do not require high security should be placed in the domain OU. Those servers should have security set to Server (Respond Only). All requests for secure communications through those servers from clients would use the highest level of security possible.

    C. Upgrade all computers in the Chicago domain to Windows 2000. All servers that require high security should be placed in an OU. All servers in that OU should have Server Secure (Require Security) enabled.

    D. Upgrade all computers in the Chicago domain to Windows 2000. All servers in the domain should be placed in an OU. That OU should have Server Secure (Require Security) enabled. All clients should be placed in a domain computer group and use Client (Respond Only) security.

15. The administrator of the Indian domain has set a group policy that requires the use of EFS for all laptop computers. The staff in India shares files regularly with staff from Chicago. After a recent security configuration change in the Chicago domain, Indian users are complaining that they cannot access the Chicago information any longer. What could be the problem? (Choose all that apply.)

    A. EFS files cannot be shared.

    B. SMB signing is required in Chicago but has not been implemented in the Indian domain yet.

    C. IPSec is not supported by India's network configuration.

    D. The trust relationship between Chicago and India was changed from two-way, transitive to one-way, non-transitive.

16. If the servers in France were migrated to Windows 2000, what would be the optimal configuration for replication?

    A. Create two sites, France1 and France2. Set up one server as a bridgehead server and schedule replication for just after business hours in France.

    B. Create one OU, France1. Set up two sites within France1 called France_(Site1) and France_(Site 2). Set replication between OU France1 and corporate for midnight corporate time. Set replication for France_(Site1) and France_(Site 2) to occur when replication between the OU and corporate is completed.

    C. Create one site, France1. Set replication between France1 and corporate for a time of low network usage.

    D. Create one OU, France1. Set replication between France1 and corporate for midnight local time. Monitor network bandwidth to ensure that replication is completed.

17. What type of authentication will occur on the network as it is currently configured? (Choose all that apply.)

    A. Kerberos

    B. NTLM

    C. MS-CHAP

    D. Digest

18. Corporate is currently providing VPN access to corporate resources to members of the SALES group (each country has a sales team with members of the SALES group). How is this currently configured? (Choose all that apply.)

    A. Using PPP and CHAP for authentication

    B. Using L2TP with IPSec and NTLM for authentication

    C. Using L2TP with IPSec and Kerberos for authentication

    D. Using PPTP with MS-CHAP for authentication

19. The operations in Sweden rarely require connections to other corporate resources. However, when those resources are needed, they must be available. In implementing VPN, what solution could save money and work with the existing infrastructure to meet this need?

    A. Demand-dial router-to-router VPN

    B. ATM switched networks

    C. Multihomed servers

    D. X.509 circuits

20. If all domains in your company were upgraded to Windows 2000–based servers, what CA strategy would you implement to improve worldwide network security for your company? (Choose all that apply.)

    A. Third-party or stand-alone CA for trusted partner authentication and access

    B. Enterprise or stand-alone CA for trusted partner authentication

    C. Root CA for corporate. Subordinate CAs for each country (United States, Sweden, France, and India).

    D. Root CA for corporate. Subordinate CAs for email and network authentication.

TESTLET 2: SOUTHWEST GIFTS CASE STUDY

Company Profile and History

Southwest Gifts is a Phoenix-based, family-owned company with retail stores throughout Arizona and New Mexico. Southwest Gifts has been selling southwestern memorabilia, non-perishable food, and gift baskets from their retail stores since 1976. Since then, they have gone from 1 retail outlet in Phoenix to 23 outlets throughout Arizona and 6 outlets in New Mexico. In 1988, the company launched a separate catalog and telephone fulfillment business under the same name and began shipping their catalogs throughout the United States and Canada. Their growth has been steady over the past 25 years and their dedication to quality and customer service has made them the leading retailer of southwestern gifts in North America.

At the Phoenix headquarters, there are 120 employees, 12 of whom work in the Information Technology Department. In Phoenix, they occupy two buildings on the same lot. One building houses administration and the telephone order fulfillment center, and the other building houses the warehouse and shipping functions. Each of their retail stores has 10 to 15 employees and one IT administrator.

In Phoenix, the company operates a 100-Mbps LAN and four Windows NT 4.0 servers (SGRAS, SGDC1, and two application servers). There is a fiber backbone connecting the administration and warehouse buildings. Each retail store operates two Windows NT 4.0 servers (one for the cash register and one for inventory, word processing, and dial-up to corporate HQ via a 56-Kbps modem). In all locations, the only protocol used is TCP/IP.

Systems and Technology Needs

Southwest Gifts has realized that the only way to stay competitive and reach out to a broader array of customers is to fully embrace the Internet and develop an e-commerce Web site to augment their thriving catalog business. Unfortunately, their previous IT manager was slow to develop new technology to help position the company strategically. As a result, they fired him and hired you, a veteran with several years of experience in e-commerce and business-to-business Internet solutions. With the new fiscal year approaching, the CEO has decided to increase the IT budget so that rapid development and implementation of an e-commerce solution can occur. The CEO has also tasked you to look at the existing IT infrastructure and make a recommendation to upgrade existing legacy systems.

In your first 60 days, you create a report detailing the e-commerce plan and an upgrade of existing systems. The plan is to upgrade to a Windows 2000 forest in Native mode. You detail plans for a secure Web site. The Web site will allow only authorized users to view information. An ActiveX control will be downloaded by the visitors for them to input their name and address, so that they can become customers. A customer ID and password will be generated so customers can become authorized users of the Web site. The full e-commerce solution will include shopping, checkout, and logging of all transactions. A transaction-tracking file with credit card numbers will be integrated with the existing billing and order fulfillment system for billing and customer service employees. It is imperative that user IDs, passwords, and customer financial information not be intercepted. Downloads of the ActiveX control must not damage user software or violate licensing agreements. To accomplish the daunting task of developing and maintaining an e-commerce Web site, you will be hiring a new webmaster, several Web developers, and technical authors to bolster the IT staff. In addition, one of the new servers being purchased will be dedicated to development and testing of Web applications.

Another goal is to secure communication between the branch offices and corporate headquarters. In order to accomplish this task and reduce long-distance charges, you've decided to implement a VPN between each branch office and corporate headquarters. However, to keep costs under budget, you will not be changing any WAN hardware or any hardware at the retail stores at this time.

In addition, each retail store manager accesses corporate offices at least once per day to upload daily sales figures to a shared SALES folder, as well as submit warehouse orders to a shared ORDERS folder. Branch managers are not given the ability to see other stores' daily sales figures. Every month, the chief financial officer produces monthly consolidated financial reports using the sales information for distribution to administration.

Technical Specifications and Considerations

Your company's current IT infrastructure and planned upgrades are as follows:

Location	Current IT Infrastructure
Phoenix (headquarters)	4 Windows NT 4.0 servers (SGRAS, SGDC1, SGAPP1, and SGAPP2)

Location	Current IT Infrastructure
Phoenix (headquarters)	140 clients running Windows 98 Fast Ethernet LAN, TCP/IP, and fiber backbone between buildings
Retail stores	2 Windows NT 4.0 servers (1 for cash register, 1 for inventory, word processing, and dial-up connectivity to Phoenix) Ethernet LAN, TCP/IP, 56-Kbps dial-up to Phoenix

The current network layout is shown in the following diagram:

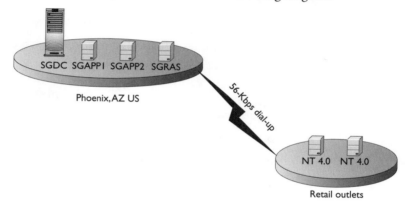

Location	Planned Upgrades
Phoenix (headquarters)	New Windows 2000 servers: SGDC1, SGDATA (running SQL 7.0), SGDC2 (running internal DNS server), SGDEV, SGVPN, SGWEB, SGAPP1, and SGAPP2. Upgrade all clients to Windows 2000 Professional.
Retail stores	No changes.
LAN	No changes.
WAN	Implement a T1 connection to the Internet from HQ and an external and internal firewall. Contract ISP to provide external DNS name resolution. Lease swgifts.com as company domain.

TESTLET 2: QUESTIONS

Based on the information in the case study, answer the multiple-choice questions with the best answer.

1. What Windows 2000 domain model should you implement?
   A. One domain for each retail store and one domain for headquarters
   B. One domain for company
   C. One domain for all retail stores and one domain for headquarters
   D. One domain for headquarters, one domain for the Arizona region, and one domain for the New Mexico region

2. Which business requirements have the most impact on Windows 2000 security design? (Choose all that apply.)
   A. Improved network performance
   B. Projected number of retail outlets
   C. E-commerce Web site
   D. Continued use of Windows NT 4.0 servers in Windows 2000 environment
   E. Remote access to corporate headquarters from retail outlets
   F. Cost

3. What is the primary security risk?
   A. Remote hackers directly connected to an internal computer via a modem
   B. Remote hackers directly connected to an internal computer via the Internet
   C. Another Southwest Gifts employee connected to an internal computer via the LAN
   D. A DOS attack launched from the Internet targeting an internal computer

4. What is Southwest Gift's tolerance for risk?

    A. Willing to try new approaches

    B. Willing to try only approaches they have tried before

    C. Willing to risk entire company for large rewards

    D. Very conservative, does not take any chances

5. How should you inform customers who want to download the ActiveX control that the control is unaltered?

    A. Use code signing.

    B. Use RADIUS.

    C. Use IAS.

    D. Use Kerberos authentication.

6. What changes should the retail stores make to support the VPN connection to corporate headquarters?

    A. Configure the connection type to dial in to HQ and use L2TP over IPSec to communicate with the VPN server.

    B. Dial into a local ISP and use L2TP over IPsec.

    C. Dial into a local ISP and use PPTP.

    D. Dial into HQ and use PPTP.

7. Between which objects will you implement SSL over TCP/IP? The objects are Customer, HQ, SGVPN, SGWEB, and Retail Stores. (Choose all that apply.)

    A. Between the Retail Stores and HQ

    B. Between Customer and SGWEB

    C. Between SGWEB, SGVPN, and HQ

    D. Between SGWEB and HQ

8. What type of CA should you use to digitally sign an ActiveX control?

    A. Enterprise subordinate CA

    B. Enterprise root CA

    C. Third-party CA

    D. Stand-alone root CA

9. Which technology should you use to securely connect the retail store to headquarters?

   A. EAP-TLS

   B. L2TP

   C. IPSec

   D. PPTP

   E. MS-CHAP

10. Which audit policy should you use to detect possible intrusion into the Southwest Gifts network?

    A. Success and failure audit for logon events

    B. Success and failure audit for policy change

    C. Success and failure audit for privilege use

    D. Success and failure audit for process tracking

11. Which methods should you use to identify and authorize existing customers on the Web site?

    A. SSL, NTLM logon, and database validation

    B. SSL, anonymous logon, and database validation

    C. SSL, anonymous logon, and CHAP

    D. SSL, NTLM logon, and CHAP

12. Where should you store the transaction tracking files?

    A. SGDATA

    B. SGWEB

    C. SGRAS

    D. SGDEV

13. Which authentication protocol should you use for the VPN connection from the retail stores to HQ?

    A. PAP

    B. MS-CHAP

   C. EAP

   D. SPAP

14. How should you authenticate visitors to the Web site?

   A. Authenticate visitors to an anonymous account.

   B. Authenticate visitors by requiring them to enter a user ID and password.

   C. Authenticate visitors by using cookies.

   D. Authenticate visitors that place an order as new or existing customers.

15. What type of disaster recovery protection should you implement at Southwest Gifts?

   A. Implement clustering where 100 percent availability is required; use software-level RAID5 for all critical data volumes; and create daily backups of all critical data, including System State data on Windows 2000 domain controllers.

   B. Implement RADIUS and IAS; use software RAID10 for all critical data volumes; and create daily backups of all critical data, including System State data on Windows 2000 domain controllers.

   C. Implement IPSec on all LAN workstations; use software RAID5 for all critical data volumes; and back up the System State data on all Windows 2000 domain controllers.

   D. Implement DFS Replicas for all critical data and back up all data nightly to tape.

16. What servers should be placed in a DMZ between an external and internal firewall? (Choose all that apply.)

   A. SGVPN

   B. SGDATA

   C. SGWEB

   D. SGDC1

   E. SGDC2

   F. SGDEV

17. Which permissions should you grant for the SALES folder?

   A. Network Administrators (FC), CFO (Read), Store Managers (Read and Write)

   B. Network Administrators (FC), CFO (Read and Write), Store Managers (Read)

   C. Network Administrators (FC), CFO (Read and Execute), Store Managers (Write and List Contents)

   D. Network Administrators (FC), CFO (Read and Write), Store Managers (No Access)

18. How should you configure the external firewall to allow secure access to SGWEB and SGVPN?

   A. Allow TCP and UDP ports 135 to 139

   B. Block access to TCP port 80

   C. Block access to connected TCP ports

   D. Allow only TCP ports 80, 443, and 1723, and IP protocol 47

19. How would you separate intranet resources from publicly visible Internet servers?

   A. Create a child domain called CORP.SWGIFTS.COM to manage all internal resources. Configure both internal and external DNS servers to resolve both internal and external names.

   B. Use a private IP address space. Configure both internal and external DNS servers to resolve both internal and external names.

   C. Create a child domain called CORP.SWGIFTS.COM to manage all internal resources. Use CORP.SWGIFTS.COM as suffix for all internal sites. Configure internal DNS server to resolve internal names, but do not include these names in the authorized Internet-based DNS server.

   D. Use a private IP address space. Configure the authorized Internet-based DNS server to resolve internal names, but do not include these names in the internal DNS server.

20. Assuming Southwest Gifts were to acquire another company to broaden its product offerings or otherwise strengthen its position in the market, how would you modify the AD (Active Directory) structure for Southwest Gifts? Assume the newly acquired company already has an Internet presence of some kind.

    A. Create a new child domain in the forest for the newly acquired company.

    B. Leave the forest intact and create a one-way trust with the newly acquired company's domain.

    C. Create a separate domain for the newly acquired company in its own tree. Place the new domain tree in the same forest as Southwest Gifts.

    D. Create a new domain for the newly acquired company in its own forest. Do nothing else.

TESTLET 1: ANSWERS

1. ☑ **B** and **C** are correct. The director of marketing, Amy Blondelle, mentioned the heightened security at the Chicago location. With a top-secret project underway and a very competitive environment, this clearly is a top-security concern for Blue Hound. The human resource director, Foster Russell, wants to implement self-service options on the Web site. Security of employee data is also very important. This data can be damaging whether it lands in the hands of a competitor, a recruiter, or simply another employee with a different compensation structure.

    ☒ **A** is not correct. External attacks on the Web site may pose a security risk, but no one you interviewed indicated this was a top concern. There is no data in the case study to indicate it is a problem at this time. **D** is not correct. Although most attacks come from inside an organization, there is no indication that internal security of employee data is at risk. **E** is also not correct. Although the human resources director is concerned about inappropriate use of the Internet, this is not a security risk for the company.

2. ☑ **C.** Based on the interviews, the following priorities have been set forth:

    Human Resources   Allow employees to manage stock options and benefits, monitor and control Internet usage to prevent unauthorized sites from being viewed at work.

    Marketing   Register site visitors, use the newest technologies, keep Chicago resources secure.

    Trusted Partner   Access to internal company database

    Chief Financial Officer   Use existing infrastructure where possible, look for cost-effective solutions.

    Therefore, answer C addresses all the concerns outlined in the interviews.

    ☒ **A** and **D** are not correct. The solution does not need to manage employees but rather allow employees to manage their benefits. **B** is not correct. Improving Web site traffic and tracking Web site usage were not a problem. Amy

Blondelle, the marketing director, asked you to provide a better solution for signing up visitors.

3. ☑ **C.** The trust relationship is shown as a two-way, transitive trust. Creating a one-way, non-transitive trust between Chicago and corporate would reduce some of the security risks. Users from the corporate domain would not automatically be trusted to access resources from the Chicago domain. Chicago users, however, would be trusted on the corporate domain.

☒ **A** is not correct. Chicago is currently connected to the Internet. However, the diagram does not specify how the site is connected. In any case, you would not place servers from the Chicago site between the firewall and the Internet. You might place a firewall between the Chicago servers and the Internet. **B** is not correct. Chicago should be its own domain in order to implement higher security measures than are needed elsewhere on the network. However, the naming convention will not add or reduce network risk significantly. **D** is not correct. Shortcut trusts are used to reduce the number of servers or domains a user must go through to gain authentication. It improves the efficiency of authentication and reduces the time it takes for a user to be authenticated, but it does not have any impact on overall security.

4. ☑ **A.** Windows 2000 can interoperate with a variety of operating systems. When non–Windows 2000 servers are present in the domain, the domain must run in Mixed mode. However, in Mixed mode the network can still run effectively. Chicago would require its own domain to accommodate the heightened security requirements. The other locations could all be part of the corporate domain. To fully utilize the advanced features of Windows 2000, your plan should include migration strategies for all non–Windows 2000 networks and servers. This will enable you to run in Native mode and fully utilize features such as Active Directory.

☒ **B** is not correct. Sweden and France both have non-Windows servers. Sweden has Windows servers as well as two Linux servers. This configuration does not require a separate domain, unless Sweden has a strong Internet presence, which is not indicated in this case study. France has two Unix servers, which may support Kerberos authentication and which can be used with Windows 2000 servers. The Unix servers are currently participating in a realm (equivalent of a Windows 2000 domain). However, they could be incorporated into the domain structure, if desired. **C** is not correct. India is currently running Windows 2000

Advanced Server. There is no reason India could not be part of the corporate domain. The partner domain is a separate domain managed by a separate company. You generally would not create a domain for an external partner. **D** is not correct for the reasons given for B and C.

5. ☑ **D.** The solution would have to work with whatever Web browsers are either currently in use by your organization or supported by the various operating systems. For instance, Internet Explorer can be used on Windows-based systems as well as Unix- and Linux-based systems. Ensuring the solution works with the common browsers used will be a primary concern unless the company standardizes on Windows 2000–based servers.

   ☒ **A** is not correct. Each operating system would not require a unique solution. Unix and Linux both utilize TCP/IP and can connect to the Internet. Microsoft Internet Explorer runs on both Unix and Linux. Therefore, the solution does not need to be created for each operating system. **B** is not correct. Web connectivity and domain structure are not relevant to connecting to a Web-based solution except in cases where Web connectivity is so slow or insufficient that data cannot easily be managed via the Web. **C** is not correct. Although Internet Explorer interoperates with all the operating systems currently in use by Blue Hound, your solution would not require a standardized browser. Although you could require the use of Internet Explorer, your solution could also work with Netscape Navigator or other Web browsers, as long as certain functionality was available in the browser.

6. ☑ **B** and **C** are correct. The SQL server contains data that is used inside the company. However, the human resources director wants this data to be available to employees via the Web. To implement this solution, the SQL server should remain internal to the company and it should allow the Web server to access it for information. Employees would connect via a VPN connection to the Web server, which will interact with the SQL server to provide data to employees who are authorized users. The presence of Unix and Linux servers on the network makes the connection method somewhat different. Through the VPN server, you can establish different types of connections. Therefore, for Unix or Linux clients, you could use PPP and CHAP. Otherwise, you could implement PPTP with MS-CHAP for Windows NT clients and L2TP with IPSec for Windows 2000 clients.

☒ **A** is not correct. There is no reason to export the data from SQL to an Access database. SQL is a secure and robust solution for Web-based database needs. **D** is not correct. The SQL data should reside on the SQL server. The database should not be set to Read and Write access for all users. Fields that should not be changed should be set to Read-Only. Fields that should not be viewed can be excluded from the view in SQL, or the Read attribute can be disabled. For better security, you would want users to connect using a VPN connection, not directly through the Web site.

7. ☑ **C** and **D** are correct. Proxy Server provides the capability to filter by IP or URL address. Blocking access provides one method of avoiding inappropriate Internet access. However, in the company's current configuration, not all users are running Windows 2000 (or Windows NT 4.0). Therefore, you may not be able to use Proxy Server. In cases where you cannot, you can use the Internet Explorer Administration Kit (IEAK) to modify IE5 so that users can only connect to zones you have permitted or defined. IE5 can be used with Windows, Unix, and Linux installations.

☒ **A** is not correct. Integrated Windows Authentication, formerly WindowsNT Challenge/Response, is a method of user authentication. This cannot be used to prevent connection to unwanted Internet locations. **B** is not correct. Digest Authentication is also a method of user authentication used on the Internet. It provides added security because the username and password are sent over the network as a hash value. Digest Authentication works through proxy servers and firewalls.

8. ☑ **B.** Windows 2000 currently only supports RAID Levels 0, 1, and 5 via the software. Therefore, you would implement RAID5, which provides disk striping with parity written across the set. This provides the ability to recover from a single disk failure without impacting users.

☒ **A** is not correct. A RAID10 hardware solution could be implemented in Windows 2000. While this is generally the preferred method because it is much faster, it is also far more costly than implementing a software solution. Since the CFO, Lorraine, specifically asked you to save money where possible, implementing RAID5 meets both the company's needs and Lorraine's desire to save money. **C** is not correct. Windows 2000 does not currently support RAID10 as a software solution. **D** is not correct. RAID5 does not use disk mirroring. Mirroring is implemented as part of RAID1. Disk duplexing involves installing two disk controllers to avoid a single point of failure for the disk subsystem. This could be implemented, if desired.

9. ☑ **A.** Remember that L2TP with IPSec works with a larger number of connection types than PPTP does. L2TP supports ATM, Frame Relay, X.25 and other connection types that utilize IP at the Transport layer. Therefore, a VPN connection using L2TP with IPSec will provide the greatest security for the Chicago site. However, L2TP with IPSec requires Windows 2000 (it is not supported in Windows NT). Chicago's servers would have to be upgraded to Windows 2000 before this solution could be implemented.

☒ **B** and **C** are not correct. Keeping existing Windows NT 4.0 servers in Chicago would require you to use PPTP instead of L2TP. However, PPTP does not support Frame Relay connections. Therefore, this solution would not work. **D** is not correct. Windows Advanced Server is not required. More important, however, is that demand-dial is a dial-up function as is callback. These are not VPN options.

10. ☑ **B** and **C** are correct. Having prospective clients download an ActiveX control or Java applet that gathers information for registration (such as user name), generates Customer ID and Password, and adds user to database is one solution. ActiveX controls work natively with Internet Explorer. For browsers that do not support Active X controls, Java applets can be used. This would automate the process and allow Marketing to gather information from registered clients. A second viable solution is to have prospective clients access a secure Web site that uses SSL. Using SSL will protect user information and provide a method of secure sign-on.

☒ **A** is not correct. Prospective clients would not use a tunneling protocol, such as PPTP to connect to your Web site. This method would be used for internal employees, not for general public access. This method also does not support the use of certificates. **D** is not correct. ActiveX controls are not encrypted, but they can (and should) contain digital certificates. This authenticates the source and content of the ActiveX control.

11. ☑ **B.** If you want to improve security at Vilbig as well as provide secure access to your knowledge database resource, you would need to implement some form of added security in the Vilbig domain. If Vilbig implements CAs within their domain, they improve security for their company. Since you will be able to recognize and trust certificates from Vilbig, you could map all certificates from

Vilbig to a user account called VilbigSupport. This would not only improve security for Vilbig but would provide a secure access method to your knowledge database as well.

☒ **A** is not correct. Implementing stand-alone CAs in your organization would not improve Vilbig's security. Although this solution would work, it does not meet the criteria. **C** is not correct. Creating a two-way transitive trust between Vilbig and your corporate domain does not improve Vilbig's security and may compromise your own. **D** is not correct. Creating a one-way, non-transitive trust between Vilbig and corporate may be one way to provide access, but mutual access is not at issue. Employees of BHE do not have any need to access Vilbig's network, so creating a trust relationship here doesn't address any issues. Finally, this solution would not improve Vilbig's network security.

12. ☑ **A.** Server Message Block (SMB) signing is also known as Common Internet File System (CIFS). It is used to authenticate both the sender and the receiver of information on a network. SMB/CIFS defines a series of commands used to pass information back and forth between computers on a network. This is supported natively in Windows 2000 and can be used with Windows NT 4.0 (Service Pack 3 or higher), or Windows 98 clients. CIFS works with Unix/Linux and can interoperate with Windows 2000. The only limitation is that this solution cannot be used with Windows 95. Since none of the clients listed in the Technical Specifications in the case study are Windows 95 clients, this solution could work.

☒ **B** is not correct. IPSec performs a similar function as SMB signing, but is not supported by down-level Windows clients such as Windows NT 4.0. **C** is not correct. MPPE is used as part of the PPTP protocol and is used for remote access tunnel encryption. **D** is not correct. IP encryption is enabled through using the IP Security (IPSec) protocol. This is supported in Windows 2000, but not in down-level operating systems.

13. ☑ **C.** SMB signing or CIFS, requires more processing per packet. Therefore, the network will experience a 10 to 15 percent decrease in performance.

☒ **A** and **B** are not correct. SMB signing requires more processing time but does not increase disk space requirements or network bandwidth requirements. **D** is not correct. The disk drive is not involved with preparing packets using SMB signing.

14. ☑ **D.** Chicago has implemented some very high security measures. Not all servers at that location contain sensitive information. However, the site clearly is at high risk if retinal scanners have been installed. Therefore, the very highest security measures are reasonable in this situation. To implement the best security measures, upgrading all computers (clients and servers) to Windows 2000 will allow you to fully use these features. All servers should be set to require security. This will slow the network response down but will ensure that all communications with servers in this domain are fully secure. Clients are set to Respond only so that if they are communicating with servers outside their domain, they will use security if it is required. This is a reasonable safeguard.

☒ **A** is not correct. Upgrading all servers in the company to Windows 2000 Server is not the right solution. This change will not address client computers in the Chicago domain. Additionally, not all servers in the company must be upgraded, only those in the Chicago domain. Others may not be able to communicate with those servers, but since these servers will be very restricted anyway, this is not a concern. **B** is not correct. Upgrading all servers in the Chicago domain to Windows 2000 Professional would disable the server features. The servers should run Windows 2000 Server and the clients should run Windows 2000 Professional. **C** is not correct. All servers in that OU should have Server Secure (Require Security) enabled. However, in order to implement this, it must also be enabled on the client side. If not, the clients will not be able to communicate with the servers.

15. ☑ **B** and **D** are correct. If SMB signing has been implemented in Chicago, it must be supported by both the client and the server for communications to occur. If India has not implemented this solution and Chicago is set to require it, communications will not occur. In addition, if the trust relationship has been changed for increased security in Chicago, users of the India domain may no longer have access to resources in the Chicago domain. Increasing security through managing trust relationships could include setting a one-way, non-transitive trust relationship. In this case, users of the Chicago domain would be trusted to access resources in the India domain, but not the reverse.

☒ **A** is not correct. Although EFS files are encrypted and cannot be shared, this is not the problem. Indian users are complaining that they can no longer access Chicago resources. Implementing EFS on laptops in the India domain would not cause this problem. **C** is not correct. IPSec would be supported on the Indian domain. It contains only Windows 2000 Advanced servers and Windows 2000 Professional desktops and laptops. IPSec would not be supported in the Chicago domain because it is running Windows NT 4.0 Server, which does not support the use of the IP Security protocol. This would not prevent Indian users from accessing Chicago resources.

16. ☑ **A.** France is connected via the equivalent of a fractional T1 line. This could pose a problem with replication traffic if the use of this Internet connection is already strained. Replication should be scheduled in a way to minimize the resources it demands. By using a bridgehead server, replication can occur among French servers after it has been replicated to the bridgehead server from corporate. In addition, France currently has two locations. Since they are connected to the Internet via the equivalent of fractional T1 lines (called E1 in Europe), they would be considered two separate sites in Windows 2000.

☒ **B** is not correct. OUs should be created based on how the company is organized or how IT is organized. Replication does not occur between OUs, but between sites. **C** is not correct. Creating one site would not be a viable solution since there are two physical locations in France. Also, the site names must conform to DNS naming standards and cannot contain any special characters, such as parentheses. **D** is not correct. Creating one OU is not a viable solution.

17. ☑ **A** and **B** are correct. Kerberos authentication is used with Windows 2000 clients. Kerberos can also be used with Unix systems that support version 5 of Kerberos. For clients that do not support Kerberos, Kerberos authentication in Windows 2000 will fail and NTLM authentication will automatically be used.

☒ **C** is not correct. MS-CHAP is used for remote access authentication. **D** is not correct. Digest authentication is used for secure Web authentication through proxy servers and firewalls.

18. ☑ **C** and **D** are correct. There are Windows 2000 clients and servers, Windows NT clients and servers, and Unix and Linux servers on this network. All clients are Windows-based. Clients are connecting using a VPN connection, thus, they are external to the network. All laptops in the technical specifications show that they are running Windows-based operating systems (98, NT, or 2000). Therefore, you can set up different VPN connections for your different clients.

☒ **A** is not correct. Although you would have to use PPP to support Unix or Linux clients (assuming they did not have third-party add-ons installed), you do not have these as clients. Therefore, PPP would not be a recommended solution, as it provides only basic security. If you installed third-party add-ons for Unix or Linux clients, they could utilize L2TP. However, you do not have these types of clients in your network. **B** is not correct. NTLM is used with down-level clients. L2TP with IPSec is not supported at all in those clients. Therefore, L2TP with IPSec would not use NTLM for authentication. You could set up VPN connections on your VPN server to use PPTP with MPPE for those down-level clients.

19. ☑ **A.** When a permanent WAN link is not feasible for location or cost reasons, you can use on-demand router-to-router VPN connections as an alternative. The answering router must be configured with a single demand-dial interface, and it must be permanently connected to the Internet. You can use an existing analog line to dial into the answering router to establish this connection. This would meet Sweden's requirement to connect, as needed, to corporate resources. It would also minimize costs by avoiding maintenance of a permanent connection to corporate that is rarely used.

☒ **B** is not correct. ATM networks are the physical method of transferring data. This solution requires additional hardware, which translates into higher costs. This would not meet the need of lowering costs and using existing infrastructure. **C** is not correct. Multihomed computers are those that have two or more network interface cards. They can act as routers in a networked environment. However, this, in itself, does not provide a solution for Sweden to connect to corporate resources on demand and at a reasonable cost. **D** is not correct. X.509 is the specification that describes certificates used for secure communications. It does not describe a circuit type. Certificates can be used to secure communications but do not provide a solution for on-demand resources.

20. ☑ **A, C,** and **D** are not correct. Using third-party certificate authorities is one way to work with certificates with parties external to your organization. Another method is to use a stand-alone CA. A stand-alone CA requires that your IT administrative staff manage the certificate processes and policies, but it also provides a greater degree of control. Stand-alone CAs do not rely upon Active Directory services, which is why they are suited to dealing with external parties. You could implement your CAs in several ways. You could use a root

CA at corporate. This root CA can then trust subordinate CAs to manage certificates. This maintains control at corporate but delegates some of the administration of these certificates to other servers. Another method is to use subordinate CAs for different organizational or geographic divisions (answer C). There may be different policies for issuing certificates, depending on the role or location of the division within the organization. Another viable solution is to use subordinate CAs to manage certificates issued for different company purposes (answer D). You may have a different policy for secure email than you do for network authentication. Separating these types of certificate policies by using subordinate CAs is a legitimate solution.

☒   **B** is not correct. An enterprise CA relies upon the use of Active Directory. Therefore, you would not use this type of CA for issuing certificates externally, such as to members of a trusted partner's organization.

TESTLET 2: ANSWERS

1. ☑ **B.** You should implement one domain for the company. The only reasons to implement more than one domain for an enterprise are (1) there are more than one IT administrative functions that define account policies for the organization, (2) the organization has a decentralized IT structure, or (3) the domain namespace is separate for various entities within the company. With Windows 2000, one domain is scalable to millions of objects.

   ☒ **A** and **C** are not correct. Retail stores will not have any Windows 2000 computers nor will they have control over their own account policy. **D** is not correct. IT functions are not decentralized by region, nor does each region require control over its own account policy.

2. ☑ **C, D,** and **E** are correct. The implementation of an e-commerce Web site, continued use of existing hardware at the retail outlets, and remote access to corporate headquarters all have the most impact on security design. Each of these requirements will impact how to secure network communication, choice of authentication protocols, and how to secure resources.

   ☒ **A** is not correct. Improved network performance is not a stated business objective. **B** is not correct. There are no plans to increase the number of retail outlets, nor would such an increase impact the overall security design. **F** is not correct. Cost does not seem to be an major issue, considering the IT budget was increased this fiscal year to accommodate the company's e-commerce solution and targeted upgrades.

3. ☑ **B.** The primary security risk for Southwest Gifts is an Internet hacker directly connected to an internal server, such as SGDATA or SGDEV. Since sensitive customer data and intellectual property are kept on these, direct access to this data from the Internet would cause the biggest potential threat to the company.

   ☒ **A** is not correct. The company will not have any internal computers connected directly to a modem. **C** is not correct. Employees establishing client/server connections via the LAN are authenticated using Kerberos, which is very secure. **D** is not correct. A DOS (denial of service) attack on an internal computer could create a problem, but it would not expose sensitive or intellectual property data to a hacker. A DOS attack might cause a server to shut down or slow down, but would not compromise security.

4. ☑ **A.** The company is willing to try new approaches and has taken risks in the past, such as with the start of their catalog business. In addition, the CEO recently fired the previous IT director due to lack of performance and is increasing the IT budget to implement a full-fledged e-commerce solution.

   ☒ **B** is not correct. The company developed a catalog business in the 1980s and wants fast implementation of an e-commerce solution. **C** is not correct. Development of an e-commerce solution does not jeopardize the retail or catalog businesses. **D** is not correct. The company has proven it has taken chances in the past, as with the development of the catalog business and the change in IT management.

5. ☑ **A.** Using code signing, you can protect downloaded software from being altered and ensure users that the code has been tested and will not damage user software. It is recommended that you sign your code before distributing it. Signing your code with a digital signature assures your users that the programs are from a known source and have not been altered. Users may be prevented from installing ActiveX controls and Java packages that are not signed.

   ☒ **B** and **C** are not correct. RADIUS is used to provide authentication, authorization, and accounting services for distributed dial-up authentication. IAS is a RADIUS server that uses user data stored in a Windows 2000 domain controller or SAM to verify requests submitted through the RADIUS protocol. **D** is not correct. Kerberos is the authentication protocol used in a Windows 2000 domain to authenticate both users and network services.

6. ☑ **C.** Since the dial-up machines at the retail stores will remain as Windows NT 4.0 servers, you cannot use L2TP over IPSec to secure the VPN tunnel. Windows NT 4.0 servers support PPTP tunnels using MPPE encryption provided by PPP. Dialing into a local ISP to gain access to the Internet will lower long-distance costs and will provide the necessary Internet access to create a VPN tunnel to headquarters.

   ☒ **A** is not correct. You do not dial directly into a RRAS server to establish a VPN tunnel. Also, the Windows NT 4.0 servers at the retail outlets do not support L2TP tunnels or IPSec encryption. **B** is not correct. The Windows NT 4.0 servers at the retail outlets do not support L2TP tunneling or IPSec encryption. **D** is not correct. You do not dial directly into a RAS server to establish a VPN tunnel. VPN tunnels are established through wide area networks typically owned by a local or national carrier (such as the Internet). One benefit of a VPN solution is that it reduces long-distance charges incurred with direct dial-up.

7. ☑ **B.** SSL (Secure Sockets Layer) over TCP/IP provides application-layer encryption over an unsecure network connection (such as the Internet). SSL is primarily used when accessing public Web sites for the protection of personal or sensitive data submitted to Web sites, such as credit card information. SSL can only be used with applications that are SSL-aware, such as IIS and the vast majority of Internet Explorer and Netscape browsers in use today. SSL uses private-key encryption technology to encrypt data before it is transmitted over an unsecure connection.

☒ **A** is not correct. VPN tunnels do not use SSL encryption. Rather, they use lower-level encryption technology, such as IPSec for L2TP tunnels or PPP/MPPE for PPTP tunnels. **C** and **D** are not correct. SSL encryption is not required to secure LAN communication. It has a limited implementation footprint because both the client and server applications must be SSL-aware. On a LAN containing Windows 2000 machines, communication can be secured at the IP layer, for instance, using IPSec, where applications do not have to be IPSec-aware (and, in fact, are not IPSec-aware).

8. ☑ **C.** Third-party CAs (certificate authorities) should be used to sign ActiveX controls downloaded from a public Web site, since public users might be prevented from installing ActiveX controls on their desktops unless the CA is trusted. For the purposes of downloaded Web content or secure Web communication between the public and the company, third-party CAs that are widely trusted, such as GTE or AT&T, must be used.

☒ **A, B,** and **D** are not correct. CAs implemented within a company are only trusted by that company's employees and trusted business partners. These types of CAs are used to digitally sign company email, for instance, or to authenticate on a company network using smart card technology. They are not practical for securing public Web content or for signing software downloaded from public Web sites.

9. ☑ **D.** By allowing PPTP tunnels on the SGVPN server at corporate, you allow the Windows NT 4.0 servers located at each retail store to securely establish a VPN tunnel to corporate headquarters. PPTP is supported with Windows NT 4.0, but L2TP and IPSec are not.

☒ **A** is not correct. EAP-TLS is not supported in Windows NT 4.0. EAP-TLS is an extension of PPP and allows for a variety of authentication schemes, such as token cards and public key devices (for example, smart cards and other forms of certificate-based authentication). EAP-TLS can be used to provide a high level of security for VPN tunnels, but it requires both the client and the server to mutually authenticate each other. If either the client or the server cannot authenticate using EAP-TLS, the connection is dropped. EAP-TLS provides more security against brute-force or dictionary attacks, and therefore, provides a higher level of security than CHAP, for instance. **B** and **C** are not correct. Neither L2TP nor IPSec is supported in Windows NT 4.0. Although L2TP over IPSec provides significant advantages over PPTP, it cannot be used in this case. L2TP over IPSec provides triple DES encryption for connections within North America, which is more secure than PPTP encryption (such as MPPE). L2TP can also be used to tunnel over X.25 and Frame Relay networks, whereas PPTP requires IP. **E** is not correct. MS-CHAP is an authentication protocol, and is not used to establish a secure connection (encrypt data) over an unsecure network such as the Internet. Secure authentication protocols ensure that logon credentials are not transmitted across the wire unencrypted, but they do not encrypt data transmission after authentication is complete. This is the function of IPSec or MPPE. MS-CHAP, MS-CHAP v2, and EAP-TLS are all authentication protocols that can be used to authenticate to a VPN server for the purposes of establishing a VPN tunnel. In the case of Southwest Gifts, MS-CHAP would be used to authenticate to SGVPN, as this is the strongest authentication protocol supported by Windows NT 4.0. MS-CHAP v2 and EAP-TLS are the only authentication protocols that require mutual authentication of both client and server; both of these can be used or are required in Windows 2000.

10. ☑ **A.** Success and failure audit for logon events will allow you to track who has successfully and/or unsuccessfully attempted to authenticate on the network. Attempts at brute-force attacks or dictionary attacks can be audited if this policy setting is enabled. Audit of failed logon events will also tell you the reason for the failure, such as account locked out or account currently disabled.

☒ **B** is not correct. Policy change events apply to successful or unsuccessful attempts to change security. If you enable auditing of policy change successes and failures, you will enable the following events on Windows 2000: user right assigned, user right removed, new trusted domain, removing trusted domain, audit policy change, IPsec policy agent started, IPSec policy agent disabled, IPSec policy changed, IPSec policy agent encountered a potentially serious failure, Kerberos policy changed, encrypted data recovery policy changed, Quality of Service (QoS) policy changed, and trusted domain information modified. **C** is not correct. Privilege use events deal with the successful or unsuccessful use of a user right, such as the right to change the system time or the right to back up files and directories. **D** is not correct. Process tracking enables auditing of the following events: a new process has been created, a process has exited, a handle to an object has been duplicated, and indirect access to an object has been obtained. The downside of monitoring this category of events is that the events are rarely useful by themselves, plus there will be a large number of them. You will need some type of analysis tool to associate object access events with a process tracking event, in order to gain more insight into what a particular user was doing.

11. ☑ **B.** SSL will encrypt all data to and from a secure Web site, including logon credentials. Since you don't know what type of client will be requesting authentication, you cannot use NTLM authentication. In addition, NTLM authentication is not available in IIS 5.0 on Windows 2000. Integrated Windows Authentication, formerly called NTLM or Windows NT Challenge/Response, is the new standard and will only work with IE 2.0 or later and will not work across an HTTP Proxy. CHAP is not used to authenticate browser-to-HTTP server connections, but rather is used to authenticate dial-up or VPN clients. Database validation will provide anonymous access from any browser, but will enable you to validate customers through the customer database using ODBC drivers and server-side scripts. This method will allow the Web site to integrate fully with the customer and order-tracking database.

☒ **A** is not correct. NTLM authentication is no longer an authentication method on IIS 5.0 in Windows 2000. NTLM has been replaced by Integrated Windows Authentication, which cannot be used in this scenario. **C** and **D** are not correct. CHAP cannot be used to authenticate against an IIS 5.0 server. CHAP is used to authenticate to a RAS server in the case of a dial-up or VPN client.

12. ☑ **A.** The SQL Server 7.0 database will be used to store the transaction tracking files. It is the database server for this organization.

☒ **B** is not correct. You would not store sensitive data on a public Web server that is accessible from the Internet. **C** is not correct. You would not store sensitive data on a RAS server that will be accessible from dial-up clients. **D** is not correct. You would not store customer data on the development server used by the Web developers. Customer data will be accessed frequently by SGWEB and should be on a dedicated server for performance reasons.

13. ☑ **B.** MS-CHAP provides the most secure authentication mechanism, in the case of a Windows NT 4.0 machine authenticating over a VPN or dial-up connection to a Windows 2000 RAS server. Although Windows NT 4.0 can use both PAP and SPAP to authenticate over a VPN connection, these authentication protocols are discouraged because they are less secure than MS-CHAP. EAP is not supported in Windows NT 4.0.

☒ **A** is not correct. PAP is the least secure authentication protocol, uses plaintext passwords, and is typically negotiated if the remote access client and server cannot negotiate a more secure authentication protocol. **C** is not correct. EAP, although more secure than any of the other authentication methods, requires mutual client/server authentication and is not supported in Windows NT 4.0. **D** is not correct. SPAP is less secure than MS-CHAP and is typically used by Shiva clients when connecting to a Windows 2000 server. SPAP uses the same password each time authentication occurs in the same reversibly encrypted form. This makes SPAP susceptible to replay attacks and, for this reason, is especially discouraged for use over VPN connections.

14. ☑ **A.** All visitors, as opposed to authorized users, should be authenticated using an anonymous account (such as IUSR_*computername*)—as defined on the Web server. Visitors will be authenticated as anonymous then will be asked to provide basic information in order to become a customer for the purposes of viewing products and placing orders.

☒ **B** and **C** are not correct. Visitors will not have a user ID or password at first, nor will they have a cookie stored on their browser client. **D** is not correct. Authorized users are the only ones allowed to view Web site information, as specified in the technical requirements.

15. ☑ **A.** The only way to provide true disaster recovery is to implement and regularly test a backup plan. The System State data on each domain controller should be backed up regularly, as should any critical data. In addition, RAID5 provides fault tolerance and high availability, should a disk fail in a RAID5 volume. Better throughput and greater efficiency could be realized using hardware RAID5 or RAID10, although at a higher cost. Where maximum availability is required, clustering can provide fault tolerance at the machine level, as well as load balancing for greater performance and response time. If a machine in the cluster fails, clustering will allow duplicate services on the other members of the cluster to handle the load.

    ☒ **B** is not correct. RADIUS and IAS do not provide any disaster recovery capability. Instead, the RADIUS protocol and IAS are used to provide authentication, authorization, and accounting services for distributed dial-up authentication. IAS is a RADIUS server that uses user data stored in a Windows 2000 domain controller or SAM to verify requests submitted through the RADIUS protocol. **C** is not correct. IPSec does not provide disaster recovery capability. IPSec is used to secure IP traffic between clients and servers in high security environments. **D** is not correct. All data does not need to be backed up nightly, only data that is critical to company operations. In addition, although DFS replicas provides fault tolerance and load balancing for DFS shares on a local-area network, they should not be implemented as a substitute for RAID 5 volumes or clustering, where possible.

16. ☑ **A** and **C** are correct. Servers that should be placed inside a DMZ between an internal and external firewall are servers that must be contacted directly via the Internet, as is the case with Web servers and VPN servers.

    ☒ **B** is not correct. SGDATA houses the SQL server, which should be accessible only to internal clients. **D** and **E** are not correct. SGDC1 and SGDC2 are domain controllers. Domain controllers should never be accessible directly via a public network. **F** is not correct. SGDEV is the developer's server, which should not be publicly accessible.

17. ☑ **C.** Access to resources should be granted to users based on the minimum required to do a particular job. In this case, the CFO requires Read and Execute permission in order to pull data from the SALES folder to build the monthly, consolidated financial report. Store Managers require Write and List Contents permission in order to open up the SALES folder and upload daily

sales data, but they should not have Read permission since they are not permitted to view other stores' daily sales data. Network administrators should have full control over the SALES folder so that they can assign permissions and take ownership of documents in the event personnel leave or a problem arises.

☒ **A** is not correct. Store managers should not have the ability to view other stores' sales figures, which would be allowed if Read permission was granted. **B** is not correct. The CFO does not require Write permission, nor do store managers require Read permission. **D** is not correct. No Access would prevent store managers from being able to upload daily sales data.

18. ☑ **D.** The Web server requires that TCP ports 80 and 443 be open so that HTTP and HTTPS requests can be made to the Web server. PPTP traffic to the SGVPN server requires that TCP port 1723 and IP protocol 47 (GRE) be open, as PPTP requires both of these to function properly.

☒ **A** is not correct. TCP and UDP ports 135 to 139 are used for NetBIOS. Enabling these ports on the external firewall would actually create a security hole in your network. **B** is not correct. Blocking access to TCP port 80 would prohibit all HTTP requests to the Web server over the Internet and effectively render the Web server useless. **C** is not correct. Blocking access to connected TCP ports would prohibit any TCP traffic from entering the external gateway, thus rendering both the Web and VPN servers useless.

19. ☑ **C** is not correct. By using CORP.SWGIFTS.COM as the domain name for all internal servers and having only the internal DNS server resolve CORP.SWGIFTS.COM addresses, you separate the internal and external namespace. Thus, you separate intranet resources from publicly available Internet servers, such as SGWEB and SGVPN.

☒ **A** and **B** are not correct. Configuring external DNS servers to resolve internal names weakens security on your internal network and can potentially allow hackers to see information about your internal name and IP address space. **D** is not correct. Configuring external DNS servers to resolve internal names would weaken security. In addition, excluding internal names from the internal DNS server would render Active Directory useless and your internal network unusable. Active Directory requires the DNS server to resolve internal host names to IP addresses.

20. ☑ **C.** By creating a separate domain for the newly acquired company in its own tree, you are able to preserve the existing name space of the newly acquired company. By placing the new tree in the same forest as Southwest Gifts, you are able to manage IT resources for the newly acquired company and maintain a single schema for all company resources. All domains within a forest have transitive trusts established so that users from any one domain can access resources in any other domain.

☒ **A** is not correct. Configuring a child domain in the forest would not preserve the newly acquired company's namespace. Since it already has an established Internet domain, this would prove too cumbersome to implement. **B** is not correct. Excluding the newly acquired company's domain from the forest would prevent centralized IT administration and the use of a single, forest-wide schema for all objects under the control of IT. This solution would be too cumbersome to manage. **D** is not correct. Creating a new forest for the newly acquired company and doing nothing else would cause the same problems as choice B. What's more, having no trusts established would prevent access to resources in the newly acquired domain, and vice versa.

MICROSOFT CERTIFIED SYSTEMS ENGINEER

Glossary

A *TO* *Z*

Access Control Entry (ACE)   An Access Control List (ACL) is a list of who has permission to an object and what that permission is. The granular permission in ACL is called an ACE.

Access Control List (ACL)   Servers use ACLs to control access to resources on the network, whether they reside on a Windows NT server or a Windows 2000 server. These ACLs are contained on the object, and that object may or may not be in Active Directory. An example of an object not contained in Active Directory is a file sitting in a directory on a file server. ACLs are attached to that file that state who can access the file and what they can do with it. An ACL is a list of who has permission to an object and what that permission is.

account lockout policy   The account lockout policy dictates the behavior for locking and unlocking user accounts.

ACE   *See* Access Control Entry.

ACL   *See* Access Control List.

ACPI   *See* Advanced Configuration and Power Interface.

Active Directory (AD)   The Active Directory is implemented on Windows 2000 domain controllers, and the directory can be accessed from Windows 2000 Professional as an Active Directory client. The Active Directory arranges objects—including computer information, user and group information, shared folders, printers, and other resources—in a hierarchical structure, in which domains can be joined into trees (groups of domains that share a contiguous namespace). Trees can be joined into forests (groups of domain trees that share a common schema, configuration, and global catalog).

Active Directory Service   This service provides the means for locating the Remote Installation Service (RIS) servers and the client computers on the network. The RIS server must have access to the Active Directory.

Active Directory Services Interface (ADSI)   This is a set of COM interfaces that enables Windows 9x, Windows NT, and Windows 2000 applications to access Active Directory and other directory services.

Add Printer Wizard   All clients running a version of the Windows operating system (Windows 2000, Windows NT, Windows 98, and Windows 95) can use the

Add Printer Wizard to create a printer entry on the client. This Add Printer Wizard can create and share a printer on a print server. The Windows 2000 version of the Add Printer Wizard has more options than the wizard in other versions of Windows, but many of the same methods can be used to get the printer set up on the client.

administration   The word *administer* is generally used as a synonym for *manage,* which in turn means to exert control. One of the many enhancements to Windows 2000—both the Professional and Server incarnations—is the ability Microsoft has given administrators to apply the degree of control desired, in a flexible and granular manner.

ADSI   *See* Active Directory Services Interface.

Advanced Configuration and Power Interface (ACPI)   ACPI combines Plug-and-Play (PnP) capability with Power Management, and places these functions under complete control of the operating system.

Advanced Power Management (APM)   An Intel/Microsoft application program interface (API) allowing programs to indicate their requirements for power to regulate the speed of components.

alerts   Alerts allow some action to be performed when a performance counter reaches a particular threshold. A common action is to log the event in the application event log. You can also send a network message to a specified computer. You can have the alert start a performance log to start logging when the alert occurs. And finally, you can configure the alert to start a program.

analysis   Analysis is the process of comparison, contrast, diagnosis, diagramming, discrimination, and/or drawing conclusions.

analysis phase   During the analysis stage, you put together the information gathered during phase one and draw conclusions based on the totality of the data. In the analysis phase, you determine what the problems are.

answer file   An answer file is a file containing the information you would normally have to key in during the setup process. Answer files help automate the installation process as all the queries presented to you during installation are answered by the answer files. With careful planning, you can prepare answers that eliminate the possibility of incorrect answers typed in by the person performing the installation, thus reducing the chances of setup failure. You can use the Setup Manager Wizard to create a customized answer file. This technique minimizes the chances of committing syntax-related errors while manually creating or editing the sample answer files.

API *See* Application Program Interface.

APIPA *See* Automatic Private Internet Protocol Addressing.

APM *See* Advanced Power Management.

AppleTalk The AppleTalk protocol suite was developed by Apple Computer for use in its Macintosh line of personal computers. AppleTalk is a local area networking system that was developed by Apple Computer Inc. AppleTalk networks can run over a variety of networks that include Ethernet, FDDI, and Token Ring, as well as Apple's proprietary media system LocalTalk. Macintosh computers are very popular in the education and art industries, so familiarity with the way they communicate using their native protocol is very useful.

AppleTalk printing device Another type of remote printer is the AppleTalk printing device. Like a Transmission Control Protocol/Internet Protocol (TCP/IP) printer, an AppleTalk printer can be connected directly to an AppleTalk network or shared across the network through an AppleShare print server. Like the TCP/IP printers, a large number of modern, high-capacity PostScript printers can be configured to communicate with an AppleTalk network as well as a TCP/IP network. In fact, many Hewlett-Packard LaserJet printers have JetDirect cards that will speak to TCP/IP and AppleTalk at the same time.

application A program designed to perform a specific function directly for the user or for another application program. An application would be, for example, word processors, database programs, graphics/drawing programs, Web browsers, email programs.

Application Program Interface (API) A set of routines used by a program to request and carry out lower level services performed by the computer's operating system or other component, which provides the program with a way to communicate with the system.

application service provider (ASP) ASPs are companies that manage applications and provide organizations with application hosting services. Analysts expect the ASP market will be a six billion-dollar industry by the year 2001. The application-hosting model offers organizations the option of outsourcing application support and maintenance.

ASP *See* application service provider.

assessment and evaluation phase Often forgotten, the last and very important phase is the assessment and evaluation phase. In this phase, you test the security plan you've set in place and determine whether you have accomplished your goals and whether the cost (both monetary and otherwise) of the higher security level is justified by the benefits to the company.

asymmetric encryption Two different but corresponding keys (called a key pair) are used; one—the public key—is used to encrypt the data and is not kept secret but is published to all wishing to send an encrypted message to the owner. The second key—the private key—is known only by the owner and is used to decrypt data that was encrypted with the corresponding public key. Also called public key encryption.

auditing Windows 2000 gives the ability to audit security-related events, track access to objects and use of user rights, and detect attempted and successful access (authorized and unauthorized) to the network. Auditing is not enabled by default, but once enabled, a security log that provides information in regard to specific activities performed on the computer is generated.

authentication The process of validating the identity of a user or a device such as a server or router. There are a number of different methods of authenticating identity, including Kerberos, NTLM, RADIUS, and others.

Authentication Header (AH) An AH allows authentication of the sender of data, but it does not provide privacy.

Automatic Private Internet Protocol Addressing (APIPA) APIPA, or Automatic Client Configuration, is a new feature initially available in Windows 98. The feature has been extended to Windows 2000 and allows Dynamic Host Control Protocol (DHCP) client computers to self-configure their IP addressing information in the event a DHCP server is not available when the computer issues a DHCPDISCOVER message. It also allows self-configuration when it senses that it has been moved from a previous network via Windows 2000 media sensing capabilities.

backup domain controller (BDC)   A backup file or copy of the primary domain controller (PDC). Periodically, the BDC is synchronized with the PDC.

backup logs   Windows Backup generates a backup log file for every backup job. These files are the best place to review the backup process in case some problem is encountered by the program. The backup log is a text file that records all the events during the backup process.

BACP   *See* Bandwidth Allocation Control Protocol.

Bandwidth Allocation Control Protocol (BACP)   Bandwidth Allocation Control Protocol (BACP) is a Point-to-Point Protocol (PPP) network control protocol that negotiates the election of a favored peer for a multiprocessing connection. If both ends of the connection issue a connection request at the same time, then the connection request of the favored peer is performed.

Bandwidth Authentication Protocol (BAP)   Bandwidth Allocation Protocol (BAP) is a PPP control protocol that is used on a multiprocessing connection to dynamically add and remove links.

BAP   *See* Bandwidth Allocation Protocol.

basic encryption   Uses a 40-bit Microsoft Point-to-Point Encryption (MPPE) key. This is a good option for servers working as Virtual Private Network (VPN) servers. The Point-to-Point Tunneling Protocol (PPTP) protocol is also available at this level. Security is bumped up to a 56-bit key if the Layer 2 Tunneling Protocol (L2TP) protocol is used.

basic input/output system (BIOS)   A set of programs encoded in ROM on IBM PC-compatible computers programs handle startup operations such as power on self test (POST) and low-level control for hardware such as disk drives, keyboards, etc.

BDC   *See* backup domain controller.

BIOS   *See* basic input/output system.

boot   The process of loading an operating system into the computer's memory (RAM) so those applications can be run on it.

boot ROM   A boot ROM is a chip on the network adapter that helps the computer boot from the network. Such a computer need not have a previously installed operating system. The BIOS of the computer that has a PXE-based boot ROM must be configured to boot from the network. Windows 2000 Server RIS supports PXE ROM versions 99 or later.

bottleneck   A bottleneck in computer terms is also a component of the system as a whole that restricts the system from operating at its peak. When a bottleneck occurs, the component that is a bottleneck will have a high rate of usage and other components will have a low rate of usage. A lack of memory is a common cause of bottleneck when your computer doesn't have enough memory for the applications and services that are running.

branch office model   The branch office model is one in which there is a primary office or headquarters and multiple small branch offices that are distributed across a region. The main difference between this and a regional model is that the connectivity that is employed is typically on-demand LAN connectivity. Each site has a LAN where the primary connectivity with the main office is accomplished through a modem, DSL, or cable modem connection to an ISP a utilizing either PPTP or L2TP to create a secure VPN connection.

business model   A business model refers to the ways in which a company conducts its business.

CA   *See* certificate authority.

CAL   *See* Client Access License.

CAPI   *See* CryptoAPI.

Centralized model   This model consolidates administrative control of group policies. A single team of administrators is responsible for managing all Group Policy Objects (GPOs) no matter where they are. This is usually applied by giving all the top-level organizational unit (OU) administrators full control to all GPOs no matter where they are located. They give each second-level OU administrator Read permission only to each GPO. You can also decentralize other resources or keep all resources centralized, depending on the environment.

centralized organization A centralized organization gives very little autonomy to units within the organization. Most decisions are made at the corporate offices, and units are expected to abide by those decisions. The military is a good example of a centralized organization. Centralized organizations are often said to be command-and-control style organizations.

certificate A message that has a digital signature that is associated with the private key of a trusted third party, and confirms that a particular public key belongs to the party (user or device) that claims to own it.

certificate authority (CA) An authority/organization that produces digital certificates with its available public key. A certificate authority (CA) is a public key certificate issuer (for example, Verisign). To use a public key certificate, you must trust the issuer (CA). This means that you have faith in the CA's authentication policies. The CA is used for doing things such as authorizing certification authenticity, revoking expired certificates, and responding to certification requests. Windows 2000 offers an alternative to a third-party CA. You can become a CA within your own Intranet. Thus, you can manage your own certificates rather than relying on a third-party certification authority.

certificate service Provides security and authentication support, including secure email, Web-based authentication, and smart card authentication.

Challenge Handshake Authentication Protocol (CHAP) A protocol used for authentication over a Point to Point Protocol (PPP) connection. The Challenge Handshake Authentication Protocol verifies the identity of the peer, using a three-way handshake. The authenticator sends a challenge message to the peer. The peer returns the user name and an MD5 hash of the challenge, the session ID, and the client's password. The authenticator then checks this response, and if the values match, the authentication is acknowledged; if not, the connection is ended. CHAP provides protection against playback attack because the challenge value changes with every message. Because the password is never sent unencrypted over the network or link, it is considered very difficult to crack.

Change permission This permission allows users the ability to change permissions on files and folders without giving them the Full Control permission. You can also use this permission to give a user or group access to modify permissions on file or folder objects without giving them the ability to have complete control over the object.

child domains   Domains connected to the root on the tree are referred to as child domains.

cipher   An algorithm used to encrypt text to make it unreadable to unauthorized persons.

Cipher command   The Cipher command is another way to encrypt and decrypt data. You can use it from the command line, and it has many switches that you can use to define exactly what you want to have done. The Cipher.exe command syntax is simply CIPHER, followed by the switches that you would like to use, followed by the path and directory/file name. The most common switches are the /E switch (encrypts the specified directories) and the /D switch (decrypts the specified directories). You can also use wildcards with the Cipher command.

CIW   *See* Client Installation Wizard.

Client Access License (CAL)   The CAL allows clients to access the Windows 2000's network services, shared folders, and printers. There are two types of CAL modes: Per Seat and Per Server. It's important to understand the difference between these two modes. When you use the Per Seat mode, each computer that accesses the server must have a CAL. The Per Server mode requires a CAL for each connection to the server. This is a subtle but significant difference. The licensing modes are the same as under Windows NT 4.0.

Client Installation Wizard (CIW)   When a client computer boots using either the Remote Boot Disk or the PXE-based boot ROM, it tries to establish a connection to the Remote Installation Service (RIS) server. If the RIS server is pre-configured to service the RIS clients, it helps the client get an Internet Protocol (IP) address from the Dynamic Host Control Protocol (DHCP) service. The CIW is then downloaded from the RIS server. This wizard has four installation options. The options that are presented to the user depend on the group policy set in the Active Directory. A user may get all four options, or may not get any of the options when starting an automatic setup.

cloning   *See* disk imaging/cloning.

comprehension   The process of distinguishing between situations, discussing, estimation, explaining, indicating, paraphrasing, and giving examples.

computer account   A computer account is an account that is created by a domain administrator and uniquely identifies the computer on the domain. A newly created account is used so that a computer may be brought into a Windows 2000 Domain.

configuration   Configuration of an operating system involves specifying settings that will govern how the system behaves.

Container object   Container objects can contain other objects. A special type of Container object you can create in the Active Directory is the organizational unit (OU).

containers   Containers are used to describe any group of related items, whether they are objects, containers, domains, or an entire network.

Control Panel Accessibility options   These are options that include StickyKeys, FilterKeys, ToggleKeys, SoundSentry, ShowSounds, High Contrast, MouseKeys, and SerialKeys.

cooperative multitasking   An environment in which an application relinquishes its use of the computer's Central Processing Unit (CPU) so that another application can use the CPU.

Copy backup   This type of backup simply copies the selected files. It neither looks for any markers set on the files nor does it clear them. The Copy backup does not affect the other Incremental or Differential backup jobs and can be performed along with the other types of backup jobs.

CryptoAPI (CAPI)   CryptoAPI (CAPI) architecture is a collection of tasks that permit applications to digitally sign or encrypt data while providing security for the user's private key data.

cryptography   The study of creating and deciphering encoded or encrypted messages.

Daily backup   This type of backup does not use any markers to back up selected files and folders. The files that have changed during the day are backed up every day at a specified time. This backup will not affect other backup schedules.

data backup   A backup and disaster protection plan is an essential part of a network administrator's duties. Windows 2000 provides a built-in the Backup utility used to back up data to tape or file, or to create an emergency repair disk (ERD). An ERD can be used to repair a computer with damaged system files.

data compression   Windows 2000 offers the capability of compressing data on a file-level basis, so long as the files and folders are located on an NT File System (NTFS) formatted partition or volume. Compression saves disk space; however, NTFS compression cannot be used in conjunction with file encryption.

data confidentiality   The ability to encrypt data before it is transferred over the network so that it cannot be read by someone eavesdropping or "tapping" the network.

Data Encryption Standard (DES)   A method of cryptography that uses a secret (private) key, originated by IBM and later adopted by the U.S. government.

Data Link Control (DLC)   DLC is a non-routable protocol used for connecting to IBM mainframes and some network-connected laser printers.

DC   *See* domain controller.

Debugging mode   This is the most advanced startup option of all. To use this option you will need to connect another computer to the problematic computer through a serial cable. With proper configuration, the debug information is sent to the second computer.

Decentralized model   This model is appropriate for companies that rely on delegated levels of administration. They decentralize the management of Group Policy Objects (GPOs), which distributes the workload to a number of domains. To apply this model, simply give all organizational unit (OU) administrators full control of their respective GPOs.

decentralized organization   In these organizations, units within the company have most of the decision-making authority. The parent company may exist only to provide common infrastructure needs for the units. Companies are often organized in this way to improve both their flexibility and their response to changing market conditions. Holding companies and cartels like OPEC are good examples of decentralized organizations.

dedicated server A dedicated printer server is a Windows 2000 server whose only role is to provide printing services. The server does not provide directory space for users other than storage for spooled print jobs. It does not provide authentication services, does not host database services, does not act as a Domain Name System (DNS) server, and so on. A dedicated print server can host several hundred printers and print queues, however. Though it may not be obvious, the printing process does have an impact on the performance of the server providing the printing services. An environment with a large number of printers or print jobs should strongly consider using at least one dedicated print server.

defragmentation The task of finding fragmented files and moving them into contiguous space is called defragmentation.

denial of service attacks The server is flooded with numerous requests that use all the bandwidth or resources so that the server cannot communicate.

Deny permission Unlike the Allow permission, the Deny permission overrides all other permissions set for a file or folder. If a user is a member of one group with a Deny Write permission for a folder and is a member of another group with an Allow Full Control permission, the user will be unable to perform any of the Write permission tasks allowed because it has been denied. The Deny permission should be used with extreme caution, as it can actually lock out all users, even administrators, from a file or folder. The proper way to remove a permission from a user or group on a file or folder is to uncheck the Allow permission for that user or group, not to check the Deny permission.

DES *See* Data Encryption Standard.

design phase The design phase is where you put forth a solution or solutions to the problems identified in phase two. How can you best address the issues within the parameters of your organization's budget, philosophy, and priorities? There may be more than one possible solution, and you will need to assess the pros and cons of each and decide on a plan of action. It is a good idea to also have in place a contingency plan if Plan A does not work.

Dfs *See* Distributed File System.

DHCP *See* Dynamic Host Control Protocol.

Differential backup   The Differential backup checks and performs a backup of only those files that are marked. It does not clear the markers after the backup, which means that any consecutive Differential backups will back up the marked files again. When you need to restore from a Differential backup, you will need the most current Full backup and the Differential backup performed after that.

Digest Authentication (DA)   DA prompts a user of a browser for an ID and a password. The ID and password are protected in transit from the server to the browser by a hash—created from the user ID and password and coupled with the server's public ID. DA can only be used on servers running Windows 2000; earlier versions of Windows or other operating systems do not have DA integration, so it cannot be used.

digital signatures   These are message digests that are encrypted and attached to a document, and used to verify the identity of the sender and the fact that the data in the document has not been tampered with.

digital subscriber line (DSL)   There are many variants of digital subscriber line (xDSL). All versions utilize the existing copper loop between a home and the local telco's Central Office (CO). Doing so allows them to be deployed rapidly and inexpensively. However, all DSL variants suffer from attenuation, and speeds drop as the loop length increases. Asymmetrical DSL (ADSL) and Symmetrical DSL (SDSL) may be deployed only within 17,500 feet of a CO, and Integrated Services Digital Network emulation over DSL (IDSL) will work only up to 30,500 feet. All DSL variants use Asynchronous Transfer Mode (ATM) as the Data-Link layer.

Direct Memory Access (DMA)   DMA is a microprocessor capable of transferring data between memory units without the aid of the Central Processing Unit (CPU). Occasionally, built-in circuitry can do this same function.

directory   A directory is a database that contains information about objects and their attributes.

directory service   The directory service is the component that organizes the objects into a logical and accessible structure, and provides for a means of searching and locating objects within the directory. The directory service includes the entire directory and the method of storing it on the network.

Directory Services Restore mode   This startup mode is available on Windows 2000 Server domain controller computers only. This mode can be used to restore the SYSVOL directory and Active Directory on the domain controller.

discover   A Dynamic Host Control Protocol (DHCP) client begins the lease process with a DHCPDISCOVER message. The client broadcasts this message after loading a minimal Transmission Control Protocol/Internet Protocol (TCP/IP) environment. The client does not know the address of the DHCP server, so it sends the message using a TCP/IP broadcast, with 0.0.0.0 as the source address and 255.255.255.255 as the destination address. The DHCPDISCOVER message contains the clients network hardware address, its computer name, a list of DHCP options the client supports, and a message ID that will be used in all messages between the client and server to identify the particular request.

disk compression   This compression allows you to compress folders, subfolders, and files to increase the amount of file storage, but slow down access to the files.

Disk Defragmenter   Disk Defragmenter can analyze your volumes and make a recommendation as to whether or not you should defragment it. It will also give you a graphical display showing you the fragmented files, contiguous files, system files, and free space. Disk Defragmenter does not always completely defragment free space; instead, it often moves it into just a few contiguous areas of the disk, which will still improve performance. Making the free space one contiguous space would have little added benefit.

disk imaging/cloning   The deployment of a new operating system is one of the most challenging and time-consuming tasks that a network administrator has to perform. The disk duplication methods are particularly useful when you need to deploy Windows 2000 Professional on a large number of computers. This is also known as disk imaging or cloning. These tools make the rollout fast and easy.

Disk Quota   Windows 2000 comes with a Disk Quota feature that allows you to control users' disk consumption on a per user/per partition basis. To begin setting disk quotas for your users, right-click any partition in either Windows Explorer or the My Computer object. Click Properties and then click the Quota tab. Also, a disk quota allows you to limit the amount of disk space used by each user.

Distributed File System (Dfs)   The Windows 2000 Distributed File System provides a method to centralize the organization of the shared resources on your network. In the past, shared resources were most often accessed via the Network Neighborhood applet, and users would have to wade through a number of domains and servers in order to access the shared folder or printer that they sought. Network users also had to remember where the obscure bit of information was stored, including both a cryptic server name and share name. The Distributed File System (Dfs) allows you to simplify the organization of your network resources by placing them in central shares accessed via a single server. Also, the Dfs allows you to create a central share point for shared resources located through the organization on a number of different servers.

Distribution Server   This is a server on which the Windows 2000 installation files reside. When you install the operating system over the network, the client machine does not need a CD-ROM drive. The first requirement for network installation is a Distribution Server that contains the installation files. The Distribution Server can be any computer on the network to which the clients have access.

DLC   *See* Data Link Control.

DMA   *See* Direct Memory Access.

DNS   *See* Domain Name System.

domain   A collection of connected areas. Routing domains provide full connectivity to all end systems within them. Also, a domain is a collection of accounts and network resources that are grouped together using a single domain name and security boundary. Domains harbor all objects on a network, where objects are defined as users, computers, printers, and anything else that can attach to the network. Windows 2000 networks can be based on one domain or several.

domain controller (DC)   Domain controllers validate logons, participate in replication of logon scripts and policies, and synchronize the user account database. This means that domain controllers have an extra amount of work to perform. Since the Terminal Server already requires such heavy resources, it is not a good idea to burden a Terminal Server with the extra work of being a domain controller. Also, all user accounts, permissions, and other network details are all stored in a centralized database on the domain controllers.

domain local groups   Domain local groups are used for granting access rights to resources such as file systems or printers that are located on any computer in the domain where common access permissions are required. The advantage of domain local groups being used to protect resources in that a member of the domain local group can come from both inside the same domain and from outside as well.

Domain Name System (DNS)   Because the actual unique Internet Protocol (IP) address of a Web server is in the form of a number difficult for humans to work with, text labels separated by dots (domain names) are used instead. DNS is responsible for mapping these domain names to the actual Internet Protocol (IP) numbers in a process called resolution. Sometimes called a Domain Name Server.

domain-naming master   This is the domain controller that oversees the addition or removal of domains within the forest. Like the schema master, this is a forest-wide role.

domain restructure   Domain restructure, or domain consolidation, is the method of changing the structure of your domains. Restructuring your domains can allow you to take advantage of the new features of Windows 2000, such as greater scalability. Windows 2000 does not have the same limitation as the Security Accounts Manager (SAM) account database in Windows NT. Without this limitation, you can merge domains into one larger domain. Using Windows 2000 organizational units (OUs), you have finer granularity in delegating administrative tasks.

domain tree   A domain tree is a hierarchical collection of the child and parent domains within a network. The domains in a domain tree have contiguous namespaces. Domain trees in a domain forest do not share common security rights, but can access one another through the global catalog.

Driver Signing   One of the most frustrating things about Windows operating systems is that any software vendors can overwrite critical system-level files with their own versions. Sometimes the vendor's version of a system-level file is buggy or flawed, and it prevents the operating system from functioning correctly, or in the worst case, prevents it from starting at all. Windows 2000 uses a procedure called Driver Signing that allows the operating system to recognize functional, high-quality files approved by Microsoft. With this seal of approval, you should be confident that installing applications containing signed files would not disable your computer. Windows 98 was the first Microsoft operating system to use digital signatures, but Windows 2000 marks the first Microsoft operating system based on NT technology to do this.

DSL   *See* digital subscriber line.

dynamic disks   Dynamic disks introduce conceptual as well as technical changes from traditional basic disk structure. Partitions are now called volumes, and these can be created or changed without losing existing data on the disk. Recall that when using basic disks, you must first create primary partitions (up to a maximum of four), then extended partitions (a maximum of one) with logical drives. Dynamic disks allow you to create volume after volume, with no limit on the number or type that can exist on a single disk; you are limited only by the capacity of the disk itself.

Dynamic Host Configuration Protocol (DHCP)   A software utility that is designed to assign Internet Protocol (IP) addresses to clients and their stations logging onto a Transmission Control Protocol/Internet Protocol (TCP/IP) and eliminates manual IP address assignments.

EAP   *See* Extensible Authentication Protocol.

EDI   *See* Electronic Data Interchange.

EFS   *See* Encrypting File System.

Electronic Data Interchange (EDI)   EDI is the computer-to-computer electronic exchange of business documents using standard formats that are widely recognized both nationally and internationally. The use of standardized data formats allows organizations to exchange common business documents without having to customize their hardware or software system for each organization they do business with.

Encapsulating Security Payload (ESP)   With IPSec, there are two choices of security service: Authentication Header (AH), and Encapsulating Security Payload (ESP). An AH allows authentication of the sender of data, but it does not provide privacy. ESP supports both authentication of the sender and encryption of the data as well.

Encrypting File System (EFS)   Unlike Windows NT 4.0, Windows 2000 provides the Encrypting File System (EFS) that allows you to encrypt and decrypt data on a file-by-file basis without the need for third-party software, as long as it is stored on an NTFS formatted partition or volume. If data packets are intercepted when sent over the network, the data will not be readable. EFS is based on public key cryptography.

encryption   Scrambling of data so as to be unreadable; therefore, an unauthorized person cannot decipher the data.

ESP   *See* Encapsulating Security Payload.

Ethernet   A networking protocol and shared media (or switched) local area network (LAN) access method linking up to 1K nodes in a bus topology.

evaluation   Evaluation is the process of assessing, summarizing, weighing, deciding, and applying standards.

extended partitions   Although extended partitions cannot be used to host operating systems, they can store other types of data and provide an excellent way to create more drives above the four-partition limit. Extended partitions do not represent one drive; rather, they can be subdivided into as many logical drives as there are letters in the alphabet. Therefore, one extended partition can contain several logical drives, each of which appears as a separate drive letter to the user.

Extensible Authentication Protocol (EAP)   EAP allows the administrator to "plug in" different authentication security providers outside of those included with Windows 2000. EAP allows your organization to take advantage of new authentication technologies including "smart card" logon and Certificate-based authentication.

FAT   *See* file allocation table.

fault tolerance   Fault tolerance is high-system availability with enough resources to accommodate unexpected failure. Fault tolerance is also the design of a computer to maintain its system's performance when some internal hardware problems occur. This is done through the use of backup systems. Fault tolerance is not a replacement for regular backups. Instead, fault tolerance provides a higher level of availability of network services and data in the event of failure.

FEK   *See* File Encryption Key.

file allocation table (FAT)   A FAT is an area on a disk that indicates the arrangement of files in the sectors. Because of the multi-user nature of Terminal Server, it is strongly recommended that the NTFS file system be used rather than the FAT file system. FAT does not offer file and directory security, whereas with NTFS you can limit access to subdirectories and files to certain users or groups of users.

file allocation table 16 (FAT16)   The earlier version of the FAT file system implemented in MS-DOS is known as FAT16, to differentiate it from the improved FAT32.

file allocation table 32 (FAT32)   FAT32 is the default file system for Windows 95 OSR2 and Windows 98. The FAT32 file system was first implemented in Windows 95 OSR2, and was supported by Windows 98 and now Windows 2000. While FAT16 cannot support partitions larger than 4GB in Windows 2000, FAT32 can support partitions up to 2TB (Terabytes) in size. However, for performance reasons, the creation of FAT32 partitions is limited to 32GB in Windows 2000. The second major benefit of FAT32 in comparison to FAT16 is that it supports a significantly smaller cluster size—as low as 4K for partitions up to 8GB. This results in more efficient use of disk space, with a 15 to 30 percent utilization improvement in comparison to FAT16.

File Encryption Key (FEK)   A random key called a File Encryption Key (FEK) is used to encrypt each file and is then itself encrypted using the user's public key. At least two FEKs are created for every encrypted file. One FEK is created with the user's public key, and one is created with the public key of each recovery agent. There could be more than one recovery agent certificate used to encrypt each file, resulting in more than two FEKs. The user's public key can decrypt FEKs created with the public key.

File Transfer Protocol (FTP)   An Internet protocol allowing the exchange of files. A program enables the user to contact another computer on the Internet and exchange files.

firewall   Either hardware or software that provides a security boundary or barrier between two networks by filtering incoming and outgoing packets.

FireWire   Also known as IEEE 1394. An Apple/Texas Instruments high-speed serial bus allowing up to 63 devices to connect; this bus supports hot swapping and isochronous data transfer.

forest   A forest is a grouping of one or more domain trees that do not share a common namespace but do share a common schema, configuration, and global catalog; in fact, it forms a noncontiguous (or discontiguous) namespace. The users in one tree do not have global access to resources in other trees, but trusts can be created that allow users to access resources in another tree.

forward lookup query   A forward lookup query occurs when a computer needs to get the Internet Protocol (IP) address for a computer with an Internet name. The local computer sends a query to a local Domain Name System (DNS) name server, which resolves the name or passes the request on to another server for resolution.

FQDN   *See* fully qualified domain name.

FSP   *See* Full Service Provider.

FTP   *See* File Transfer Protocol.

full service provider (FSP)   FSPs offer multilayer suites of help that are sandwiched between a company's application and the data center. The service is a packaged solution of hardware, software, and hosting facilities. As an extra safety measure, the service providers guarantee 100 percent uptime with 24/7 checking on the security, backup, and hosting of the Web site. The strategy for FSP business solutions for growing enterprises is to free companies from the headaches of managing back-end infrastructure so they can focus on their core business. FSPs provide storage and networking equipment, software, bandwidth allotment, and round-the-clock technical support, with help from blue-chip suppliers.

fully qualified domain name (FQDN)   A full site name of a system rather than just its host name. The FQDN of each child domain is made up of the combination of its own name and the FQDN of the parent domain. The FQDN includes the host name and the domain membership of that computer.

gateway   In networking, gateway refers to a router or a computer functioning as one, the "way out" of the network or subnet, to get to another network. You also use gateways for software that connects a system using one protocol to a system using a different protocol, such as the Systems Network Architecture (SNA) software (allows a local area network (LAN) to connect to an IBM mainframe). You can also use Gateway Services for NetWare used to provide a way for Microsoft clients to go through a Windows NT or Windows 2000 server to access files on a Novell file server.

GC   *See* Global Catalog.

Global Catalog (GC)   The GC holds a replica of every object in Active Directory, but it only includes some of the objects' attributes—those most often used in search operations. The GC allows users and administrators to find directory information without having to know which server or domain actually contains the data.

Global Catalog (GC) server   The GC server is a domain controller that contains a partial replica of every domain in Active Directory. Generally, a user must have access to a global catalog server to successfully log on to the network because the global catalog is needed to determine what groups the user belongs to.

global groups   Global groups are used for combining users who share a common access profile based on job function or business role. Typically organizations use global groups for all groups in which membership is expected to change frequently. These groups can have as members only user accounts defined in the same domain as the global group.

globally unique identifier (GUID)   The globally unique identifier (GUID) is a unique numerical identification created at the time the object is created. An analogy would be a person's social security number, which is assigned once and never changes, even if the person changes his or her name, or moves.

GPC   *See* Group Policy Container.

GPO   *See* Group Policy Object.

GPT   *See* Group Policy Template.

graphical user interface (GUI)   An overall and consistent system for the interactive and visual program that interacts (or interfaces) with the user. GUI can involve pull-down menus, dialog boxes, on-screen graphics, and a variety of icons.

group policy   Group policy provides for change management and desktop control on the Windows 2000 platform. You are familiar with the control you had in Windows NT 4.0 using system policies. Group policy is similar to system policies but allows you a much higher level of granular configuration management over your network. Some of the confusion comes from the change of names applied to different groups in Windows 2000. You can apply group policy to sites, domains, and organizational units. Each of these represents a group of objects, so group policy is applied to the group of objects contained in each of these entities. Group policy cannot be directly applied to security groups that are similar to the groups you are used to working with in Windows NT 4.0. However, by using group policy filtering, you can successfully apply group policy to individual security groups.

Group Policy Container (GPC)   The Active Directory object Group Policy Containers (GPCs) store the information for the Folder Redirection snap-in and the Software Deployment snap-in. GPCs do not apply to local group policies. They contain component lists and status information, which indicate whether Group Policy Objects (GPOs) are enabled or disabled. They also contain version information, which insures that the information is synchronized with the Group Policy Template (GPT) information. GPCs also contain the class store in which GPO group policy extensions have settings.

Group Policy Object (GPO)   After you create a group policy, it is stored in a Group Policy Object (GPO) and applied to the site, domain, or organizational unit (OU). GPOs are used to keep the group policy information; essentially, it is a collection of policies. You can apply single or multiple GPOs to each site, domain, or OU. Group policies are not inherited across domains, and users must have Read permission for the GPO that you want to have applied to them. This way, you can filter the scope of GPOs by adjusting who has read access to each GPO.

Group Policy Template (GPT)   The subset of folders created on each domain controller that store Group Policy Object (GPO) information for specific GPOs are called Group Policy Templates (GPTs). GPTs are stored in the SysVol (System Volume) folder, on the domain controller. GPTs store data for Software Policies, Scripts, Desktop File and Folder Management, Software Deployment, and Security settings. GPTs can be defined in computer or user configurations. Consequently, they take effect either when the computer starts or when the user logs on.

GUI   *See* graphical user interface.

GUID   *See* globally unique identifier.

HAL   *See* Hardware Abstraction Layer.

Hardware Abstraction Layer (HAL)   The Windows NT's translation layer existing between the hardware, kernel, and input/output (I/O) system.

Hardware Compatibility List (HCL)   The Hardware Compatibility List is published by Microsoft for each of its operating systems, and is updated on a monthly basis. There is a copy of the HCL on the Windows 2000 Professional CD, located in the Support folder and named Hcl.txt.

hardware profile   A hardware profile is a set of instructions that tells your computer how to boot the system properly, based on the setup of your hardware. Hardware profiles are most commonly used with laptops. This is because laptops are frequently used in at least two different settings: stand-alone and in a docking station on a network. For example, when the laptop is being used at a docking station, it requires a network adapter. However, when the laptop is used away from the network, it does not. The hardware profile dialog manages these configuration changes. If a profile is created for each situation, the user will automatically be presented these choices on Windows startup.

hash   A mathematical calculation applied to a string of text, resulting in a string of bits of a fixed size, which cannot be done in reverse to arrive back at the original source data.

HCL   *See* Hardware Compatibility List.

HKEY_CLASSES_ROOT   Contains information used for software configuration and object linking and embedding (OLE), as well as file association information.

HKEY_CURRENT_CONFIG   Holds data about the current hardware profile that is in use.

HKEY_CURRENT_USER   Has information about the user who is currently logged on.

HKEY_LOCAL_MACHINE   Stores information about the hardware, software, system devices, and security information for the local computer.

HKEY_USERS   Holds information and settings for the environments of all users of the computer.

HTML   *See* HyperText Markup Language.

HTTP   *See* HyperText Transfer Protocol.

HyperText Markup Language (HTML)   The format used to create documents viewed on the World Wide Web (WWW) by the use of tags (codes) embedded within the text.

HyperText Transfer Protocol (HTTP)   HTTP is an Internet standard supporting World Wide Web (WWW) exchanges. By creating the definitions of Universal Resource Locators (URLs) and their retrieval usage throughout the Internet.

IAS   *See* Internet Authentication Services.

ICS   *See* Internet Connection Sharing.

IDE   *See* Integrated Drive Electronics.

identity interception   Unauthorized access is gained by using the valid credentials of someone else.

IIS *See* Internet Information Service.

impersonation The ability of an unauthorized person to present credentials that appear to be valid.

implementation phase The implementation phase is the phase in which you actually put the plan into action. Implementation may require hiring outside personnel, or you may be able to implement your plan with your current IT staff.

inbound connection Inbound connections are those where access to the intranet or resources within the intranet are being accessed by users outside of it. These users could be dialing in using a modem and connecting directly to the intranet or they could make use of an existing public network, such as the Internet, to gain access to resources within. Either way, security must be in the forefront of any such implementation.

Incremental backup This backup process is similar to the Differential backup, but it clears the markers from the selected files after the process. Because it clears the markers, an Incremental backup will not back up any files that have not changed since the last Incremental backup. This type of backup is fast during the backup but is very slow while restoring the files. One needs the last Full backup and all of the subsequent Incremental backups to fully restore data. The positive side of this backup type is that it is fast and consumes very little media space.

indexing service Provides indexing functions for documents stored on disk, allowing users to search for specific document text or properties.

Industry Standard Architecture (ISA) A PC's expansion bus used for peripheral's plug-in boards.

infrastructure An underlying base or foundation for an organization or system.

infrastructure master There is an infrastructure master for each domain, and it updates the group-to-user references when group members are changed.

inheritance When you nest an organizational unit (OU) within another OU, by default, the properties of the parent OU flow down the hierarchy. This is called inheritance. These properties can consist of security or group policies. Inheritance allows an object in an OU to inherit the permissions applied to the OU or parent object. In most cases, the parent object is an OU. One of the advantages and disadvantages of inheritance is that it can be blocked. Inheritance lets a given Access Control Entry (ACE) propagate from the container where it was applied to all children of the container. Inheritance can be combined with delegation to grant administrative rights to a whole subtree of the directory in a single operation.

Integrated Drive Electronics (IDE) drive   An IDE drive is a hard disk drive for processors containing most controller circuitry within the drive. IDE drives combine Enhanced System Device Interface (ESDI) speed with small computer system interface (SCSI) hard drive interface intelligence.

Integrated Services Digital Network (ISDN)   Integrated Services indicates the provider offers voice and data services over the same medium. Digital Network is a reminder that ISDN was born out of the digital nature of the intercarrier and intracarrier networks. ISDN runs across the same copper wiring that carries regular telephone service. Before attenuation and noise cause the signal to be unintelligible, an ISDN circuit can run a maximum of 18,000 feet. A repeater doubles this distance to 36,000 feet.

International model   In this model, a global enterprise does business in more than one country and perhaps has offices in different nations as well. In addition, a company is operating with an international business model if it has operations that are located in more than one country. The company will have business operations that will consist of a Worldwide Headquarters, possibly divisional headquarters that are based around the country or continent that is being serviced as well as offices, production and distribution facilities located to take advantage of the economic advantages of being located in multiple international locations.

Internet Authentication Services (IAS)   IAS performs authentication, authorization, and accounting of dial-up and virtual private network (VPN) users. IAS supports the Remote Access Dial-In User Service (RADIUS) protocol.

Internet Connection Sharing (ICS)   ICS can be thought of as a less robust version of Network Address Translation (NAT lite). ICS uses the same address translation technology. ICS is a simpler version of NAT useful for connecting a few computers on a small local area network (LAN) to the Internet or useful for a remote server through a single phone line and account.

Internet Information Service (IIS)   Windows NT Web browser software that supports Secure Sockets Layer (SSL) security protocol from Netscape. IIS provides support for Web site creation, configuration, and management, along with Network News Transfer Protocol (NNTP), File Transfer Protocol (FTP), and Simple Mail Transfer Protocol (SMTP).

Internet Packet Exchange (IPX)   Novell NetWare's built-in networking protocol for local area network (LAN) communication derived from the Xerox Network System protocol. IPX moves data between a server and/or workstation programs from different network nodes. Sometimes called an Internetwork Packet Exchange.

Internet Protocol Security (IPSec)   IPSec is a new feature included in Windows 2000 and provides for encryption of data as it travels between two computers, protecting it from modification and interpretation if anyone were to see it on the network.

Internet service provider (ISP)   The organization allowing users to connect to its computers and then to the Internet. ISPs provider the software to connect and sometimes a portal site and/or internal browsing capability.

Internetworking   Internetworking refers to connecting two or more networks. This concept is the foundation of the global Internet, as well as private large enterprise networks. With Internet connectivity becoming a necessity rather than a luxury, and most major (and many, many minor) companies "on the net," it is important to know how to secure your internal, private LAN from unauthorized access originating on the public network to which it is connected.

interrupt request (IRQ)   An electronic signal that is sent to the computer's processor requiring the processor's attention. Also, a computer instruction designed to interrupt a program for an input/output (I/O).

IPSec   *See* Internet Protocol Security.

IPX   *See* Internet Packet Exchange.

IRQ   *See* interrupt request.

ISA   *See* Industry Standard Architecture.

ISDN   *See* Integrated Services Digital Network.

ISP   *See* Internet service provider.

Kerberos   Kerberos guards against username and password safety vulnerability by using tickets (temporary electronic credentials) to authenticate. Tickets have a limited life span and can be used in place of usernames and passwords (if the software supports this). Kerberos encrypts the password into the ticket. It uses a trusted server called the Kerberos Distribution Center (KDC) to handle authentication requests. Kerberos speeds up network processes by integrating security and rights across network domains and also eliminates workstations' need to authenticate themselves repeatedly at every domain they access. Kerberos security also makes maneuvering around networks simple using multiple platforms such as Unix or NetWare easier.

knowledge   Knowledge is the very lowest level of learning. It is, of course, important that a network administrator have this knowledge. Knowledge involves the processes of defining, location, recall, recognition, stating, matching, labeling, and identification.

L2TP   *See* Layer Two Tunneling Protocol.

Last Known Good Configuration   This mode starts the system using the configuration that was saved in the registry during the last system shutdown. This startup option is useful when you have changed some configuration parameters and the system fails to boot. When you use this mode to start the system, all changes that were made after the last successful logon are lost. Use this option when you suspect that some incorrect configuration changes are causing the system startup failure. This mode does not help if any of the installed drivers have been corrupted or any driver files are deleted by mistake.

Layer Two Tunneling Protocol (L2TP)   L2TP offers better security through the use of IPSec and creates virtual private networks (VPNs). Windows 2000 uses L2TP to provide tunneling services over Internet Protocol Security (IPSec)–based communications. L2TP tunnels can be set up to traverse data across intervening networks that are not part of the VPN being created. L2TP is used to send information across intervening and nonsecure networks.

LDAP   *See* Lightweight Directory Access Protocol.

legend   The legend displays information about the counters that are being measured. It is the set of columns at the bottom of System Monitor.

life cycle   The phase that a business will progress through when implementing a change from the beginning to the end of use is known as the life cycle. Depending on the topic, there are various phases that a process goes through until it begins to repeat itself again. Products tend to go through various stages such as new technology, state of the art, advanced, mainstream, mature, and obsolete.

Lightweight Directory Access Protocol (LDAP)   A simplified Directory Access Protocol (DAP) accessing a computer's directory listing. LDAP is able to access to X.500 directories.

Line Printer Daemon (LPD)   LPD is the server process that advertises printer queues and accepts incoming print submissions, which are then routed to the print device.

Line Printer Remote (LPR)   LPR is a process that spools a print job to a remote print spool that is advertised by the Line Printer Daemon (LPD).

link parameter negotiation   An Agreement between the client and the server on the size of the packets as well as how they are framed.

local model   The local model is the "mom and pop" corner store model, in which all or most business comes from members of the immediate neighborhood or community, or within a city.

local policy   A group policy stored locally on a Windows 2000 member server or a Windows 2000 professional computer is called a local policy. The local policy is used to set up the configuration settings for each computer and for each user. Local policies are stored in the \%systemroot%\system32\grouppolicy folder on the local computer. Local policies include the auditing policy, user rights and privilege assignment, and various security options.

local printer   A print device that is directly attached, via a parallel or serial cable, to the computer that is providing the printing services. Drivers for the print device must reside on the computer that connects to the printer.

local user profiles (local profiles)   Local user profiles are kept on one local computer hard drive. When a user initially logs on to a computer, a local profile is created for them in the \%systemdrive%\Documents and Settings\<username> folder. When users log off the computer, the changes that they made while they were logged on will be saved to their local profile on that client computer. This way, subsequent logons to that computer will bring up their personal settings. When users log on to a different computer, they will not receive these settings, as they are local to the computer in which they made the changes. Therefore, each user that logs on to that computer receives individual desktop settings. Local profiles are ideal for users who only use one computer. For users that require access to multiple computers, the roaming profile would be the better choice.

LogicalDisk object   The LogicalDisk object measures the transfer of data for a logical drive (i.e., C or D) or storage volumes. You can use the PhysicalDisk object to determine which hard disk is causing the bottleneck. Then, to narrow the cause of the bottleneck, you can use the LogicalDisk object to determine which, if any, partition is the specific cause of the bottleneck. By default, the PhysicalDisk object is enabled and the LogicalDisk object is disabled on Windows 2000 Server.

LPD   *See* Line Printer Daemon.

LPR   *See* Line Printer Remote.

macro viruses   Macros are small programs that run inside other programs; for example, macros can be written to automate commonly used functions in Microsoft Word and other word processing programs. A macro virus uses this capability to invade a system and cause damage or gain unauthorized access to data.

malicious code   This is a method of attacking a network by embedding ActiveX, VB script, or a Java applet in a Web page or e-mail message. When the page or message is executed, it will provide the intruder with a way to access information on the network which he or she is not authorized to access.

management model   An important facet of the overall business model is the company's management model. How does the "chain of command" work within the company? Is management paternalistic, where control emanates from one person who may see him or herself as a benevolent dictator? Is the management style more team-oriented, in which upper-level employees run the operation (management by committee)?

mandatory roaming profiles   Mandatory roaming profiles are mandatory user profiles the user cannot change. They are usually created to define desktop configuration settings for groups of users in order to simplify administration and support. Users can make changes to their desktop settings while they are logged on, but these changes will not be saved to the profile, as mandatory profiles are read-only. The next time they log on, their desktop will be set back to the original mandatory profile settings.

man-in-the-middle attacks   An intruder intercepts packets in transit and changes the security credentials to administrator, thereby allowing administrative functions on the server.

masquerading   This is where an unauthorized user uses the IP address of a trusted system account or device.

Master File Table (MFT)   The MFT stores the information needed by the operating system to retrieve files from the volume. Part of the MFT is stored at the beginning of the volume and cannot be moved. Also, if the volume contains a large number of directories, it can prevent the free space from being defragmented.

master image   After configuring one computer with the operating system and all the applications, Sysprep is run to create an image of the hard disk. This computer serves as the master or model computer that will have the complete setup of the operating system, application software, and any service packs. This hard disk image is the master image and is copied to a CD or put on a network share for distribution to many computers. Any third-party disk-imaging tool can then be used to replicate the image to other identical computers.

MCSE   *See* Microsoft Certified Systems Engineer.

Message Queuing Services   Provides a communication infrastructure and a development tool for creating distributed messaging applications. Such applications can communicate across heterogeneous networks and with computers that might be offline. Message queuing provides guaranteed message delivery, efficient routing, security, transactional support, and priority-based messaging.

MFT   *See* Master File Table.

Microsoft Certified Systems Engineer (MCSE)   An engineer who is a technical specialist in advanced Microsoft products, specifically NT Server and NT Workstation.

Microsoft Challenge Handshake Authentication Protocol (MC-CHAP)
The Microsoft Challenge Handshake Authentication Protocol is similar to CHAP but is considered more secure. As with CHAP, the authenticator sends a challenge to the peer. The peer must return the user name and an MD4 hash of the challenge string, the session ID, and the MD4-hashed password. This sort of design manipulates a hash of the MD4 hash of the password, and provides an additional level of security because it allows the authenticator to store hashed passwords instead of clear-text passwords.

Microsoft Management Console (MMC)   The MMC provides a standardized interface for using administrative tools and utilities. The management applications contained in an MMC are called snap-ins, and custom MMCs hold the snap-ins required to perform specific tasks. Custom consoles can be saved as files with the .msc file extension. The MMC was first introduced with NT Option Pack. Using the MMC leverages the familiarity you have with the other snap-ins available within MMC, such as SQL Server 7 and Internet Information Server 4. With the MMC, all your administrative tasks can be done in one place.

Mini-Setup Wizard   The purpose of this wizard is to add some user-specific parameters on the destination computer. These parameters include: end-user license agreement (EULA); product key (serial number); username, company name, and administrator password; network configuration; domain or workgroup name; and, date and time zone selection.

mirror set   In a mirror set, all data on a selected partition or drive are automatically duplicated onto another physical disk. The main purpose of a mirror set is to provide fault tolerance in the event of missing or corrupt data. If one disk fails or contains corrupt files, the data is simply retrieved and rebuilt from the other disk.

mirrored volume   Like basic disks, dynamic disks can also be mirrored and are called mirrored volumes. A continuous and automatic backup of all data in a mirrored volume is saved to a separate disk to provide fault tolerance in the event of a disk failure or corrupt file. Note that you cannot mirror a spanned or striped volume.

mirroring   Also called RAID1. RAID1 consists of two drives that are identical matches, or mirrors, of each other. If one drive fails, you have another drive to boot up and keep the server going.

Mixed mode When in Mixed mode, the domain still uses master replication with a Windows 2000 PDC. The Windows NT backup domain controllers (BDCs) replicate from the Windows 2000 server, as did the Windows NT primary domain controller (PDC). When you are operating in Mixed mode, some Windows 2000 functionality will not be available. You will not be able to use group nesting or transitive trusts. Mixed mode is the default mode.

MMC *See* Microsoft Management Console.

NAT *See* Network Address Translation.

national model In the national model, the company does business all over the country, but rarely or never conducts business outside the national boundaries. The company will have business operations that will consist of a corporate headquarters, regional offices, production and distribution facilities located in multiple regions of a country.

Native mode Native mode allows only Windows 2000 domain controllers to operate in the domain. When all domain controllers for the domain are upgraded to Windows 2000 Server, you can switch to Native mode. This allows you to use transitive trusts and the group-nesting features of Windows 2000. When switching to Native mode, ensure you no longer need to operate in Mixed mode because you cannot switch back to Mixed mode once you are in Native mode.

NDS *See* NetWare Directory Service.

NetBEUI *See* Network Basic Input/Output System Extended User Interface.

NetBIOS *See* Network Basic Input/Output System.

NetWare Directory Service (NDS) NDS (created by Novell) has a hierarchical information database allowing the user to log on to a network with NDS capable of calculating the user's access rights.

Network Address Translation (NAT) With NAT, you can allow internal users to have access to important external resources while still preventing unauthorized access from the outside world.

Network Basic Input/Output System (NetBIOS)   A program in Microsoft's operating system that links personal computers to a local area network (LAN).

Network Basic Input/Output System Extended User Interface (NetBEUI)   The transport layer for the Disk Operating System (DOS) networking protocol called Network Basic Input/Output System (NetBIOS).

network   Two or more computers connected together by cable or wireless media for the purpose of sharing data, hardware peripherals, and other resources.

network authenticator   A network authenticator is a special packet that contains information that is unique to the sender or client; and incidentally, one of the most important aspects of network security. By authenticating a user you give that user rights within the network. When it is done properly, authenticating once will get the user through your network without any hitches—the user can go about their normal work and not be interrupted by needing to authenticate again for access to certain areas of the network with higher security.

network interface card (NIC)   A board with encoding and decoding circuitry and a receptacle for a network cable connection that, bypassing the serial ports and operating through the internal bus, allows computers to be connected at higher speeds to media for communications between stations.

network printer   A print device that has a built-in network interface or connects directly to a dedicated network interface. Both workstations and servers can be configured to print directly to the network printer, and the network printer controls its own printer queue, determining which jobs from which clients will print in which order. Printing clients have no direct control over the printer queue and cannot see other print jobs being submitted to the printer. Administration of a network printer is difficult. Drivers for the print device must reside on the computer that connects to the printer.

network layer protocol negotiation   The act of negotiating and obtaining a valid IP address.

NIC   *See* network interface card.

nondedicated server   A nondedicated print server is a Windows 2000 server that hosts printing services in addition to other services. A domain controller, database server, or Domain Name System (DNS) server can provide printing services as well, but should be used only for a smaller number of printers or for printers that are not heavily used. Anyone setting up a nondedicated print server should monitor the performance of the printing process and the other tasks running on the server and be prepared to modify the server configuration if the performance drops below acceptable levels.

nonmandatory roaming profiles   Roaming user profiles are stored on the network file server and are the perfect solution for users who have access to multiple computers. This way their profile is accessible no matter where they log on in the domain. When users log on to a computer within their domain, their roaming profile will be copied from the network server to the client computer and the settings will be applied to the computer while they are logged on. Subsequent logins will compare the roaming profile files to the local profile files. The file server then copies only any files that have been altered since the user last logged on locally, significantly decreasing the time required to logon. When the user logs off, any changes that the user made on the local computer will be copied back to the profile on the network file server.

Normal backup   This is the most common type and is also known as a Full backup. The Normal backup operation backs up all files and folders that are selected irrespective of the archive attributes of the files. This provides the easiest way to restore the files and folders but is expensive in terms of the time it takes to complete the backup job and the storage space it consumes. The restore process from a Normal backup is less complex because you do not have to use multiple tape sets to completely restore data.

NT File System (NTFS)   The NT File System (with file names up to 255 characters) is a system created to aid the computer and its components in recovering from hard disk crashes.

NT LAN Manager (NTLM)   NTLM was the default authentication system in Windows NT 4.0 and is backward compatible with Windows 2000 for networks that run earlier versions of the operating system (OS).

NTFS   *See* NT File System.

NTLM   *See* NT LAN Manager.

NWLink IPX/SPX/NetBIOS Compatible Transport Protocol (NWLink)
Microsoft's implementation of Novell's Internet Packet eXchange/Sequenced Packet eXchange (IPX/SPX) protocol stack, required for connecting to NetWare servers prior to version 5. NWLink can also be used on small networks that use only Windows 2000 and other Microsoft client software. NWLink is a Network Driver Interface Specification (NDIS) compliant, native 32-bit protocol. The NWLink protocol supports Windows sockets and NetBIOS.

ODBC *See* Open Database Connectivity.

offer After the Dynamic Host Control Protocol (DHCP) server receives the DHCPDISCOVER message, it looks at the request to see if the client configuration request is valid. If so, it sends back a DHCPOFFER message with the client's network hardware address, an IP address, a subnet mask, the length of time the lease is valid, and the IP address of the server that provided the DHCP information. This message is also a Transmission Control Protocol/Internet Protocol (TCP/IP) broadcast, as the client does not yet have an Internet Protocol (IP) address. The server then reserves the address it sent to the client so that it is not offered to another client making a request. If there are more than one DHCP servers on the network, all servers respond to the DHCPDISCOVER message with a DHCPOFFER message.

Open Database Connectivity (ODBC) A database programming interface that allows applications a way to access network databases.

Open Systems Interconnection (OSI) model This is a model of breaking networking tasks into layers. Each layer is responsible for a specific set of functionality. There are performance objects available in System Monitor for analyzing network performance.

operations master This is a domain controller that takes on the role of handling a single master operation.

Organizational Chart The Organizational Chart is a logical description of the structure of a business organized by groups, divisions and, often, individuals. This structure is depicted in the context of who performs the work and who manages the workers and who manages the managers, etc. Equally important is how each business unit, division, department, etc., fits into the "Big Picture" of how the business as a whole operates.

organizational unit (OU)   OUs in Windows 2000 are objects that are containers for other objects, such as users, groups, or other organizational units. Objects cannot be placed in another domain's OUs. The whole purpose of an OU is to have a hierarchical structure to organize your network objects. You can assign a group policy to an OU. Generally, the OU will follow a structure from your company. It may be a location, if you have multiple locations. It can even be a department-level organization. Also, OUs are units used to organize objects within a domain. These objects can include user accounts, groups, computers, printers, and even other OUs. The hierarchy of OUs is independent of other domains.

OSI   *See* Open Systems Interconnection model.

OU   *See* organizational unit.

outbound connections   Connecting to and accessing private network resources through the Internet or some other public network is where Virtual Private Networks (VPNs) take over. This allows the administrator to centrally maintain security from outbound connections while also allowing users to make use of local Internet Service Providers (ISPs). This prevents the users from having to make long distance calls and racking up very large phone bills.

paging   When enough memory is not available for the running applications, pages of memory can be swapped from physical memory to the hard disk too much and slow the system down. This is also known as paging because pages of memory are swapped at a time. Windows 2000 separates memory into 4KB pages of memory to help prevent fragmentation of memory. Swapping can even get bad enough that you can hear your hard disk running constantly.

paging file   A file on the hard disk (or spanning multiple disks) that stores some of the program code that is normally in the computer's RAM. This is called virtual memory, and allows the programs to function as if the computer had more memory than is physically installed.

password   A string of characters (text, numbers, or symbols) that is kept private and used to authenticate a user's identity.

Password Authentication Protocol (PAP)   A simple authentication method used over Point-to-Point Protocol (PPP) connections, which is less secure than Challenge Handshake Authentication Protocol (CHAP).

password policy   A password policy regulates how your users must establish and manage their passwords. This includes password complexity requirements and how often passwords must change. There are several settings that can be used to implement a successful password policy. You can enforce password uniqueness so those users cannot simply switch back and forth between a few easy-to-remember passwords. This can be set to low, medium, or high security. With low security, the system remembers the user's last 1 to 8 passwords (it is your choice as administrator to decide how many); with medium, it remembers the last 9 to 16 passwords; with high, it remembers the last 17 to 24 passwords.

PCMCIA   *See* Personal Computer Memory Card Interface Adapter.

PDC   *See* primary domain controller.

peer-to-peer network   A workgroup is also referred to as a peer-to-peer network, because all the computers connected together and communicating with one another are created equal. That is, there is no central computer that manages security and controls access to the network.

performance logging   Performance logging has many features. The data collected are stored in a comma-delimited or tab-delimited format, which allows for exportation to spreadsheet and database applications for a variety of tasks such as charting and reports. The data can also be viewed as collected. You can configure the logging by specifying start and stop times, the name of the log files, and the maximum size of the log. You can start and stop the logging of data manually or create a schedule for logging. You can even specify a program to run automatically when logging stops. You can also create trace logs. Trace logs track events that occur rather than measuring performance counters.

permissions inheritance   By default, all permissions set for a folder are inherited by the files in the folder, the subfolders in the folder, and the contents of the subfolders. When the permissions on a folder are viewed in the Security tab of the file or folder Permissions window, inherited permissions are indicated with a gray check box.

Personal Computer Memory Card Interface Adapter (PCMCIA)   An interface standard for plug-in cards for portable computers; devices meeting the standard (for example, fax cards, modems) are theoretically interchangeable.

physical memory   Physical memory is the actual random access memory (RAM) on the computer. When the physical memory becomes full, the operating system can also use space on the hard disk as virtual memory. When memory becomes full, rather than locking up the computer, the operating system stores unused data on the hard disk in a page file (also called paging or swap file). Data are swapped back and forth between the hard disk and physical memory as needed for running applications. If memory is needed that is in virtual memory, it is swapped back into physical memory.

physical security   Physical security consists of protecting of the network's physical assets (servers, workstations, cable, hubs, and so on) from intruders.

PhysicalDisk object   The PhysicalDisk object measures the transfer of data for the entire hard disk. You can use the PhysicalDisk object to determine which hard disk is causing the bottleneck. By default, the PhysicalDisk object is enabled and the LogicalDisk object is disabled on Windows 2000 Server.

PKI   *See* Public Key Infrastructure.

Plug-and-Play (PnP)   A standard requiring add-in hardware to carry the software to configure itself in a given way supported by Microsoft Windows 95. Plug-and-Play can make peripheral configuration software, jumper settings, and Dual In-line Package (DIP) switches unnecessary. PnP allows the operating system to load device drivers automatically and assign system resources dynamically to computer components and peripherals. Windows 2000 moves away from this older technology with its use of Kernel-mode and User-mode PnP architecture. PnP auto-detects, configures, and installs the necessary drivers in order to minimize user interaction with hardware configuration. Users no longer have to tinker with IRQ and I/O settings.

PnP   *See* Plug-and-Play.

Point-to-Point Protocol (PPP)   A serial communication protocol most commonly used to connect a personal computer to an Internet Service Provider (ISP). PPP is the successor to Serial Line Internet Protocol (SLIP) and may be used over both synchronous and asynchronous circuits. Also, PPP is a full-duplex, connectionless protocol that supports many different types of links. The advantages of PPP made it de facto standard for dial-up connections.

Point-to-Point Tunneling Protocol (PPTP)   One of two standards for dial-up telephone connection of computers to the Internet, with better data negotiation, compression, and error corrections than the other Serial Line Internet Protocol (SLIP), but costing more to transmit data and unnecessary when both sending and receiving modems can handle some of the procedures.

policy inheritance   Group policies have an order of inheritance in which the policies are applied. Local policies are applied first, then group policies are applied to the site, then the domain, and finally the organizational unit (OU). Policies applied first are overwritten by policies applied later. Therefore, group policies applied to a site overwrite the local policies and so on. When there are multiple Group Policy Objects (GPOs) for a site, domain, or OU, the order in which they appear in the Properties list applies. This policy inheritance order works well for small companies, but a more complex inheritance strategy may be essential for larger corporations.

ports   A channel of a device that can support single point-to-point connections is known as a port. Devices can be single port, as in a modem.

Power options   Power options entail the computer hardware power usage and are dependent on the particular hardware. Power options include Standby and Hibernation modes. Standby mode turns off the monitor and hard disks to save power. Hibernation mode turns off the monitor and disks, saves everything in memory to disk, turns off the computer, and then restores the desktop to the state in which you left it when the computer is turned on.

PPP   *See* Point-to-Point Protocol.

PPTP   *See* Point-to-Point Tunneling Protocol.

Preboot Execution Environment (PXE)   The PXE is a new Dynamic Host Control Protocol (DHCP)–based technology used to help client computers boot from the network. The Windows 2000 Remote Installation Service (RIS) uses the PXE technology along with the existing Transmission Control Protocol/Internet Protocol (TCP/IP) network infrastructure to implement the RIS-based deployment of Windows 2000 Professional. The client computer that has the PXE-based ROM uses its Basic Input/Output System (BIOS) to contact an existing RIS server and get an Internet Protocol (IP) address from the DHCP server running on the network. The RIS server then initializes the installation process on the client computer.

preemptive multitasking   An environment in which timesharing controls the programs in use by exploiting a scheduled time usage of the computer's Central Processing Unit (CPU).

primary domain controller (PDC)   Performs NT security management for its local domain. The PDC is periodically synchronized to its copy, the backup domain controller (BDC). Only one PDC can exist in a domain. In an NT 4.0 single domain model, any user having a valid domain user account and password in the user accounts database of the PDC has the ability to log onto any computer that is a member of the domain, including MetaFrame servers.

Primary Domain Controller (PDC) emulator   This domain controller (DC) emulates a Windows NT PDC if there are Windows NT backup domain controllers (BDCs) in the domain, processing password changes and replicating the information to the BDCs. If the domain operates in native mode, with only Windows 2000 DCs, the PDC emulator receives preferential replication of password changes performed by other DCs, serving as a sort of clearinghouse for password medications.

Primary Domain Name System (DNS) server   The Primary DNS server maintains the master copy of the DNS database for the zone. This copy of the database is the only one that can be modified, and any changes made to its database are distributed to secondary servers in the zone during a zone transfer process. The server can cache resolution requests locally, so a lookup query does not have to be sent across the network for a duplicate request. The primary server contains the address mappings for the Internet root DNS servers. Primary servers can also act as secondary servers for other zones.

primary partitions   Primary partitions are typically used to create bootable drives. Each primary partition represents one drive letter, up to a maximum of four on a single hard disk. One primary partition must be marked as active in order to boot the system, and most operating systems must be loaded on a primary partition to work.

print device   The hardware that actually does the printing. A print device is one of two types as defined in Windows 2000: local or network-interface. A local print device connects directly to the print server with a serial or parallel interface. A network-interface print device connects to the printer across the network and must have its own network interface or be connected to an external network adapter.

print driver   A software program used by Windows 2000 and other computer programs to connect with printers and plotters. It translates information sent to it into commands that the print device can understand.

print server   A print server is a computer that manages printing on the network. A print server can be a dedicated computer hosting multiple printers, or it can run as one of many processes on a nondedicated computer.

Printer permission   Printer permission is established through the Security tab in the printer's Properties dialog. The security settings for printer objects are similar to the security settings for folder shares.

private   A digital code that can be used to decrypt information which works in conjunction with a corresponding public key.

protocols   Protocols are sets of rules that computers use to communicate with one another. Protocols usually work together in stacks, so called because in a layered networking model, they operate at different layers or levels. These protocols govern the logic, formatting, and timing of information exchange between layers.

public key   A digital code used to encrypt information, which is then decrypted by a private key.

public key encryption   The public key is used to encrypt the data and is not kept secret but is published to all wishing to send an encrypted message to the owner.

public key cryptography   A public key, published and made widely available, is used to encrypt data and a corresponding private key, kept secret, is used for decryption.

Public Key Infrastructure (PKI)   A PKI is a system of digital certificates, certificate authorities, and other registration authorities that verify and authenticate the validity of each party involved in an electronic transaction.

publishing resources   Resources, such as folders and printers, which are available to be shared on the network, can be published to the Active Directory. The resources are published to the directory and can be located by users, who can query the directory based on the resource's properties (for example, to locate all color printers).

PXE   *See* Preboot Execution Environment.

QoS   *See* Quality of Service.

Quality of Service (QoS) Admission Control   Admission control allows you to control how applications are allotted network bandwidth. You can give important applications more bandwidth, less important applications less bandwidth.

RADIUS   *See* Remote Authentication Dial-In User Service.

RAID   *See* redundant array of inexpensive disks.

RAS   *See* Remote Access Service.

RDP   *See* Remote Desktop Protocol.

recovery agent   The recovery agent restores the encrypted file on a secure computer with its private recovery keys. The agent decrypts it using the cipher command line and then returns the plain text file to the user. The recovery agent goes to the computer with the encrypted file, loads the recovery certificate and private key, and performs the recovery. It is not as safe as the first option because the recovery agent's private key may remain on the user's computer.

Recovery console   The Recovery console is a new command-line interpreter feature in Windows 2000 that helps in system maintenance activities and resolving system problems. This program is separate from the Windows 2000 command prompt.

redundant array of inexpensive disks (RAID)   Although mirroring and duplexing are forms of RAID, most people think of RAID as involving more than two drives. The most common form of RAID is RAID5, which is the striping of data across three or more drives, providing fault tolerance if one drive fails. For the best disk performance, consider using a SCSI RAID (redundant array of independent disks) controller. RAID controllers automatically place data on multiple disk drives and can increase disk performance. Using the software implementation of RAID provided by NT would increase performance if designed properly, but the best performance is always realized through hardware RAID controllers.

redundant array of inexpensive disks5 (RAID5) Volume   A RAID5 volume on a dynamic drive provides disk striping with parity, and is similar to a basic stripe set with parity. This disk configuration provides both increased storage capacity and fault tolerance. Data in a dynamic RAID5 volume are interleaved across three or more disks (up to 32 disks), and parity information is included to rebuild lost data in the event of an individual disk failure. Like a spanned or striped volume, a RAID5 volume cannot be mirrored.

regional model   A company is operating with a regional business model if it has operations that are not merely local to a metropolitan area. The company will have business operations that are located in multiple parts of a state or a country.

registry   The registry is the hierarchical database that stores operating system and application configuration information. It was introduced in Windows 9x and NT and replaced much of the functionality of the old initialization, system, and command files used in the early versions of Windows (.INI, .SYS, and .COM extensions). The registry is also a Microsoft Windows program allowing the user to choose options for configuration and applications to set them; it replaces confusing text-based .INI files.

relationships model   Another consideration involved in analyzing the business requirements of your organization hinges on the company's relationships with the outside world—business partners, vendors and customers. This is especially important if the company wishes to make information available to some or all of these through direct access to the company's network.

remote   The word "remote" can take on a number of different meanings depending on the context. In the case of an individual computer, the computer you are sitting in front of is sometimes referred to as being "local" while any other computer is considered "remote." In this context any machine but your own is considered a remote computer. In discussions related to network configuration and design, "remote" may refer to segments and machines that are on the far side of a router. In this context, all machines on your physical segment are considered "local" and machines located on other physical segments are referred to as remote.

remote access policy   Remote access policies allow you to create demand-dial connections to use specific authentication and encryption methods. In Windows NT versions 3.5x and Windows NT 4.0, authorization was much simpler. The administrator simply granted dial-in permission to the user. The callback options were configured on a per-user basis.

Remote Access Service (RAS)   Remote Access Service is a built-in feature of the Microsoft NT operating system. It allows users to establish a connection to an NT network over a standard phone line. Remote Access allows users to access files on a network or transfer files from a remote PC, over a Dial-up Networking connection. The performance of transferring files over a dial-up connection is very similar to the performance you would get if you were downloading a file from the Internet.

Remote Authentication Dial-In User Service (RADIUS) A client/server protocol used for authentication of dial-in clients that allows centralized authentication and control of remote users.

Remote Desktop Protocol (RDP) Remote Desktop Protocol (RDP) is the application protocol between the client and the server. It informs the server of the keystrokes and mouse movement of the client and returns to the client the Windows 2000 graphical display from the server. RDP is a multi-channel, standard protocol that provides various levels of compression so that it can adapt to different connection speeds and encryption levels from 40 to 128 bit. Transmission Control Protocol/Internet Protocol (TCP/IP) carries the messages, and RDP is the language in which the messages are written. Both are needed to use Microsoft's implementation of Terminal Services.

Remote Installation Preparation (RIPrep) RIPrep is a disk duplication tool included with Windows 2000 Server. It is an ideal tool for creating images of fully prepared client computers. These images are the customized images made from the base operating system, local installation of applications such as Microsoft Office, and customized configurations.

Remote Installation Preparation (RIPrep) Wizard The RIPrep Wizard enables the network administrator to distribute to a large number of client computers a standard desktop configuration that includes the operating system and the applications. This not only helps in maintaining a uniform standard across the enterprise; it also cuts the costs and time involved in a large-scale rollout of Windows 2000 Professional.

Remote Installation Service (RIS) The RIS, part of Windows 2000 Server, allows client computers to install Windows 2000 Professional from a Windows 2000 Server with the service installed. The Remote Installation Service (RIS) facilitates installation of Windows 2000 Professional remotely on a large number of computers with similar or dissimilar hardware configurations. This not only reduces the installation time but also helps keep deployment costs low. Also, the Windows 2000 Remote Installation Service allow you a way to create an image of Windows 2000 Professional you can use to install Windows 2000 Professional on your network client systems. This image actually consists of the installation files from the Windows 2000 Professional CD-ROM.

remote local printer   A print device connected directly to a print server but accessed by another print server or by workstations. The queue for the print device exists on the server, and the print server controls job priority, print order, and queue administration. Client computers submit print jobs to the server and can observe the queue to monitor the printing process on the server. Drivers for the print device are loaded onto the client computer from the print server.

remote network printer   A network printer connected to a print server that is accessed by client workstations or other print servers. Like the remote local printer, the printer queue is controlled by the print server, meaning that the client computers submit their print jobs to the print server, rather than to the print device directly. This allows for server administration and monitoring of the printer queues. Drivers for the print device are loaded onto the client computers from the print server.

replay attack   An attack in which the unauthorized user records the exchange of packets between an authorized user and the server, and plays it back later.

replication service   Distributes directory data across the enterprise network.

repudiation   The identity of the sender cannot be verified.

request   After the client receives the DHCPOFFER message and accepts the Internet Protocol (IP) address, it sends a DHCPREQUEST message out to all Dynamic Host Control Protocol (DHCP) servers indicating that it has accepted an offer. The message contains the IP address of the DHCP server that made the accepted offer, and all other DHCP servers release the addresses they had offered back into their available address pool.

reverse lookup query   A reverse lookup query resolves an Internet Protocol (IP) address to a Domain Name System (DNS) name, and can be used for a variety of reasons. The process is different, though, because it makes use of a special domain called in-addr.arpa. This domain is also hierarchical, but is based on IP addresses and not names. The sub-domains are organized by the *reverse* order of the IP address. For instance, the domain 16.254.169.in-addr.arpa contains the addresses in the 169.254.16.* range; the 120.129.in-addr.arpa domain contains the addresses for the 129.120.*.* range.

RID master   The RID master is a domain-wide role, and this domain controller (DC) allocates relative ID sequences to the domain controllers in its domain. A RID is a unique security identifier assigned each time a user, group, or computer object is created.

RIPrep   *See* Remote Installation Preparation.

rollback strategy   As with any upgrade, problems can sometimes require going back to the previous state. This possibility also applies to upgrading your domain to Windows 2000. You need to create a plan to "roll back" your network to its previous state if the upgrade to Windows 2000 fails.

Routing and Remote Access Service (RRAS)   Within Windows NT, a software routing and remote access capability combining packet filtering, Open Shortest Path First (OSPF) support, etc.

RRAS   *See* Routing and Remote Access Service.

Safe mode   Safe mode starts Windows 2000 using only some basic files and device drivers. These devices include monitor, keyboard, mouse, basic VGA video, CD-ROM, and mass storage devices. The system starts only those system services that are necessary to load the operating system. Networking is not started in this mode. The Windows background screen is black in this mode, and the screen resolution is 640 by 480 pixels with 16 colors.

Safe Mode with Command Prompt   This option starts the operating system in a safe mode using some basic files only. The Windows 2000 command prompt is shown instead of the usual Windows desktop.

Safe Mode with Networking   This mode is similar to Safe mode, but networking devices, drivers, and protocols are loaded. You may choose this mode when you are sure that the problem in the system is not due to any networking component.

SAM   *See* Security Accounts Manager.

schema   A set of rules which defines the classes of objects and attributes contained in the directory, the constraints and limits on instances of these objects, and the format of their names.

schema master   The domain controller (DC) designated as schema master controls updates and modifications to the schema. This role is forest-wide, because a common schema is shared by all domains in a forest. There can be only one schema master in the forest, and changes to the schema can be made only through that machine.

scripted method   This method for Windows 2000 Professional installation uses an answer file to specify various configuration parameters. This is used to eliminate user interaction during installation, thereby automating the installation process. Answers to most of the questions asked by the setup process are specified in the answer file. Besides this, the scripted method can be used for clean installations and upgrades.

SCSI   *See* small computer system interface.

Secondary Domain Name System (DNS) server   Secondary DNS servers provide fault tolerance and load balancing for DNS zones. Secondary servers contain a read-only copy of the zone database that it receives from the primary server during a zone transfer. A secondary server will respond to a DNS request if the primary server fails to respond because of an error or a heavy load. Since secondary servers can resolve DNS queries, they are also considered authoritative within a domain, and can help with load balancing on the network. Secondary servers can be placed in remote locations on the network and configured to respond to DNS queries from local computers, potentially reducing query traffic across longer network distances. While there can be only one primary server in a zone, multiple secondary servers can be set up for redundancy and load balancing.

secret key   A digital code or password shared by two parties, used for both encryption and decryption of messages.

secret key encryption   When two parties use the same shared secret key to encrypt and decrypt data.

Secure Sockets Layer (SSL)   A protocol that provides security at the socket level and used for securing Web access.

Security Accounts Manager (SAM)   The Security Accounts Manager (SAM) is the portion of the Windows NT Server registry that stores user account information and group membership. Attributes that are specific to Terminal Server can be added to user accounts. This adds a small amount of information to each user's entry in the domain's SAM.

security groups The Windows 2000 security groups allow you to assign the same security permissions to large numbers of users in one operation. This ensures consistent security permissions across all members of a group. Using security groups to assign permissions means the access control on resources remains fairly static and easy to control and audit. Users who need access are added or removed from the appropriate security groups as needed, and the access control lists change infrequently.

security templates Windows 2000 comes with several predefined security templates. These templates address several security scenarios. Security templates come in two basic categories: default and incremental. The default or basic templates are applied by the operating system when a clean install has been performed.; they are not applied if an upgrade installation has been done.

segment In discussions of Transmission Control Protocol/Internet Protocol (TCP/IP), segment often refers to the group of computers located on one side of a router, or sometimes a group of computers within the same collision domain. In TCP/IP terminology, "segment" can also be used to describe the chunk of data sent by TCP over the network (roughly equivalent to the usage of "packet" or "frame").

Sequenced Packet Exchange (SPX) The communications protocol (from NetWare) used to control network message transport.

server The word "server" can take on a variety of different meanings. A server can be a physical computer. A server can also represent a particular software package. For example, Microsoft Exchange 2000 is a mail and groupware server application. Often, server applications are just referred to as "servers," as with mail servers. The term "server" is also used to refer to any computer that is currently sharing its resources on the network. In this context, all computers, whether Windows 3x or Windows 2000, can be servers on a network.

Server Message Block (SMB) signing SMB signing requires that every packet in the stream be verified. Enabling SMB signing can result in decreased performance on the server. This may be an acceptable tradeoff in an environment where sensitive data is subject to attack, but is a side effect of which you should be aware if your network's functions require optimum performance.

Service Level Agreement (SLA) The SLA is a document that is created by the Information Technology (IT) department that describes the roles and responsibilities of the IT department, outlines the scope of services to be performed, and attempts to set expectations for the end user.

service pack   A service pack typically contains bug fixes, security fixes, systems administration tools, drivers, and additional components. Microsoft recommends installing the latest service packs as they are released. As a new feature in Windows 2000, you do not have to reinstall components after installing a service pack.

Setup Manager   The Setup Manager is the best tool to use when you have no idea of the answer file syntax or when you do not want to get into the time-consuming task of creating or modifying the sample answer file. When you choose to use the Setup Manager for unattended installations, you need to do a lot of planning beforehand. It is understood that you will not be using Setup Manager for automating installations on one or two computers; that would be a waste of effort. Setup Manager is useful for mass deployments only.

SETUPACT.LOG   The Action log file contains details about the files that are copied during setup.

SETUPAPI.LOG   This log file contains details about the device driver files that were copied during setup. This log can be used to facilitate troubleshooting device installations. The file contains errors and warnings along with a time stamp for each issue.

SETUPCL.EXE   The function of the SETUPCL.EXE file is to run the Mini-Setup Wizard and to regenerate the security IDs on the master and destination computers. The Mini-Setup Wizard starts on the master computer when it is booted for the first time after running Sysprep.

SETUPERR.LOG   The Error log file contains details about errors that occurred during setup.

SETUPLOG.TXT   This log file contains additional information about the device driver files that were copied during setup.

shared folders   Sharing folders so that other users can access their contents across the network is easy in Windows 2000, as easy as right-clicking the folder name in Windows Explorer, selecting the Sharing tab, and choosing Share This Folder. An entire drive and all the folders on that drive can be shared in the same way.

Shared Folders permission   As only folders, not files, can be shared, Shared Folder permission is a small subset of standard NT File System (NTFS) permissions for a folder. However, securing access to a folder through share permissions can be more restrictive or more liberal than standard NTFS folder permissions. Shared Folder permission is applied in the same manner as NTFS permissions.

shared printers   The process for sharing a printer attached to your local computer is similar to that for sharing a folder or drive. If the users who will access your printer will do so from machines that don't run the Windows 2000 operating system, you will need to install drivers for the other operating system(s).

shared resource   A shared resource is a device, data, or program that is made available to network users. This can include folders, files, printers, and even Internet connections.

Simple Network Management Protocol (SNMP)   A standard for managing hardware devices connected to a network, approved for Unix use, that lets administrators know, for example, when a printer has a paper jam or is low on toner.

simple volume   A simple volume is a volume created on a dynamic disk that is not fault tolerant, and includes space from only one physical disk. A simple volume is just that—it is a single volume that does not span more than one physical disk, and does not provide improved drive performance, extra capacity or fault tolerance. One physical disk can contain a single, large simple volume, or several smaller ones. Each simple volume is assigned a separate drive letter. The number of simple volumes on a disk is limited only by the capacity of the disk and the number of available letters in the alphabet.

single master operation   This is an operation in which a single domain controller is in charge of a particular operation for a period of time.

Single-Instance-Store (SIS) Volume   When you have more than one image on the Remote Installation Service (RIS) server, each holding Windows 2000 Professional files, there will be duplicate copies of hundreds of files. This may consume a significant hard drive space on the RIS server. To overcome this problem, Microsoft introduced a new feature called the Single-Instance-Store, which helps in deleting all the duplicate files, thus saving on hard drive space.

single sign-on   The ability of users to provide one username and password to access all authorized network resources rather than having to be authenticated separately for multiple servers and applications.

SIS   *See* Single-Instance-Store.

Site Server Internet Locator Server (ILS) Service   This service supports Internet Protocol (IP) telephony applications, publishes IP multicast conferences on a network, and can also publish user IP address mappings for H.323 IP telephony. Telephony applications, such as NetMeeting and Phone Dialer in Windows Accessories, use Site Server ILS Service to display user names and conferences with published addresses. Site Server ILS Service depends on Internet Information Services (IIS).

SLA   *See* Service Level Agreement.

small computer system interface (SCSI)   A complete expansion bus interface that accepts such devices as a hard disk, CD-ROM, disk drivers, printers, or scanners.

smart card   A device similar to a credit card, which contains an embedded chip (also called a token) that stores digital certificates and is used for authentication. By adding a chip to the card, it becomes a smart card with the power to serve many different purposes. As an access-control device, smart cards protect personal and business data so that only the appropriate users are granted access.

SMB   *See* Server Message Block.

SMP   *See* Symmetric Multiprocessing.

SMS   *See* Systems Management Server.

SNA   *See* Systems Network Architecture.

snap-ins   The management applications that are contained in a Microsoft Management Console (MMC) are called snap-ins, and custom MMCs hold the snap-ins required to perform specific tasks.

SNMP   *See* Simple Network Management Protocol.

social engineering attack   This is the term used for breaking into a network by simply "outwitting" employees and convincing them to reveal their passwords. Often the intruder pretends to be with the company's IT department and tells the users that he is verifying their password or that there is a problem with their network account.

spanned volume   A spanned volume is similar to a volume set in NT 4.0. It contains space from multiple disks (up to 32), and provides a way to combine small "chunks" of disk space into one unit, seen by the operating system as a single volume. It is not fault tolerant. When a dynamic volume includes the space on more than one physical hard drive, it is called a spanned volume. Spanned volumes can be used to increase drive capacity, or to make use of the leftover space on up to 32 existing disks. Like those in a basic storage volume set, the portions of a spanned volume are all linked together and share a single drive letter.

SPX   *See* Sequenced Packet Exchange.

stack   A data structure in which the first items inserted are the last ones removed, unlike control structure programs that use the Last In First Out (LIFO) structure.

static Internet Protocol (IP) address   A static IP address allows users to use a domain name that can be translated into an IP address. The static IP address allows the server to always have the same IP address, so the domain name always translates to the correct IP address. If the address was assigned dynamically and occasionally changed, users might not be able to access the server across the Internet using the domain name.

stripe set   The term "striping" refers to the interleaving of data across separate physical disks. Each file is broken into small blocks, and each block is evenly and alternately saved to the disks in the stripe set. In a two-disk stripe set, the first block of data is saved to the first disk, the second block is saved to the second disk, and the third block is saved to the first disk, and so on. The two disks are treated as a single drive, and are given a single drive letter.

stripe set with parity   A stripe set with parity requires at least three hard disks, and provides both increased storage capacity and fault tolerance. In a stripe set with parity, data is interleaved across three or more disks and includes parity (error checking) information about the data. As long as only one disk in the set fails, the parity information can be used to reconstruct the lost data. If the parity information itself is lost, it can be reconstructed from the original data.

striped volume   Like a stripe set in NT 4.0, a striped volume is the dynamic storage equivalent of a basic stripe set and combines free space from up to 32 physical disks into one volume by writing data across the disks in stripes. This increases performance but does not provide fault tolerance. A striped volume improves drive performance and increases drive capacity. Because each data block is written only once, striped volumes do not provide fault tolerance.

striping   Striping is when the data are striped across the drives and there is parity information along with the data. The parity information is based on a mathematical formula that comes up with the parity based on the data on the other drives.

strong encryption   Uses a 56-bit DES key. There are 72 quadrillion possible combinations—this is to say that strong encryption is fairly safe.

subnetting   Using several data paths to reduce traffic on a network and avoid problems if a single path should fail; usually configured as a dedicated Ethernet subnetwork between two systems based on two Network Interface Cards (NICs).

subsidiary model   A subsidiary model is one in which there exists a parent company that owns in whole or in part other companies. The core business that each subsidiary services can be completely different or subsidiaries can be in competition with each other. A company that has a subsidiary model will typically choose to implement Active Directory (AD) with multiple domains in a single tree. The reasons for this are that each subsidiary will probably want retain complete control over their environment. With the creations of multiple domains each subsidiary can maintain it own autonomy. They are able to deploy their own set of requirement for there users.

Symmetric Multiprocessing (SMP)   SMP is a system in which all processors are treated as equals, and any thread can be run on any available processor. Windows 2000 also supports processor affinity, in which a process or thread can specify which set of processors it should run on. Application Programming Interfaces (APIs) must be defined in the application.

synthesis   The process of design, formulation, integration, prediction, proposal, generalization, and show relationships.

Sysprep.inf   Sysprep.inf is an answer file. When you want to automate the Mini-Setup Wizard by providing predetermined answers to all setup questions, you must use this file. This file needs to be placed in the %Systemroot%\Sysprep folder or on a floppy disk. When the Mini-Setup Wizard is run on the computer on which the image is being distributed, it takes answers from the Sysprep.inf file without prompting the user for any input.

System Monitor   The System Monitor is part of this Administrative Tools utility, and allows you to collect and view data about current memory usage, disk, processor utilization, network activity, and other system activity. The System Monitor replaces the Performance Monitor used in Windows NT. System Monitor allows you to collect information about your hardware's performance as well as network utilization, and can be used to measure different aspects of a computer's performance on one's own computer or on other computers on the network.

system policy   The system policy editor is used to provide user and computer configuration settings in the Windows NT registry database. The system policy editor is still used for the management of Windows 9x and Windows NT server and workstations and stand-alone computers using Windows 2000.

System Preparation (Sysprep)   Sysprep provides an excellent means of saving installation time and reducing installation costs. Sysprep is the best tool to copy the image of a computer to other computers that have identical hardware configurations. It is also helpful in standardizing the desktop environment throughout the organization. Since one Sysprep image cannot be used on computers with identical hardware and software applications, you can create multiple images when you have more than one standard. It is still the best option where the number of computers is in hundreds or thousands and you wish to implement uniform policies in the organization.

Systems Management Server (SMS)   This Windows NT software analyzes and monitors network usage and various network functions.

Systems Network Architecture (SNA)   Systems Network Architecture (SNA) was developed by IBM in the mainframe computer era (1974, to be precise) as a way of getting its various products to communicate with each other for distributed processing. SNA is a line of products designed to make other products cooperate. In your career of designing network solutions, you should expect to run into SNA from time to time because many of the bigger companies (banks, healthcare institutions, government offices) bought IBM equipment and will be reluctant to part with their investment. SNA is a proprietary protocol that runs over SDLC exclusively, although it may be transported within other protocols, such as X.25 and Token Ring. It is designed as a hierarchy and consists of a collection of machines called nodes.

Take Ownership permission   This permission can be given to allow a user to take ownership of a file or folder object. Every file and folder on an NT File System (NTFS) drive has an owner, usually the account that created the object. However, there are times when ownership of a file needs to be changed, perhaps because of a change in team membership or a set of new responsibilities for a user.

Task-based model   This model is appropriate for companies in which administrative duties are functionally divided. This means that this model divides the management of Group Policy Objects (GPOs) by certain tasks. To apply this model, the administrators that handle security-related tasks will also be responsible for managing all policy objects that affect security. The second set of administrators that normally deploy the companies' business applications will be responsible for all the GPOs that affect installation and maintenance.

TCO   *See* Total Cost of Operation.

TCP/IP   *See* Transmission Control Protocol/Internet Protocol.

Terminal Services   In application server mode, Terminal Services provides the ability to run client applications on the server, while "thin client" software acts as a terminal emulator on the client. Each user sees an individual session, displayed as a Windows 2000 desktop. The server manages each session, independent of any other client session. If you install Terminal Services as an application server, you must also install Terminal Services Licensing (not necessarily on the same computer). However, temporary licenses can be issued for clients that allow you to use Terminal servers for up to 90 days. In remote administration mode, you can use Terminal Services to log on remotely and manage Windows 2000 systems from virtually anywhere on your network (instead of being limited to working locally on a server). Remote administration mode allows for two concurrent connections from a given server and minimizes impact on server performance. Remote administration mode does not require you to install Terminal Services Licensing.

TFTP   *See* Trivial File Transfer Protocol.

Theory X   Theory X is the so-called traditional model, often used in government agencies, where there is a strict chain of command that employees are expected to follow. Going "over the heads" of superiors is frowned upon, or even formally prohibited, and the structure of the organization is paramilitary in nature. Employees are expected to follow the rules that are handed down from on high.

Theory Y   Theory Y is the modern management theory that offers a kinder, gentler atmosphere in which employee input in decision-making is encouraged or even required. The company presents itself as one big, happy family where each member is equally valued (although not, of course, equally compensated in monetary terms). Creativity is considered a more valuable asset than going "by the book."

token ring   A local area network (LAN) specification that was developed by IBM in the 1980s for PC-based networks and classified by the (Institute of Electrical and Electronics Engineers) IEEE as 802.5. It specifies a star topology physically and a ring topology logically. It runs at either 4 Mbps or 16 Mbps, but all nodes on the ring must run at the same speed.

Total Cost of Operation (TCO) analysis   The whole idea of TCO analysis is to expose the hidden costs of a product over its projected life cycle.

Transmission Control Protocol/Internet Protocol (TCP/IP)   A set of communications standards created by the U.S. Department of Defense (DoD) in the 1970s that has now become an accepted way to connect different types of computers in networks because the standards now support so many programs.

trees   Trees are groups of domains that share a contiguous namespace. They allow you to create a hierarchical grouping of domains that share a common contiguous namespace. This hierarchy allows global sharing of resources among domains in the tree. All the domains in a tree share information and resources with a single directory, and there is only one directory per tree. However, each domain manages its own subset of the directory that contains the user accounts for that domain. So, when a user logs into a domain, the user has global access to all resources that are part of the tree, providing the user has the proper permissions.

Trivial File Transfer Protocol (TFTP)   A simplified version of the File Transfer Protocol (FTP), associated with the Transmission Control Protocol/Internet Protocol (TCP/IP) family, that does not provide password protection or a user directory.

Trojan horse A virus or malicious program is disguised as a harmless program.

trust The users in one tree do not have global access to resources in other trees, but trusts can be created that allow users to access resources in another tree. A trust allows all the trees to share resources and have common administrative functions. Such sharing capability allows the trees to operate independently of each other, with separate namespaces, yet still be able to communicate and share resources through trusts.

trust relationship A trust relationship is a connection between domains in which users who have accounts in and log on to one domain can then access resources in other domains, provided they have proper access permissions.

UDF *See* Unique Database File.

UDP *See* User Datagram Protocol.

Unattended method The Unattended method for Windows 2000 Server installation uses the answer file to specify various configuration parameters. This method eliminates user interaction during installation, thereby automating the installation process and reducing the chances of input errors. Answers to most of the questions asked by the setup process are specified in the answer file. In addition, the scripted method can be used for clean installations and upgrades.

UNATTEND.TXT The creation of customized UNATTEND.TXT answer files is the simplest form of providing answers to setup queries and unattended installation of Windows 2000. This can either be done using the Setup Manager or by editing the sample UNATTEND.TXT file using Notepad or the MS-DOS text editor. The UNATTEND.TXT file does not provide any means of creating an image of the computer.

UNATTEND.UDF This file is the Unique Database File, which provides customized settings for each computer using the automated installation.

UNC *See* universal naming convention.

UNICODE UNICODE is a 16-bit character encoding standard developed by the Unicode Consortium between 1988 and 1991 that uses two bytes to represent each character and enables almost all of the written languages of the world to be represented using a single character set.

uninterruptible power supply (UPS)   A battery that can supply power to a computer system if the power fails. It charges while the computer is on and, if the power fails, provides power for a certain amount of time, allowing the user to shut down the computer properly to preserve data.

Unique Database File (UDF)   When you use the WINNT32.EXE command with the /unattend option, you can also specify a Unique Database File (UDF), which has a .UDB extension. This file forces Setup to use certain values from the UDF file, thus overriding the values given in the answer file. This is particularly useful when you want to specify multiple users during the setup.

universal groups   Universal groups are used in larger, multi-domain organizations, in which there is a need to grant access to similar groups of accounts defined in multiple domains. It is better to use global groups as members of universal groups to reduce overall replication traffic from changes to universal group membership. Users can be added and removed from the corresponding global groups with their account domains, and a small number of global groups are the direct members of the universal group. Universal groups are used only in multiple domain trees or forests. A Windows 2000 domain must be in native mode to use universal groups.

Universal Serial Bus (USB)   A low-speed hardware interface (supports MPEG video) with a maximum bandwidth up to 1.5 MBps (megabytes per second).

universal naming convention (UNC)   A UNC is an identification standard of servers and other network resources.

UPS   *See* uninterruptible power supply.

USB   *See* Universal Serial Bus.

user account   The information that defines a particular user on a network, which includes the username, password, group memberships, and rights and permissions assigned to the user.

User Datagram Protocol (UDP)   A Transmission Control Protocol/Internet Protocol (TCP/IP) normally bundled with an Internet Protocol (IP) layer software that describes how messages received reached application programs within the destination computer.

value bar   The value bar is positioned below the graph area. It displays data for the selected sample, the last sample value, the average of the counter samples, the maximum and minimum of the samples, and the duration of time the samples have been taken over.

virtual private network (VPN)   A private network configured within or over a public network. Access control and encryption can provide the same security as a private network, while taking advantage of the scale and built-in management facilities of larger public networks. VPNs reduce service costs and long distance/usage fees, lighten infrastructure investments, and simplify wide area network (WAN) operations over time.

volume set   The term "volume" indicates a single drive letter. One physical hard disk can contain several volumes, one for each primary partition or logical drive. However, the opposite is also true. You can create a single volume that spans more than one physical disk. This is a good option when you require a volume that exceeds the capacity of a single physical disk. You can also create a volume set when you want to make use of leftover space on several disks by piecing them together as one volume.

VPN   *See* virtual private network.

WDM   *See* Windows32 Drive Model.

Windows 3x   Windows *3x* changed everything. It was a 16-bit operating system with a user interface that resembled the look and feel of IBM's (at that time not yet released) OS/2, with 3D buttons and the ability to run multiple programs simultaneously, using a method called cooperative multitasking. Windows *3x* also provided virtual memory, the ability to use hard disk space to "fool" the applications into behaving as if they had more RAM than was physically installed in the machine.

Windows 2000 Control Panel   The Control Panel in Windows 2000 functions similarly to the Control Panel in Windows *9x* and NT, except that "under the hood" there are now two locations that information is stored, which is modified by the Control Panel applets. The Control Panel in previous operating systems was a graphical interface for editing registry information.

Windows Backup   Windows Backup is a built-in Backup and Restore utility, which has many more features than the backup tool provided in Windows NT 4.0. It supports all five types of backup: Normal, Copy, Differential, Incremental, and Daily. Windows Backup allows you to perform the backup operation manually or you may schedule it to run at a later time in unattended mode. Included with the operating system, it is a tool that is flexible and easy to use.

Windows 9x   In August of 1995, Microsoft released its long-awaited upgrade of Windows, Windows 95. For the first time, Windows could be installed on a machine that didn't already have MS-DOS installed. Many improvements were made: the new 32-bit functionality (although still retaining some 16-bit code for backward compatibility); preemptive multitasking (a more efficient way to run multiple programs in which the operating system controls use of the processor, and the crash of one application does not bring down the others that are currently running); and support for filenames longer than the DOS-based eight-character limit.

Windows 2000   Microsoft's latest incarnation of the corporate operating system was originally called NT 5, but the name was changed to Windows 2000 between the second and third beta versions—perhaps to underscore the fact that this is truly a *new* version of the operating system, not merely an upgrade to NT.

Windows Internet Naming Service (WINS)   WINS provides name resolution for clients running Windows NT and earlier versions of Microsoft operating systems. With name resolution, users can access servers by name, instead of having to use Internet Protocol (IP) addresses that are difficult to recognize and remember. WINS is used to map NetBIOS computer names to IP addresses. This allows users to access other computers on the network by computer name. WINS servers should be assigned a static IP address, which allows clients to be able to find the WINS servers. Clients cannot find a WINS server by name because they need to know where the WINS server is in order to translate the name into an IP address.

Windows Internet Naming Service (WINS) Name Registration   Each WINS client has one or more WINS servers identified in the network configuration on the computer, either through static assignment or through DHCP configuration. When the client boots and connects to the network, it registers its name and IP address with the WINS server by sending a registration request directly to the server. This is not a broadcast message, since the client has the address of the server. If the server is available and the name is not already registered, the server responds with a successful registration message, which contains the amount of time the name will be registered to the client, the time-to-live (TTL). Then the server stores the name and address combination in its local database.

Windows Internet Naming Service (WINS) Name Release   When a WINS client shuts down properly, it will send a name release request to the WINS server. This releases the name from the WINS server's database so that another client can use the name if necessary. The release request contains the WINS name and address of the client. If the server cannot find the name, it sends a negative release response to the client. If the server finds the matching name and address in its database, it releases the name and marks the record as inactive. If the name is found but the address does not match, the server ignores the request.

Windows Internet Naming Service (WINS) Name Renewal   As with Dynamic Host Control Protocol (DHCP), WINS name registrations are temporary and must be renewed to continue to be valid. The client will attempt to renew its registration when half (50 percent) of the time-to-live (TTL) has elapsed. If the WINS server does not respond, the client repeatedly attempts to renew its lease at ten-minute intervals for an hour. If the client still receives no response, it restarts the process with the secondary WINS server, if one is defined. The client will continue attempting to renew its lease in this manner until it receives a response from a server. At that time, the server sends a new TTL to the client and the process starts over.

Windows Internet Naming Service (WINS) proxy agent   A WINS proxy agent is similar to a Dynamic Host Control Protocol (DHCP) Relay Agent. It listens for requests for non-WINS network clients and redirects those requests to a WINS server. A WINS proxy operates in two modes.

Windows Internet Naming Service (WINS) snap-in   With the snap-in, you can view the active WINS entries under the Active Registrations folder. In addition, you can supply static mappings for non-WINS clients on the network through the snap-in. To configure a static mapping, select the Active Registrations folder and select New Static Mapping from the Action menu. Once a static mapping is entered into the WINS database, it cannot be edited. If you need to make changes to a static mapping, you must be delete and recreate the entry.

Windows NT   The NT kernel (the core or nucleus of the operating system, which provides basic services for all other parts of the operating system) is built on a completely different architecture from consumer Windows. In fact, NT was based on the 32-bit preemptive multitasking operating system that originated as a joint project of Microsoft and IBM before their parting of the ways, OS/2. NT provided the stability and security features that the "other Windows" lacked, albeit at a price, and not only a monetary one; NT was much pickier in terms of hardware support, did not run all of the programs that ran on Windows 9x (especially DOS programs that accessed the hardware directly), and required more resources, especially memory, to run properly.

Windows32 Driver Model (WDM)   The Win32 Driver Model (WDM) provides a standard for device drivers that will work across Windows platforms (specifically Windows 98 and 2000), so that you can use the same drivers with the consumer and business versions of the Windows operating system.

WINNT.EXE program   The WINNT.EXE program is used for network installations that use an MS-DOS network client. The WINNT32.EXE program is used to customize the process for upgrading existing installations. The WINNT32.EXE program is used for installing Windows 2000 from a computer that is currently running Windows 95/98 or Windows NT.

WINS   *See* Windows Internet Naming Service.

workgroup   A workgroup is a logical grouping of resources on a network. It is generally used in peer-to-peer networks. This means that each computer is responsible for access to its resources. Each computer has its own account database and is administered separately. Security is not shared between computers, and administration is more difficult than in a centralized domain.

zones of authority   The Domain Name System (DNS) namespace is divided into zones, and each zone must have one name server that is the authority for the name mapping for the zone. Depending on the size of the namespace, a zone may be subdivided into multiple zones, each with its own authority, or there may be a single authority for the entire zone. For instance, a small company with only 200 to 300 computers could have one DNS server handle the entire namespace.